CAMBRIDGE LIBRARY COLLECTION

Books of enduring scholarly value

Archaeology

The discovery of material remains from the recent or the ancient past has always been a source of fascination, but the development of archaeology as an academic discipline which interpreted such finds is relatively recent. It was the work of Winckelmann at Pompeii in the 1760s which first revealed the potential of systematic excavation to scholars and the wider public. Pioneering figures of the nineteenth century such as Schliemann, Layard and Petrie transformed archaeology from a search for ancient artifacts, by means as crude as using gunpowder to break into a tomb, to a science which drew from a wide range of disciplines - ancient languages and literature, geology, chemistry, social history - to increase our understanding of human life and society in the remote past.

A Bibliographical List Descriptive of Romano-British Architectural Remains in Great Britain

First published in 1912, this volume provides a list of all Romano-British structures in the British Isles known at the time of publication, complete with references to published works on each structure, arranged by county. This volume omits burial sites and circumstantial evidence for occupation, focusing on a wide range of excavated structures ranging from military defences to foundations and pavements. The detailed references for each structure provide a valuable resource for researching the extent of previous excavations on a site, and for recovering information on structures which have since been lost or destroyed. Modern discoveries can also be placed in context with earlier excavations in the same area. The author, Arthur H. Lyell (d. 1925), was a prominent archaeologist specialising in Roman Britain.

Cambridge University Press has long been a pioneer in the reissuing of out-of-print titles from its own backlist, producing digital reprints of books that are still sought after by scholars and students but could not be reprinted economically using traditional technology. The Cambridge Library Collection extends this activity to a wider range of books which are still of importance to researchers and professionals, either for the source material they contain, or as landmarks in the history of their academic discipline.

Drawing from the world-renowned collections in the Cambridge University Library, and guided by the advice of experts in each subject area, Cambridge University Press is using state-of-the-art scanning machines in its own Printing House to capture the content of each book selected for inclusion. The files are processed to give a consistently clear, crisp image, and the books finished to the high quality standard for which the Press is recognised around the world. The latest print-on-demand technology ensures that the books will remain available indefinitely, and that orders for single or multiple copies can quickly be supplied.

The Cambridge Library Collection will bring back to life books of enduring scholarly value (including out-of-copyright works originally issued by other publishers) across a wide range of disciplines in the humanities and social sciences and in science and technology.

A Bibliographical List Descriptive of Romano-British Architectural Remains in Great Britain

Arthur Henry Lyell

CAMBRIDGE UNIVERSITY PRESS

Cambridge, New York, Melbourne, Madrid, Cape Town, Singapore,
São Paolo, Delhi, Dubai, Tokyo

Published in the United States of America by Cambridge University Press, New York

www.cambridge.org
Information on this title: www.cambridge.org/9781108008907

© in this compilation Cambridge University Press 2010

This edition first published 1912
This digitally printed version 2010

ISBN 978-1-108-00890-7 Paperback

A BIBLIOGRAPHICAL LIST

DESCRIPTIVE OF ROMANO-BRITISH ARCHITECTURAL REMAINS IN GREAT BRITAIN

CAMBRIDGE UNIVERSITY PRESS
London: FETTER LANE, E.C.
C. F. CLAY, Manager

Edinburgh: 100, PRINCES STREET
Berlin: A. ASHER AND CO.
Leipzig: F. A. BROCKHAUS
New York: G. P. PUTNAM'S SONS
Bombay and Calcutta: MACMILLAN AND CO., Ltd.

A BIBLIOGRAPHICAL LIST

DESCRIPTIVE OF ROMANO-BRITISH
ARCHITECTURAL REMAINS IN
GREAT BRITAIN

BY

ARTHUR H. LYELL, M.A., F.S.A.

Cambridge:
at the University Press
1912

𝕮𝖆𝖒𝖇𝖗𝖎𝖉𝖌𝖊:

PRINTED BY JOHN CLAY, M.A.

AT THE UNIVERSITY PRESS

PREFACE

THE description of discoveries of Roman Architectural Remains in Britain are scattered so widely that on the suggestion of the late Mr George E. Fox I commenced this Bibliographical List, in the hope that the student of the future might thus easily obtain all available information regarding any excavated site. The List may also serve two other purposes: either to prevent needless excavations on sites that have been exhaustively explored or on the other hand to stimulate the thorough exploration and planning of sites hitherto only imperfectly investigated.

It has been found necessary to omit obscure evidence of buildings, as for instance where roof tiles have been found without a trace of any foundations. Burial sites although indicating the probable proximity of dwellings, remains of which indeed may actually exist to-day and await discovery, are also excluded. On the other hand some Forts which have not been explored, but which there is every reason to believe will furnish evidence of architectural remains have been included, as well as a few minor and possibly doubtful sites.

Nearly all the publications referred to may be found in the Library of the Society of Antiquaries of London. I cannot

boast of having exhausted all works which may contain references. It is more than probable that there may be some books
and periodicals which refer to remains of buildings contained
in this list and in most cases quoted or gleaned from the books
I have cited. Newspaper notices have been generally omitted ;
but it is to be hoped that no important work will be found
missing.

To Mr Mill Stephenson I am profoundly indebted for un-
remitting kindness in advice, as well as for incalculable help in
revising and checking all the references.

A. H. L.

LONDON,
   July, 1912.

CONTENTS

BIBLIOGRAPHY AND ABBREVIATIONS

THE following list of works includes those which deal with England, Scotland and Wales.

Works dealing with particular counties will be found under the heading of the respective county; but where a publication only treats of one particular site or contains an account of only one or two sites, the title in each case is given in full under the respective name of place.

Antiquarian Repertory. Antiquarian Repertory, 4 vols. 1775—84, 1807—9.

Antiquary. The Antiquary, I.—XLV. 1880—1909.

Archaeologia, *see* London S.A.

Archaeologist. The Archaeologist. Edited by J. O. Halliwell, 1842.

Arch. Jour. The Archaeological Journal and other Volumes published by the Royal Archaeological Institute of Great Britain and Ireland:

    (*a*)   Arch. Jour. I.—LXVII. 1845—1910.

    (*b*)   Winchester Volume, 1845.

    (*c*)   York Volume, 1846.

    (*d*)   Norwich Volume, 1847.

    (*e*)   Lincoln Volume, 1848.

    (*f*)   Salisbury Volume, 1849.

    (*g*)   Oxford Volume, 1850.

    (*h*)   Bristol Volume, 1851.

    (*i*)   Newcastle Volume, 1852.

    (*j*)   Chichester Volume, 1853.

Arch. Review. Archaeological Review, A Journal of Historic and Pre-historic Antiquities, 1888—90.

Arch. Scotica, *see* Scotland S.A.

Assoc. Archit. Soc. Reports. The Associated Architectural Societies Reports and Papers, I.—XXIX. 1850—1908.

Athenaeum. The Athenaeum, Journal of Literature, 1831—1910.

Ayr and Gall. Colls. Archaeological and Historical Collections relating to the Counties of Ayr and Wigton. Published by the Ayrshire and Wigton (now Ayrshire and Galloway Archaeological Association), 9 vols. 1875—95.

B.A.A.   British Archaeological Association:
    (*a*)   Collectanea Archaeologica, 2 vols. 4to. 1862, 1871.
    (*b*)   Journal, I.—L. 1845—94 ; N.S. I.—XV. 1895—1909.
    (*c*)   Proceedings at Canterbury, 1845.
    (*d*)   Transactions at Gloucester, 1846.
    (*e*)   Transactions at Winchester, 1845.
    (*f*)   Transactions at Worcester, 1848.

Bateman's Diggings. Bateman, Thomas. Ten Years digging in the Counties of Derby, Stafford and York from 1848—58, Lond. 1861.

Bib. Topog. Brit.   Bibliotheca Topographica Britannica, 1780.

Birm. and Mid. Inst. Trans.   Birmingham and Midland Institute Transactions, Archaeological section, 1870—78.

Blome's Britannia.   Blome, R.   Britannia ; or a Geographical description of the Kingdoms of England, Scotland and Ireland, etc. 1673.

Brit. Curios.   British Curiosities in Art and Nature (printed for Sam. Illidge, 1721).

Brit. Mus.   British Museum, Pavements exhibited.

Brit. Romana, *see* London S.A.

Britton and Brayley.   Britton, J., and Brayley, E. W.   Beauties of England and Wales, 26 vols. 1801—15.

Builder.   The Builder, I.—XCVII. 1843—1909.

Camden, *see* Gough.

Carter.   Carter, J.   Ancient Architecture, 1795.

Coll. Antiq., *see* Smith, C. Roach.

Dugdale's Imbanking.   Dugdale, Sir W.   History of Imbanking and Draining Fens and Marshes.   Edited by C. N. Cole, 1772.

East Anglian N. and Q.   The East Anglian: or Notes and Queries on Subjects connected with the County of Suffolk, Cambridge, etc.   Edited by C. H. Evelyn White, I.—IV. 1864—69, N.S. I.—X. 1885—1904, 3 S. XI.—XII. 1905—8, 4 S. XIII. 1909—10.

East Anglian Miscell.   East Anglian Miscellany.

Fowler's Pav.   Fowler, W.   Mosaic Pavements of Great Britain, 1804.

Gent. Mag.   Gentleman's Magazine, vols. 1—138, 1731—1868.

Gent. Mag. Lib. Rom.   Gentleman's Magazine Library Romano-British Remains.   Edited by G. L. Gomme, 2 parts, 1887.

Godwin's Arch. Handbook.   Godwin, Henry.   The English Archaeologist's Handbook, 1867.

Gough's Brit. Top.   Gough, Richard.   British Topography, 2 vols. 1780.

Gough's Camden.   Camden, William.   Britannia.   Edited by Richard Gough, 2nd ed. 4 vols. 1806.

Grose's Antiq.   Grose, Francis.   Antiquities of England and Wales, 6 vols. 1773—87.

Hearne's Reliquiae.   Hearne, Thomas.   Reliquiae Hearnianae: the remains of T. Hearne, with notes by P. Bliss, 2 vols. 1857.

Holinshed.   Holinshed, R.   Chronicles of England, 1587.

Horsley. Horsley, John. Britannia Romana, 2 vols. 1732.

Hübner. Hübner, Aemilius. Inscriptiones Britanniae Latinae, 1873.

Illust. Arch. The Illustrated Archaeologist. Edited by J. R. Allen, vol. I. 1904 (*see* The Reliquary).

Illust. Lond. News. Illustrated London News, 1842—1911.

Kennett's Antiquities. Kennett, White. Parochial Antiquities, 1695.

King's Mun. Antiq. King, Edward. Munimenta Antiqua, 1799—1806.

Knight's England. Knight, Charles. Old England, 2 vols. 1845.

Leland's Itin. Leland, John. The Itinerary of. Edited by T. Hearne, 3rd ed. 9 vols. 1768—69.

Lewis. Lewis, Samuel. A Topographical Dictionary of England, 5th ed. 4 vols. 1845.

Lewis. Lewis, Samuel. A Topographical Dictionary of Wales, 3rd ed. 2 vols. 1845.

London Royal Inst. Proc. London, Royal Institution of Great Britain, Proceedings, 1851—1910.

London R. S. London, Royal Society
    (*a*) Philosophical Transactions, 1735—1910.
    (*b*) Classified Papers in the Archives of the Royal Society, 1606 —1741, by A. H. Church, 1907.
    (*c*) Letters and Papers in the Archives of the Royal Society, 1741 —1806, by A. H. Church, 1908.

London S.A. London, Society of Antiquaries of :
    (*a*) Archaeologia. Archaeologia, I.—LXII. 1779—1910.
    (*b*) Brit. Rom. Britannia Romana (A collection of Original Drawings, etc. belonging to the Society), 4 vols.
    (*c*) Minute Book. MS. Minute Books, I.—XXXVIII. 1718—1844.
    (*d*) Proc. Proceedings, I.—IV. 1849—59, N.S. I.—XXIII. 1859—1910.
    (*e*) Topog. Colls. Topographical Collections.
    (*f*) Vet. Mon. Vetusta Monumenta, 6 vols.

Lysons' Envir. Lond. Lysons, Daniel. The Environs of London, 4 vols. 1792—1811.

Lysons' Mag. Brit. Lysons, Daniel and Samuel. Magna Britannia, 1806 —22.

Lysons' Reliquae. Lysons, Samuel. Reliquae Britannico Romanae, 1801—17.

Mag. Brit. 1738. Magna Britannia Antiqua et Nova, 6 vols. 1738.

Midland Antiq. Midland Antiquary, Nos. 1—14, 1882—86.

Midland Co. Hist. Coll. Midland Counties History Collector. Edited by J. Thompson, 2 vols. 1854—56.

Morgan. Morgan, Thomas. Romano-British Mosaic Pavements : a History of their discovery, 1886.

Nichols' Horae Romanae. Nichols, W. L. Horae Romanae, 1838.

N. and Q. Notes and Queries, Eleven Series, 1850—1910.

Phil. Trans., *see* London R.S.

Pointer's Brit. Rom. Pointer, John. Britannia Romana, or Roman Antiquities in Britain, 1724.

Prynne's Diary. Surtees Society Publications, LIV. Diary of Abraham de la Prynne, the Yorkshire Antiquary.

Reliquary. The Reliquary. Edited by Llewellynn Jewitt, I.—XXVII. 1860—86, N.S. I.—VIII. 1887—1894.

Reliquary and Illust. Arch. The Reliquary and Illustrated Archaeologist, I.—XV. 1895—1909.

R.I.B.A. Trans. Royal Institute of British Architects, Transactions, 23 vols. 1860—84, N.S. I.—VIII. 1885—92, 3 S. I.—XVI. 1896—1909.

Roy. Roy, William. Military Antiquities of the Romans, 1793.

Royal Society, *see* London R.S.

Salmon's England. Salmon, Nathaniel. New Survey of England, 1731.

Scarth's Rom. Brit. Scarth, H. M. Roman Britain, n.d.

Scotland S. A. Scotland, Society of Antiquaries of:

    (*a*) Arch. Scot. Archaeologia Scotica, 1792—1890.

    (*b*) Proc. Proceedings, I.—XLII. 1855—1909.

Smith, C. Roach. Smith, C. Roach.

    (*a*) Coll. Antiq. Collectanea Antiqua I.—VII. 1848—80.

    (*b*) Retrospections. Retrospections, Social and Archaeological, 2 vols. 1883—85.

Strutt's Chronicle. Strutt, Joseph. Chronicles of England, B.C. 54 to A.D. 1066, 1779.

Stukeley's Itin. Curios. Stukeley, W. Itinerarum Curiosum, 2nd ed. 1776.

Stukeley's Letters. Surtees Society Publications, Vols. 73, 76, 80. W. Stukeley's Letters and Diaries, I. II. III.

Tour in Britain. Tour in the whole Island of Britain by a Gentleman, 3rd ed. 1742.

Vet. Mon., *see* London S.A.

V.C.H. Victoria History of the Counties of England.

Wren's Parentalia. Wren, C. Parentalia: or memoirs of the family of the Wrens, 1750.

Wright's Arch. Album. Wright, T. Archaeological Album or Museum of National Antiquities, 1845.

Wright's Celt, Roman and Saxon. Wright, T. The Celt, the Roman and the Saxon, 5th ed. 1892.

Wright's Wanderings. Wright, T. Wanderings of an Antiquary, 1854.

ROMAN REMAINS

BEDFORDSHIRE

V.C.H. Victoria History of the Counties of England. Bedfordshire, II. 1908.

Bedford (Castle Lane). Pavement. Building News, Oct. 7, 1881 ; V.C.H. II. 5.

Shefford. Foundations, cemetery, etc. Arch. Jour. I. 397 ; Cambs. Antiq. Soc. Pubs. 4to, I. 8th paper, 10 (plan); V.C.H. II. 11 (plan).

Yelden. Foundations. Arch. Jour. XXXIX. 82 ; Assoc. Archit. Soc. Rep. XVI. 263 ; V.C.H. II. 15.

BERKSHIRE

Berks. Bucks. and Oxon. Arch. Jour. Berkshire, Buckinghamshire and Oxfordshire Archaeological Journal, I.—XVI. 1895—1910.

Berks. Quarterly Jour. Quarterly Journal of the Berkshire Archaeological and Architectural Society, 3 vols., N.D.

King. King, Cooper. Popular History of Berkshire, 1887.

Newbury Field Club Trans. Newbury District Field Club Transactions, I.—IV. 1871—95.

V.C.H. Victoria History of the Counties of England. Berkshire, I. 1906.

Abingdon. Foundations. Lond. S.A. Proc. 2 S. III. 145, 202; V.C.H. I. 202.

Bagshot Heath (Wickham Bushes). Foundations. Lysons' Mag. Brit. I. 199 ; V.C.H. I. 206.

Basildon. Building and pavements. B.A.A. Jour. XVI. 32 ; Coll. Antiq. I. 65 ; Hedges, J. K., Hist. of Wallingford, 1881, I. 136; Hussey, R., An account of the Roman road from Alchester to Dorchester, 1841, 20 n ; Lewis, I. 161 ; Lond. S.A. Archaeologia, XXVIII. 447, and Minute Book, XXXVII. 350; Morgan, 145, 148; Newbury Field Club Trans. IV. 98 ; V.C.H. I. 203.

Blewbury (Lowborough Hill). Foundations. Arch. Jour.
v. 286; Gent. Mag. 1838, i. 48, and Lib. Rom. Brit. Rem.
i. 4; Hewett, W., Hist. of Compton, 1844, 113; V.C.H.
I. 203.

Boxford. Foundations. Newbury Field Club Trans. I. 208;
V.C.H. I. 203.

Bradfield. Foundations (?). Lond. S.A. Proc. 2 S. XVI. 276;
V.C.H. I. 203.

Brimpton. Building. Godwin's Arch. Handbook, 59; V.C.H.
I. 204.

Bucklebury (Marlstone). Building and pavement. B.A.A. Jour.
XVI. 290, XVII. 336, XXXVI. 28; King, 49; Newbury Field
Club Trans. IV. 184; V.C.H. I. 205.

Chaddleworth. Pavement. Gent. Mag. 1827, ii. 448, and Lib.
Rom. Brit. Rem. i. 6; V.C.H. I. 205.

Cranhill, *see* Letcombe Regis.

Easthampstead, *see* Bagshot Heath.

Eling, *see* Hampstead Norris.

Finchampstead. Foundations. Lond. S.A. Proc. 1 S. IV. 283;
Surrey Arch. Colls. IX. 345; V.C.H. I. 207.

Frilford. Buildings. Antiquary, IX. 42; Arch. Jour. LIV. 340
(plan); Builder, XLV. 775, 805; Oxford Archit. and Hist.
Soc. Proc. N.S. IV. 233; Times, Dec. 1, 1883; V.C.H. I. 207
(plan).

Hampstead Norris (Eling Farm). Buildings and pavements.
B.A.A. Jour. XIX. 148, XXXVI. 27; King, 49; Newbury
Field Club Trans. I. 208, IV. 183; V.C.H. I. 210.

(Well House Farm). Buildings and pavements. B.A.A.
Jour. XIX. 60; King, 49; Lewis, II. 389; Newbury and its
Environs, History of, 1839, 218; V.C.H. I. 209.

Ilsley, East. Foundations. B.A.A. Jour. XVII. 290; V.C.H. I.
210.

Lambourn (Stancombe Down). Foundations. Lond. S.A.
Proc. 2 S. XI. 410; Newbury Field Club Trans. IV. 190;
Reliquary, N.S. I. 234; V.C.H. I. 211.

Letcombe Regis (Cranhill). Buildings. Arch. Jour. XXXIII.
382 (plan); Oxford Hist. Soc. III. 78; V.C.H. I. 211
(plan).

Lowborough Hill, *see* Blewbury.

Maidenhead. Building. Antiquary, XIV. 227; Berks. Quarterly Jour. II. 75; Maidenhead and Taplow Field Club Reports, 1890—91, 50; V.C.H. I. 204.

Marlstone, *see* Bucklebury.

Newbury (Enbourne Road). Foundations. Berks. Bucks. and Oxon. Arch. Jour. XIII. 30; Reading Mercury, Apr. 6, 1907.

Pangbourn. Foundation. Arch. Jour. I. 164; V.C.H. I. 212.

Stancombe Down, *see* Lambourn.

Stanford-in-the-Vale. Pavement. Berks. Bucks. and Oxon. Arch. Jour. XIII. 60; V.C.H. I. 214.

Streatley. Foundations. Hoare, R. C., Ancient North Wilts. 53; V.C.H. I. 214.

Uffington (Woolstone). Buildings and pavements. Antiquary, X. 133, XI. 278; Berks. Bucks. and Oxon. Arch. Jour. XIII. 60; Illust. Lond. News, July 5, 1884; Lond. S.A. Proc. 2 S. XXI. 215, and Topog. Colls., brown portfolio (photos of pavements); Morgan, 149; Newbury Field Club Trans. III. 239, IV. 189; Oxford Hist. Soc. III. 78; Times, May 23, 1884; V.C.H. I. 222.

Waltham St Laurence. Buildings. Arch. Jour. VI. 114 (plan); Leland's Itin. I. preface, x; Lysons' Mag. Brit. I. 199; V.C.H. I. 216 (plan).

Waltham, White. Foundations. Leland's Itin. I. preface, ix; Lysons' Mag. Brit. I. 199.

Watchfield. Foundations. Antiquary, XLI. 403; Berks. Bucks. and Oxon. Arch. Jour. XIII. 60; Lond. S.A. Proc. 2 S. XXI. 163; V.C.H. I. 218.

Well House, *see* Hampstead Norris.

Weycock, *see* Waltham St Laurence.

Wickham Bushes, *see* Bagshot Heath.

Wittenham, Long. Foundations. Antiquary, XXIX. 56; Athenaeum, Aug. 26, 1893; Lond. S.A. Proc. 2 S. XVIII. 10 (plan); V.C.H. I. 219 (plan).

Woolstone, *see* Uffington.

BUCKINGHAMSHIRE

Bucks. Records. Records of Buckinghamshire, I.—IX. 1858—1908.
Gibbs. Gibbs, R. Buckinghamshire Miscellany, 1891.
Sheahan. Sheahan, J. J. History of Buckinghamshire, 1862.
V.C.H. Victoria History of the Counties of England. Buckinghamshire,
II. 1908.

Bletchley, *see* Shenley.
Brickhill, Bow, *see* Fenny Stratford.
Buckingham, *see* Foscott.
Chenies (Latimer). Buildings and pavement. Bucks. Records,
III. 180 (plan), IV. 276 ; Sheahan, 842 ; V.C.H. II. 8 (plan).
Ellesborough. Buildings. Bucks. Records, II. 53 (plan) ; Gibbs,
174 ; Sheahan, 132 ; V.C.H. II. 6.
Foscott, or Foxcott. Buildings and pavement. Bucks. Records,
I. Catalogue of Museum, 4, III. 240; Gent. Mag. 1838, i.
302, 1841, i. 81, 1843, i. 303, and Lib. Rom. Brit. Rem. i. 7,
8 ; Sheahan, 275 ; V.C.H. II. 7.
Kimble, Little. Foundations and pavement. Bucks. Records,
I. 39, II. 48, IV. 276; Sheahan, 131 ; V.C.H. II. 8.
Nash Lee. Foundations. V.C.H. II. 10.
Oakley. Foundations. Berks. Bucks. and Oxon. Arch. Jour.
IV. 46; V.C.H. II. 10.
Shenley. Buildings and pavement. Antiquary, XXXVII. 342 ;
V.C.H. II. 4.
Stratford, Fenny. Foundations and pavement. Gibbs, 56 ;
Lewis, I. 407 ; Lysons' Mag. Brit. I. 483 ; Sheahan, 25, 532.
Tingewick. Buildings. Arch. Jour. XX. 376 ; Bucks. Records,
III. 33 (plan), IV. 36 ; Gibbs, 334 ; V.C.H. II. 12 (plan).
Wycombe, High. Buildings and pavement. Antiquary, XLIV.
246 ; Britton and Brayley, I. 362 ; Bucks. Records, III. 160
(plan), V. 156 ; Gent. Mag. 1817, ii. 551, 1829, i. 546, and
Lib. Rom. Brit. Rem. i. 13 ; Langley, T., History of
Desborough, 1797, 29 ; Lewis, I. 407 ; Lond. S.A. Proc. 2 S.
III. 233 ; Lysons' Mag. Brit. I. 483 ; Newbury Field Club
Trans. IV. 240 ; Parker, John, Hist. of Wycombe, 1878, 1, 2
(plan), 5 ; Sheahan, 917 ; V.C.H. II. 17, 18 (plan).

CAMBRIDGESHIRE

Cambs. Antiq. Soc. Trans. Cambridge Antiquarian Society Transactions, 8vo Series, I.—XLIV. 1851—1908.

Cambs. Antiq. Soc. Proc. Cambridge Antiquarian Society Proceedings and Communications, I.—XIII. 1859—1909.

Arbury. Foundations. Cambs. Antiq. Soc. Proc. X. 284, XI. 198, 211.

Burwell. Pavement. Builder, LXXXIX. 509. Now in Sedgwick Museum, Cambridge.

Cambridge. Buildings, causeway and bridge. Cambs. Antiq. Soc. Trans. III. 3, 17, 72, XX. 3, 26; Lysons' Mag. Brit. II. 44.

Comberton. Buildings. Cambs. Antiq. Soc. Trans. III. 14 and pl. 2 (plan), XX. 22 (plan), 24; Gent. Mag. 1842, ii. 526, and Lib. Rom. Brit. Rem. i. 14.

Fleam Dyke and Mutlow Hill. Foundations. Arch. Jour. IX. 229; Cambs. Antiq. Soc. Trans. III. 40, XX. 67.

Ickleton. Buildings. Arch. Jour. VI. 14, 96; Athenaeum, Sept. 9, 1848; B.A.A. Jour. IV. 356, 365 (plan), V. 54, XXIII. 278, XXXIV. 256, and Coll. Arch. II. 248; Gent. Mag. 1848, ii. 633, and Lib. Rom. Brit. Rem. i. 15, 72.

Landwade. Buildings and pavement. Cambs. Antiq. Soc. Proc. XI. 210.

Litlington. Buildings and pavement. Arch. Jour. XXV. 30; Cambridge Chronicle, May and Dec. 1841; Cambs. Antiq. Soc. Trans. III. 37, XX. 60, 62, and Proc. VI. 310; Gent. Mag. 1829, i. 546, and Lib. Rom. Brit. Rem. i. 16; Lond. S.A. Archaeologia, XXVI. 368, 376 (plan).

Swaffham Prior. Buildings. Antiquary, XXVII. 24; Cambs. Antiq. Soc. Proc. VIII. 229 (plan); Reliquary, N.S. VII. 57.

CHESHIRE

Ches. Arch. Soc. Jour. Chester Architectural and Archaeological Society Journal, I.—III. 1850—85. N.S. I.—XV. 1887—1909.

Ches. N. and Q. Cheshire Notes and Queries, I.—VI. 1898—1903.

Hemingway. Hemingway, J. History of Cheshire, 2 vols., 1858.

Lanc. and Ches. Antiq. Soc. Trans. Lancashire and Cheshire Antiquarian Society Transactions, I.—XXI. 1884—1903.

Lanc. and Ches. Hist. Soc. Trans. Lancashire and Cheshire Historic Society Transactions, I.—XXV. 1849—1909.

Ormerod. Ormerod, J. History of Cheshire, 3 vols., 1819.

Watkin. Watkin, T. W. Roman Cheshire, 1886.

Birkenhead (Wallasey Pool). Bridge. Cambs. Antiq. Soc. Trans. III. 18, XX. 28 ; Chester Arch. Soc. Jour. I. 55 ; Watkin, 80, 81.

Bowden. Building. Watkin, 306.

Chester (*Deva*). The city, walls, gates, etc. Antiquary, XVII. 41, 242, XVIII. 86, 278, XIX. 41 ; Arch. Jour. XLIII. 265, XLIV. 52, XLV. 264, 268, XLVII. 243, XLVIII. 293 ; B.A.A. Jour. V. 212, XLIV. 129, 212, XLV. 199, XLVII. 273, L. 63 ; Britton and Brayley, II. 195 ; Builder, LXI. 248 ; Ches. Arch. Soc. Jour. II. 334, 374, III. 251, 471, 487, N.S. I. 177, 203, II. 40, III. 71, XV. 133 ; Ches. N. and Q. N.S. IV. 228 ; Coll. Antiq. VI. 42 ; Haverfield, F., Catalogue of the Roman and sculptured stones in the Grosvenor Museum, Chester, 5—15 ; King's Mun. Antiq. II. 64, 218 ; Lanc. and Ches. Antiq. Soc. Trans. IX. 203 ; Lewis, I. 566 ; Liverpool Archit. and Arch. Soc. Proc. II. 33 ; Lond. S.A. Proc. 2 S. XXII. 462 ; Lysons' Mag. Brit. II. 427 ; Ormerod, I. 295 ; Pennant's Tour in Wales, I. 114 ; Stukeley's Itin. Curios. I. 59, II. 30 ; Watkin, 86.

Black Friars Street. Buildings. Lanc. and Ches. Antiq. Soc. Trans. IV. 365 ; Lanc. and Ches. Hist. Soc. Trans. 4 S. III. 54 ; Watkin, 319.

Bridge Street. Buildings and pavement. Antiquary, XXXVI.6; B.A.A. Jour. VI. 156, XXII. 376, 388 (plan); Britton and Brayley, II. 198; Builder, XXII. 60, XXIII. 109, 157; Ches. Arch. Soc. Jour. I. 355, 435, III. 1 (plan), 106, N.S. I. 185, 212, VI. 395, VIII. 104, XIII. 139; Earwaker, J. D., Local Gleanings relating to Lanc. and Ches. II. 169; Gent. Mag. 1863, ii. 67, 209, and Lib. Rom. Brit. Rem. i. 18 ; Godwin's Arch. Handbook, 37 ; Hemingway, II. 352 ; Horsley's Brit. Rom. 318 ; Lewis, I. 566 ; Lond. S.A. Archaeologia, XL. 285

(plan), and Proc. 2 S. II. 325, XVIII. 96; Ormerod, I. 295; Pennant's Tour in Wales, I. 116; Watkin, 130.

Castle. Buildings and pavement. Gent. Mag. 1837, i. 641, and Lib. Rom. Brit. Rem. i. 17; Watkin, 192.

Commonhall Street. Buildings. B.A.A. Jour. V. 230; Watkin, 147.

Eastgate Street. Buildings. B.A.A. Jour. N.S. VI. 355; Ches. Arch. Soc. Jour. N.S. VIII. 82 (plan), 85.

Foregate Street. Buildings. Antiquary, XVIII. 124.

Northgate Street. Buildings and pavement. Antiquary, XXVI. 25, XXXIII. 361; B.A.A. Jour. XLVIII. 169, XLIX. 298 (plan); Builder, LXII. 307, LXXIII. 51, 153; Ches. Arch. Soc. Jour. III. 32, N.S. V. 105, VI. 277; Lond. S.A. Proc. 2 S. XVIII. 91 (plan), and Topog. Colls., brown portfolio (plan, etc.); Watkin, 157.

Nuns' Garden. Pavement. Ormerod, I. 295; Watkin, 192.

St Mary's Rectory. Foundations. Watkin, 197.

Watergate Street. Buildings and pavement. B.A.A. Jour. XLVI. 312, L. 197, N.S. I. 69; Britton and Brayley, II. 199; Broster, P., Chester Guide, 1872, 24; Ches. Arch. Soc. Jour. I. 52, III. 32; Hemingway, II. 358; Lysons' Mag. Brit. II. 428; Ormerod, I. 295; Pennant's Tour in Wales, I. 116; Watkin, 152.

White Friars Street. Buildings. Antiquary, X. 37; Lanc. and Ches. Hist. Soc. Trans. 3 S. XII. 10 (plan), 4 S. III. 51; Reliquary, XXV. 64, N.S. I. 233; Watkin, 148.

Wishing Steps. Foundations. Watkin, 197.

Locality not given. Buildings, etc. Antiquary, XXXVII. 13; B.A.A. Jour. II. 193; Blome's Britannia, 53; British Curiosities in Art and Nature, 93; Magna Britannia Antiqua et Nova, I. 277.

Eccleston. Pavement. Britton and Brayley, II. 238.

Farndon. Buildings. Lanc. and Ches. Hist. Soc. Trans. 4 S. III. 56.

Kinderton. Foundations. Lond. S.A. Proc. 1 S. IV. 244.

Lyme. Pavement (?). Ches. N. and Q. N.S. I. 82; Marriott, W., Hist. of Lyme, 1810, 261.

Malpas. Pavement. Watkin, 286.

Northwick.   Foundations.   Ches. Arch. Soc. Jour. I. 46;
Watkin, 253.

Statham.   Foundations.   B.A.A. Jour. VII. 12.

Tarporley (Eaton).   Foundations.   Lanc. and Ches. Hist. Soc.
Trans. 4 S. III. 57.

Wilderspool.   Station, buildings, kilns, excavations, etc.
Antiquary, XXXIV. 354, XXXVI. 258, XXXVII. 13; B.A.A.
Jour. VII. 8, XVII. 60; Beamont, W., Account of the Roman
station at Wilderspool, 1876; Kendrick, J., Guide to the
collection of Roman remains from Wilderspool, 1872, 4, 8 ;
Lanc. and Ches. Antiq. Soc. Trans. XVII. 141, 239, 269, XX.
249 ; Lanc. and Ches. Hist. Soc. Trans. 4 S. XII. 1 (plans),
XIV. 1 (plans), XVI. 1 (plans), XXI. 190, 219, XXII. 15;
May, Thos., The Roman Fortifications recently discovered
at Wilderspool, 1899, and Warrington's Roman Remains
discovered at Wilderspool, etc. 1904 (plans, etc.) ; Reliquary,
X. 88, XI. 43 ; Reliquary and Illust. Arch. N.S. VI. 263 ;
Watkin, 260.

CORNWALL

Borlase.   Borlase, W.   Antiquities of Cornwall, 1754.

Helston.   Ovens.   Arch. Jour. XX. 64.

St Erth (Bossens).   Buildings.   Lond. S.A. Minute Book, VIII.
109; Phil. Trans. LI. i. 13.

St Paul (Kerris).   Arched vault paved with stone.   Borlase, 286.

Wendron (Goldvadneck Barrow).   Stone vault and fine chequered
brick pavement found in 1700.   Borlase, 286.

CUMBERLAND

Arch. Survey.   An Archaeological Survey of Cumberland and Westmorland, by R. S. Ferguson, printed in Archaeologia, LIII. (1893), 485—531.

Bruce's Rom. Wall.   Bruce, J. Collingwood.   The Roman Wall, 3rd ed.
1867.

Bruce's Handbook.   Bruce, J. C.   Handbook to the Roman Wall, 6th ed.
1909.

Cumb. and Westm. Arch. Soc. Trans. Cumberland and Westmorland Antiquarian and Archaeological Society Transactions, I.—XVI. 1874—1900, N.S. I.—X. 1901—10.

Ferguson. Ferguson, R. S. Popular History of Cumberland, 1890.

Hodgson. Hodgson, J. History of Northumberland, 3 vols., 1820—58.

Hutchinson. Hutchinson, W. History of Cumberland, 2 vols., 1794.

Maclauchlan. Maclauchlan, Henry. Memoir on the Roman Wall, 1858.

Nicolson and Burn. Nicolson, J., and Burn, R. History of Westmorland and Cumberland, 2 vols., 1777.

Roy. Roy, W. Military Antiquities of the Romans, 1793.

Warburton. Warburton, J. Vallum Romanum, 1753.

Whellan. Whellan, W. History of Cumberland and Westmorland, 1860.

Beckfoot, *see* Mawbray.

Bewcastle. Station, buildings, etc. Arch. Jour. XI. 124 ; Arch. Survey, 493 ; Britton and Brayley, III. 115 ; Bruce's Rom. Wall, 354, and Handbook, 250 ; Cumb. and Westm. Arch. Soc. Trans. N.S. II. 242 ; Ferguson, 75 ; Gent. Mag. 1792, ii. 1074, and Lib. Rom. Brit. Rem. i. 20 ; Hutchinson, I. 92 ; Lysons' Mag. Brit. IV. cxlv ; Maughan, J. A., Memoir on the Roman station and Runic cross at Bewcastle, 1857 ; Nicolson and Burn, II. 477 ; Whellan, 630.

Birdoswald (*Amboglanna*). Station, buildings, etc. Arch. Jour. XXXIX. 454 ; Arch. Survey, 494; B.A.A. Jour. N.S. VII. 74, XII. 277, XIV. 199 ; Britton and Brayley, III. 118 ; Bruce's Rom. Wall, 253, and Handbook, 200 ; Ches. Arch. Soc. Trans. III. 333 ; Coll. Antiq. III. 200 ; Cumb. and West. Arch. Soc. Trans. XIV. 184, XV. 180, 201, 346, 351, 353 ; Dorset Field Club Proc. XIV. 32 ; Ferguson, 93 ; Gent. Mag. 1852, i. 483 ; Glasgow Arch. Soc. Trans. I. 110 ; Hodgson's Northumb. III. ii. 206, 295 ; Horsley's Brit. Rom. 107 ; Hutchinson, I. 65 ; Lysons' Mag. Brit. IV. cxxxvii; Maclauchlan, 54; Newcastle S.A. Arch. Æliana, IV. 63, 141, N.S. XXIV. 39, Proc. II. 216, VII. 225, 3 S. II. 291, and Lapid. Septen. 180 ; Nicolson and Burn, 504 ; V.C.H. London, I. 66 ; Warburton, 81 ; Whellan, 689.

Borrowdale. Part of bridge. Arch. Survey, 494 ; Lond. S.A. Proc. 1 S. III. 225.

Bowness-on-Solway. Station, etc. Arch. Survey, 494 ; Britton and Brayley, III. 191 ; Bruce's Rom. Wall, 303, and

Handbook, 242; Cumb. and Westm. Arch. Soc.Trans. I. 212 ; Hodgson's Northumb. III. ii. 225 ; Horsley's Brit. Rom. 109, 158, 267; Hutchinson, II. 484; Lewis, I. 309; Lond. S.A. Minute Book, III. 244; Lysons' Mag. Brit. IV. cxl ; Maclauchlan, 87, 88 n ; Newcastle S.A. Proc. II. 240; Nicolson and Burn, II. 214; Whellan, 149, 151.

Brampton. Foundations. Lond. S.A. Proc. 2 S. XVI. 422 ; Maclauchlan, 63, 64.

Brunstock Park. The Wall. Builder, LXVII. 87, 195 ; Cumb. and Westm. Arch. Soc. Trans. XIII. 459; Maclauchlan, 73.

Burgh-on-Sands. Station, etc. Arch. Survey, 495 ; Britton and Brayley, III. 190; Cumb. and Westm. Arch. Soc. Trans. I. 151 ; Hodgson's Northumb. III. ii. 221; Horsley's Brit. Rom. 156; Hutchinson, II. 501 ; Lysons' Mag. Brit. IV. cxxxix ; Maclauchlan, 81 ; Newcastle S.A. Arch. Æliana, N.S. XII. 171, and Proc. II. 238 ; Nicolson and Burn, II. 222 ; Whellan, 153.

Caermote. Fort and foundations. Arch. Survey, 497 ; Cumb. and Westm. Arch. Soc. Trans. III. 43, 76, VI. 191 ; Lond. S.A. Proc. 1 S. III. 224.

Cambeck, *see* Castlesteads.

Carlisle (*Luguvallium*). The city, walls, etc. Arch. Survey, 497 ; Britton and Brayley, III. 96; Bruce's Rom. Wall, 293, and Handbook, 233 ; Ferguson, 98; Hutchinson, II. 585, 650; Lond. S.A. Proc. 2 S. IV. 47 ; Lysons' Mag. Brit. IV. cxlvi ; Maclauchlan, 75 ; Newcastle S.A. Arch. Æliana, N.S. XII. 163 ; Nicolson and Burn, II. 228 ; Stukeley's Itin. Curios. II. 54 ; Whellan, 139.

Bank Street. Stockade. Arch. Survey, 497 ; B.A.A. Jour. XXXIII. 523, XXXIV. 242, 260; Cumb. and Westm. Arch. Soc. Trans. III. 134, IV. 91 ; Lond. S.A. Proc. 2 S. VII. 217, 356.

Blackfriars Street. Buildings and pavement. Arch. Survey, 498 ; Lond. S.A. Proc. 2 S. XIII. 263.

Citadel Row. Stockade. Arch. Survey, 498 ; B.A.A. Jour. XXXIII. 523, XXXIV. 260; Cumb. and Westm. Arch. Soc. Trans. III. 134, IV. 91.

Devonshire Street. Buildings. Arch.Survey,498 ; Jefferson,S.,

Hist. of Carlisle, 1838, 330; Lond. S.A. Proc. 2 S. XIII. 264, and Topog. Colls., brown portfolio (plan).

Eden river. Bridge and walk. Arch. Survey, 498; Cumb. and Westm. Arch. Soc. Trans. IX. 167; Lond. S.A. Proc. 2 S. XI. 209.

English Street. Stockading and tanks of oak. Arch. Survey, 498; B.A.A. Jour. XXXIII. 523, XXXIV. 260; Cumb. and Westm. Arch. Soc. Trans. III. 134, IV. 91, N.S. III. 412; Lond. S.A. Proc. 2 S. VII. 216, 356.

Tullie House. Stockading and timber platform. Arch. Jour. L. 20; Arch. Survey, 499; Cumb. and Westm. Arch. Soc. Trans. XII. 344; Lond. S.A. Proc. 2 S. XIV. 222; Newcastle S.A. Proc. V. 156.

Carlisle, Old, near Wigton. Station and buildings. Arch. Survey, 500; B.A.A. Jour. III. 43; Britton and Brayley, III. 196; Bruce's Rom. Wall, 362, and Handbook, 251; Cumb. and Westm. Arch. Soc. Trans. III. 64; Hodgson's Northumb. III. ii. 234; Horsley's Brit. Rom. 112; Hutchinson, II. 400; Lond. S.A. Archaeologia, X. 137; Lysons' Mag. Brit. IV. cxlii; Newcastle S.A. Proc. II. 158; Nicolson and Burn, II. 144; Stukeley's Itin. Curios. II. 54; Whellan, 267.

Castlesteads, or Cambeck Fort, Walton. Station and buildings. Arch. Survey, 500; Britton and Brayley, III. 126; Bruce's Rom. Wall, 276, 277; Coll. Antiq. IV. 148; Cumb. and Westm. Arch. Soc. Trans. I. 204, N.S. II. 391, III. 346; Gent. Mag. 1740, 171, 1742, 76, and Lib. Rom. Brit. Rem. i. 34; Hodgson's Northumb. III. ii. 211, 316; Horsley's Brit. Rom. 107; Hutchinson, I. 102; Lond. S.A. Archaeologia, XI. 63, and Minute Book, XVII. 17; Lysons' Mag. Brit. IV. cxxxviii; Maclauchlan, 62; Newcastle S.A. Proc. 3 S. II. 295; Nicolson and Burn, II. 483; Stukeley's Letters, II. 65, 105; Whellan, 694.

Denton, Nether. Fort and walls. Arch. Survey, 502; Cumb. and Westm. Arch. Soc. Trans. I. 88; Lond. S.A. Proc. 2 S. IV. 45.

Drumburgh. Station, etc. Antiquary, XXXVI. 8; Arch. Survey, 502; Britton and Brayley, III. 191; Bruce's Rom. Wall, 301, and Handbook, 240; Cumb. and Westm. Arch. Soc.

Trans. I. 209, XVI. 81 ; Hodgson's Northumb. III. ii. 223 ;
Horsley's Brit. Rom. 157; Hutchinson, II. 486; Lysons' Mag.
Brit. IV. cxl; Maclauchlan, 85 ; Newcastle S.A. Proc. II.
239, 3 S. III. 296; Nicolson and Burn, II. 214; Stukeley's
Letters, II. 64 ; Whellan, 151.

Ellenborough (Maryport). Station, buildings, etc. Arch. Jour.
XXXVII. 320 ; Arch. Survey, 503; Britton and Brayley, III.
202 ; Bruce's Rom. Wall, 365, and Handbook, 251 ; Cumb.
and Westm. Arch. Soc. Trans. V. 237 ; Ferguson, 68 ;
Hodgson's Northumb. III. ii. 238 ; Horsley's Brit. Rom. 113 ;
Hutchinson, II. 269 ; Lond. S.A. Archaeologia, II. 58, X.
140, and Proc. 2 S. VIII. 392 ; Lysons' Mag. Brit. IV. cxli,
clxxxvi ; Nicolson and Burn, II. 109; Stukeley's Itin.
Curios. II. 49 ; Whellan, 325.

Flimby, Risehow. Foundations. Arch. Jour. XXXVII. 344;
Arch. Survey, 504 ; Cumb. and Westm. Arch. Soc. Trans.
V. 124 (plan).

Gilsland. Fort and buildings. B.A.A. Jour. N.S. XV. 51 ;
Cumb. and Westm. Arch. Soc. Trans. IX. 164 (plan), XIII.
467, XIV. 401 ; Lond. S.A. Topog. Colls., brown portfolio
(plan of buildings) ; Newcastle S.A. Arch. Æliana, N.S. XII.
160 (plan).

Hardknott. Walled fort and buildings. Antiquary, XXVI. 25,
41, 90, 171, XXVIII. 137 ; Arch. Survey, 506 ; Britton and
Brayley, III. 235; Cumb. and Westm. Arch. Soc. Trans. VIII.
68, XII. 375 (plans), XIII. 449, N.S. I. 303 ; Cymmrodorion
Soc. Trans. 1908—9, 70 ; Ferguson, 63 ; Hutchinson, I. 569
(plan) ; Jefferson, S., Hist. of Allerdale, 1842, 184 ; Lysons'
Mag. Brit. IV. cxlviii ; Whellan, 411.

Harehill, near Lanercost. Turret. Arch. Survey, 506 ; Bruce's
Rom. Wall, 274 ; Lysons' Mag. Brit. IV. cxxxiii ; Maclauchlan, 58.

Harrow's Scar, near Birdoswald. Mile Castle. Cumb. and
Westm. Arch. Soc. Trans. XV. 375 (plan).

Keswick. Pavement. Arch. Survey, 509; Hutchinson, II. 155.

Kirkandrews-upon-Eden. Mile Castle. Arch. Survey, 509 ;
Maclauchlan, 80 ; Whellan, 170.

Kirksteads. Station. Arch. Survey, 509 ; Cumb. and Westm.

Arch. Soc. Trans. I. 148; Newcastle S.A. Proc. II. 237; Whellan, 171.

Lanercost. Camp and bridge. Arch. Survey, 510; Bruce's Rom. Wall, 272; Cumb. and Westm. Arch. Soc. Trans. I. 40.

Maryport, *see* Ellenborough.

Mawbray, or Mawburgh. Walled camp. Arch. Jour. XXXVI. 424, XXXVII. 230; Arch. Survey, 511; Cumb. and Westm. Arch. Soc. Trans. IV. 318, V. 136, N.S. I. 81; Ferguson, 71; Hutchinson, II. 346; Lond. S.A. Proc. 2 S. VIII. 206; Lysons' Mag. Brit. IV. cxxxvi; Whellan, 236, 238, 422.

Moresby. Station and foundations. Arch. Survey, 512; Britton and Brayley, III. 214; Bruce's Rom. Wall, 372; Ferguson, 67; Hodgson's Northumb. III. ii. 248; Hutchinson, II. 90; Jefferson, S., Hist. of Allerdale, 1842, 59; Lewis, III. 329; Newcastle S.A. Arch. Æliana, N.S. V. 138; Nicolson and Burn, II. 47; Stukeley's Itin. Curios. II. 52; Whellan, 421, 440.

Netherby. Station and buildings. Arch. Survey, 513; Britton and Brayley, III. 99; Bruce's Rom. Wall, 355, and Handbook, 251; Ferguson, 75; Gent. Mag. 1742, 76, 1750, 27, and Lib. Rom. Brit. Rem. i. 34, ii. 386; Gough's Brit. Topog. I. 287; Hodgson's Northumb. III. ii. 249, 316; Hutchinson, II. 533, 539 (plan); King's Mun. Antiq. II. 181; Lond. S.A. Archaeologia, II. 59, X. 141, and Minute Book, IX. 89, X. 179, XVI. 322, 339; Lysons' Mag. Brit. IV. cxlvi; Maitland's Scotland, I. 206; Nicolson and Burn, 469; Roy, 166, 197; Stukeley's Itin. Curios. II. 57, and Letters, II. 77, 85; Whellan, 628.

Old Wall. Foundations. Cumb. and Westm. Arch. Soc. Trans. XIII. 465 (plan).

Orton. Foundations. Arch. Survey, 513; Hutchinson, II. 516; Whellan, 175.

Papcastle. Station and buildings. Arch. Survey, 514; Britton and Brayley, III. 210; Ferguson, 68; Lewis, III. 515; Lysons' Mag. Brit. IV. cxlii; Nicolson and Burn, II. 104; Stukeley's Itin. Curios. II. 51, and Letters, II. 106; Whellan, 292, 301.

Penrith, Old, *see* Plumpton Wall.

Pike Hill, near Lanercost. Mile Castle. Arch. Survey, 514; Cumb. and Westm. Arch. Soc. Trans. I. 214 (plan).

Plumpton Wall. Station and buildings. Arch. Survey, 514; Britton and Brayley, III. 169; Bruce's Rom. Wall, 361, and Handbook, 251; Cumb. and Westm. Arch. Soc. Trans. XV. 46; Gent. Mag. 1790, ii. 982, and Lib. Rom. Brit. Rem. i. 36; Horsley's Brit. Rom. 111 (plan); Hutchinson, I. 477; Jefferson, S., Hist. of Leath Ward, 1840, 461; Lond. S.A. Archaeologia, X. 137; Lysons' Mag. Brit. IV. cxliii; Nicolson and Burn, II. 420; Warburton, 115; Whellan, 575.

Poltross Burn. Mile Castle, excavations, etc. Arch. Survey, 515; Cumb. and Westm. Arch. Soc. Trans. IX. 163, XV. 209; Lond. S.A. Proc. 2 S. XI. 209; Maclauchlan, 50; Newcastle S.A. Arch. Æliana, N.S. XII. 160.

Ravenglass, *see* Walls Castle.

Robin Hood's Butt, on Gillalees Beacon. Building. Cumb. and Westm. Arch. Soc. Trans. N.S. I. 82.

Stanwix. Station, etc. Arch. Survey, 517; Britton and Brayley, III. 97; Bruce's Rom. Wall, 290, and Handbook, 229; Cumb. and Westm. Arch. Soc. Trans. IX. 174; Ferguson, 87; Hodgson's Northumb. III. ii. 218; Horsley's Brit. Rom. 108; Hutchinson, II. 577; Lysons' Mag. Brit. IV. cxxxix; Maclauchlan, 74; Newcastle S.A. Arch. Æliana, N.S. XII. 170, and Proc. II. 234; Nicolson and Burn, II. 452; Stukeley's Itin. Curios. II. 56; Whellan, 140, 179.

Walls Castle, Ravenglass. Fort, buildings, etc. Arch. Survey, 519; Cumb. and Westm. Arch. Soc. Trans. III. 23, VI. 216; Ferguson, 61, 64; Hutchinson, I. 568; Lond. S.A. Proc. 2 S. VII. 357, IX. 61, XI. 210; Maxwell, Sir Herbert, Memories of the Month, 1 S. 1901, 119; Newcastle S.A. Proc. II. 322; Reliquary, N.S. II. 54; Whellan, 488.

Walton, *see* Castlesteads.

Watchcross. Station, etc. Arch. Survey, 520; Britton and Brayley, III. 131; Bruce's Rom. Wall, 288, and Handbook, 231; Hodgson's Northumb. III. ii. 218; Horsley's Brit. Rom. 154; Hutchinson, I. 121; Maclauchlan, 72; Nicolson and Burn, II. 485; Whellan, 681.

Willowford, Gilsland. Fort and bridge. Arch. Survey, 520;

Cumb. and Westm. Arch. Soc. Trans. IX. 166 ; Hutchinson, I. 65, 72 ; Maclauchlan, 52 ; Newcastle S.A. Arch. Æliana, N.S. XII. 162, and Proc. 3 S. II. 124.

Wolsty. Foundations. Arch. Survey, 520 ; Cumb. and Westm. Arch. Soc. Trans. V. 258.

The Wall (general), *see* Northumberland.

DERBYSHIRE

Bateman's Ten Years' Diggings. Bateman, T. Ten Years' Diggings in the counties of Derby, etc. 1861.

Bateman's Vestiges. Bateman, T. Vestiges of Antiquities in Derbyshire, 1848.

Bray. Bray, W. Tour in Derbyshire, 1783.

Derby Arch. Soc. Jour. Derbyshire Archaeological and Natural History Society Journal, I.—XXXIII. 1879—1910.

V.C.H. Victoria History of the Counties of England. Derbyshire, I. 1905.

Bradwell. Oven (?). Derby Arch. Soc. Jour. XXI. 1 (plan) ; V.C.H. I. 254 (plan).

Brough (*Anavio*). Station, buildings, excavations, etc. Antiquary, XXXIX. 291 ; Bateman's Ten Years' Diggings, 251, and Vestiges, 151 ; Bib. Top. Brit. Pt. XXIV. 39 ; Bray, 208 ; Britton and Brayley, III. 475 ; Builder, LXXXVI. 616 ; Derby Arch. Soc. Jour. VII. 80, XXVI. 177 (plans, etc.) ; Gough's Camden, II. 430 ; Lanc. and Ches. Antiq. Soc. Trans. XXI. 203 ; Lysons' Mag. Brit. V. ccxv ; V.C.H. I. 201 (plans, etc.).

Buxton (*Aquae*). Buildings and pavement. Bateman's Vestiges, 151 ; Bray, 227 ; Britton and Brayley, III. 438 ; Derby Arch. Soc. Jour. VII. 85, XXV. 159, 163, XXVI. 201 ; Gough's Camden, II. 437 ; Lewis, I. 448 ; Lond. S.A. Archaeologia, IX. 137 (plan), X. 27, and Minute Book, XXII. 332 ; Lysons' Mag. Brit. V. ccxvi ; Reliquary, III. 208 ; Reliquary and Illust. Arch. N.S. X. 54 ; V.C.H. I. 222 ; Whitaker, J., Hist. of Manchester, 2nd ed. 1773, I. 201.

Chester, Little (*Derventio*). Station, foundations, and pavements. Bateman's Vestiges, 145 ; Bray, 109 ; Britton and Brayley, III. 383 ; Derby Arch. Soc. Jour. VII. 75 ; Gough's

Camden, II. 419; Lewis, I. 567; Lond. S.A. Archaeologia, X. 26; Lysons' Mag. Brit. V. ccxv; Stukeley's Itin. Curios. I. 54 (plan); V.C.H. I. 216 (plan).

Crich. Foundations. Bateman's Vestiges, 158; Derby Arch. Soc. Jour. VIII. 226; Lysons' Mag. Brit. V. ccviii; V.C.H. I. 256.

Derby, *see* Chester, Little.

Melandra Castle. Station, buildings, excavations, gates and walls. Antiquary, XXXVI. 7; Bateman's Vestiges, 153; Britton and Brayley, III. 456; Derby Arch. Soc. Jour. VII. 87, XXIII. 90 (plans, etc.), XXIX. Appendix, the Report of the Manchester and District Branch of the Classical Association on the Excavations (plans, etc.); Gough's Camden, II. 431; King's Mun. Antiq. II. 63 (plan); Lanc. and Ches. Antiq. Soc. Trans. VI. 224, XVII. 105, 141, 258; Lond. S.A. Archaeologia, III. 236; Lysons' Mag. Brit. V. ccxvi; V.C.H. I. 210 (plans, etc.).

Parwich. Foundations. Bateman's Vestiges, 154; Lysons' Mag. Brit. V. ccxvii.

DEVONSHIRE

Devon Assoc. Trans.   Devonshire Association Transactions, I.—XLI. 1863—1909.
Oliver.   Oliver, G.   History of the city of Exeter, 1861.
Polwhele.   Polwhele, R.   History of Devonshire, 3 vols. 1793—1806.
Shortt.   Shortt, W. T. P.   Sylva Antiqua Iscana, Exeter, N.D.

Brixham (Berry Head). Walled fort. B.A.A. Coll. Arch. II. 23; Devon Assoc. Trans. XXIII. 77; Lysons' Mag. Brit. VI. cccli.

Chudleigh. Foundations of bridge. Devon Assoc. Trans. XXI. 436.

Exeter (*Isca Dumnuniorum*). Gates and walls. Polwhele, I. 184; Shortt, 55, 78, 137; Stukeley's Itin. Curios. I. 156 (plan).
Cathedral (near). Pavement. B.A.A. Jour. XVIII. 260; Devon Assoc. Trans. XXIII. 84; Gent. Mag. 1843, i. 191, and Lib. Rom. Brit. Rem. i. 44; Oliver, 2.

Fore Street. Pavement. Polwhele, I. 185.

High Street. Buildings and pavement. B.A.A. Jour. XVIII. 260; Devon Assoc. Trans. XXIII. 84; Jenkins, A., Hist. of Exeter, 1806, 6 n; Lond. S.A. Archaeologia, VI. 5; Lysons' Mag. Brit. VI. cccx; Shortt, 55, 142, and Nos. 10 and 15 on plan.

Pancras Lane. Pavement. B.A.A. Jour. XVIII. 260, and Coll. Arch. II. 28; Devon Assoc. Trans. XXIII. 84; Lysons' Mag. Brit. VI. cccx; Polwhele, I. 185; Shortt, No. 16 on plan; Stukeley's Itin. Curios. I. 158.

Queen Street. Buildings. B.A.A. Jour. I. 140, XVIII. 260.

South Street. Buildings and pavement. B.A.A. Jour. XVIII. 260; Devon Assoc. Trans. XXIII. 83; Devon and Cornwall Notes and Gleanings, III. 97; Gent. Mag. 1834, ii. 40; Oliver, 2; Shortt, 21, 23, 25, 29, 35, 41, 114, 139, 140.

Holcombe, *see* Uplyme.

Modbury. Foundations (?). Devon Assoc. Trans. XXIII. 79; Gent. Mag. 1846, ii. 517, and Lib. Rom. Brit. Rem. i. 44.

Seaton (Hannaditches). Buildings. Devon Assoc. Trans. XXIII. 48, 54, 81.

Teignbridge. Bridge. Devon Assoc. Trans. XXXIII. 81; Lond. S.A. Archaeologia, XIX. 308; Lysons' Mag. Brit. VI. cccxi.

Uplyme (Holcombe). Buildings and pavement. Arch. Jour. XI. 49; B.A.A. Jour. VI. 450; Builder, VIII. 471; Devon Assoc. Trans. XXIII. 48, 54, 82; Lond. S.A. Archaeologia, XLV. 462 (plan), Proc. 1 S. II. 265, 2 S. V. 276, and Topog. Colls., red portfolio (plan, etc.).

DORSETSHIRE

Dorset Field Club Proc. Dorset Natural History and Antiquarian Field Club Proceedings, I.—XXX. 1877—1909.

Hutchins. Hutchins, J. History of the county of Dorset, 3rd ed., 4 vols., 1861—67.

Warne's Anc. Dorset. Warne, C. Ancient Dorset, 1872.

Warne's Vestiges. Warne, C. Dorsetshire, its Vestiges, Celtic, Roman, etc., 1865.

Bere Regis (Kingston Down). Walled well. Lond. S.A. Archaeologia, XXXIX. 87.

Bradford Abbas. Floors and ovens. Dorset Field Club Proc. II. 53.

Charminster. Pavement. Dorset Field Club Proc. XIII. xxii, XVII. xxv.

Dewlish. Pavement. Arch. Jour. XXII. 345 ; Arch. Review, IV. 297 ; Hutchins, II. 607.

Dorchester (*Durnovaria*). Amphitheatre. Arch. Review, IV. 297 ; B.A.A. Jour. II. 101, XXVIII. 91 ; Britton and Brayley, IV. 341 ; Dorset Field Club Proc. I. 8 ; Stukeley's Itin. Curios. I. 163 ; Warne's Anc. Dorset, 213, and Vestiges, 22.

Walls and gates. Arch. Jour. XXII. 348 ; Barnes, W., Guide to Dorchester ; Blome's Britannia, 86 ; Britton and Brayley, IV. 339 ; Dorset Field Club Proc. XII. xxxi, 135, XIV. xxii, 44, XX. 131 ; Hutchins, II. 394 ; Lewis, II. 69, 70 ; Stukeley's Itin. Curios. I. 161 ; Warne's Anc. Dorset, 210, and Vestiges, 22.

All Saints Glebe. Pavement. Dorset Field Club Proc. XXIV. xliii.

Castle or Gaol. Buildings and pavement. Arch. Jour. XVI. 82, 183, XXII. 344, 348 ; Arch. Review, IV. 298 ; Athenaeum, Sept. 25, 1858 ; B.A.A. Jour. XXVIII. 214 ; Dorset Field Club Proc. XXIX. lxxviii ; Hutchins, II. 394 ; Lond. S.A. Archaeologia, XVII. 330, Minute Book, XXXIII. 84, and Topog. Colls., red portfolio (drawing of a pavement) ; Morgan, 211 ; Warne's Anc. Dorset, 212. Pavement now in gaol chapel.

Cedar Park. Pavement. Dorset Field Club Proc. XVI. xliii.

Durngate Street. Pavement. Antiquary, XLI. 286 ; Blandford Herald, July 13, 1905 ; Dorset Field Club Proc. XXVII. 239 ; Times, July 10, 1905. Orig. pav. in museum.

Fordington Field. Pavement. Athenaeum, Sept. 2, 1899 ; B.A.A. Jour. N.S. v. 266.

Gas Works. Pavement. Antiquary, XXXVIII. 108.

Icen Way. Pavement. Antiquary, XXXVII. 195 ; Builder, LXXX. 543.

Olga Road. Buildings and pavement. Antiquary, XXXV. 289, 364 ; Dorset Field Club Proc. XXII. xxiv, xxviii, XXIII. 110, XXVII. 239. Portion of orig. pav. in museum.

Somerleigh Court. Pavement. Antiquary, XX. 124; Arch. Review, IV. 299; Dorset County Chronicle, Aug. 1, 1899; Dorset Field Club Proc. XIV. xxiv.

South Street. Pavements. Antiquary, XXXVI. 105; Arch. Review, IV. 299; Builder, LXXVII. 602; Dorset Field Club Proc. XVIII. xxiii; Hutchins, II. 394; Lond. S.A. Proc. 2 S. XXI. 154; Warne's Anc. Dorset, 212.

S.W. angle of town. Pavement. Arch. Review, IV. 299; B.A.A. Jour. XX. 201; Gent. Mag. 1841, ii. 413, and Lib. Rom. Brit. Rem. i. 56; Hutchins, II. 396; Warne's Anc. Dorset, 212.

Mr Templeman's garden (1747). Pavement. Hutchins, II. 692; Warne's Anc. Dorset, 212.

Victoria Park. Pavement. Builder, LXXVII. 485, 602.

Locality not given. Pavements. Antiquary, XXXI. 101, XXXIII. 230; Builder, LXXIX. 470; Wright's Celt, Roman and Saxon, 253.

Fifehead Neville. Buildings and pavement. Antiquary, XXXIX. 4; Arch. Jour. XXXVIII. 433; Builder, LXXXIII. 535; Dorset Field Club Proc. XXIV. xxxix, lxxiv, 172; Lond. S.A. Proc. 2 S. VIII. 543, IX. 66, and Topog. Colls., brown portfolio (drawings); Morgan, 215.

Frampton. Buildings and pavement. Arch. Jour. XVI. 186, XXII. 345; Arch. Review, IV. 300; B.A.A. Jour. XXVIII. 217, XXXVIII. 303; Britton and Brayley, IV. 511; Dorset Field Club Proc. XXI. 176; Hutchins, II. 685-7; Lysons' Reliquiae, I. Pt. 3; Morgan, 33, 60, 201, 211; Warne's Vestiges, 10; Wright's Celt, Roman and Saxon, 250, 253, 356.

Halstock. Pavement. Arch. Review, IV. 300; Gent. Mag. 1818, i. 5, and Lib. Rom. Brit. Rem. i. 56.

Hemsworth, see Witchampton.

Hod Hill. Buildings. Warne's Anc. Dorset, 154.

Holcombe, see Uplyme, Devon.

Holwell, near Cranborne. Buildings and pavement. Arch. Jour. XLIV. 395; Warne's Anc. Dorset, 225 n.

Iwerne Minster. Buildings. Antiquary, XXXIII. 16; Dorset Field Club Proc. XII. xxxiii.

Jordan Hill, see Preston.

Maiden Newton. Pavement. Arch. Review, IV. 301; Hutchins, II. 687; Lewis, III. 205.

Milton Abbas (Bagber). Kiln. Arch. Review, IV. 296; Dorset Field Club Proc. XIII. 23, XVII. 127; Warne's Vestiges, 14, 38.

Portland. Pavement. B.A.A. Jour. XXVIII. 32.

Preston (Jordan Hill). Buildings and pavements. Arch. Jour. I. 280, 385, XXII. 345; Arch. Review, IV. 302; Athenaeum, Dec. 7, 1844; B.A.A. Jour. I. 324, XXVIII. 90, 93, 94; Buckland, F., Curiosities of Natural History, 2 S. 107, 109, 111; Builder, XCIII. 107; Dorset Field Club Proc. X. xxviii, XXI. xxxv, 205 (plan); Gent. Mag. 1844, i. 185, and Lib. Rom. Brit. Rem. i. 60; Harford, H. C., Essay on Roman remains near Weymouth, 1844 (plan); Lond. and Middsx. Arch. Soc. Trans. III. 503; Lond. S.A. Archaeologia, XLVI. 447, Proc. 1 S. I. 32, and Minute Book, XXXVIII. 381; Morgan, 214; Oxford Ashmolean Soc. I. 55; Price's Roman Antiquities, 34; Warne's Anc. Dorset, 224, 225, 227.

Rampisham. Pavement. Arch. Jour. XXII. 345; Arch. Review, IV. 302; Dorset Field Club Proc. XVII. xxxvii; Hutchins, II. 692; Warne's Vestiges, 10.

Rushmore, *see* Woodcuts and Woodyates.

Sherborne: The Abbey. Pavement. Dorset Field Club Proc. XII. xxii.

Lenthy Common. Pavement. Arch. Jour. II. 85, XXII. 345, 360; Arch. Review, IV. 301; B.A.A. Jour. I. 57; Dorset Field Club Proc. XIV. xxix; Warne's Vestiges, I. Now in the dairy of Sherborne Castle.

Tarrant Hinton. Buildings with pavement. Arch. Jour. XLIV. 392; Arch. Review, IV. 302; B.A.A. Winchester vol. 1845, 179; Dorset Field Club Proc. XXX. 3; Morgan, 201, 214.

Thornford. Buildings. Arch. Review, IV. 302; Dorset Field Club Proc. I. 41.

Tollard Green. Foundations. Arch. Jour. XXIV. 168.

Wareham. Town. Dorset Field Club Proc. XII. 115.

Creech Grange. Pavement. Dorset Field Club Proc. X. xvi, XI. xix.

Furzebrook. Pavement. Antiquary, XIX. 78; Dorset Field Club Proc. XIII. 90.

Weymouth (Newberry Terrace). Buildings and pavement. Antiquary, XXXVIII. 108; Dorset Field Club Proc. XXIII. xxvi. *See also* Preston, Jordan Hill.

Witchampton (Hemsworth). Buildings and pavement. Antiquary, XLIV. 407; Arch. Jour. XXIV. 167, XLIV. 391; Builder, XCV. 395; Dorset Field Club Proc. XI. 19, XXX. 1; Somerset and Dorset Notes and Queries, XI. 177, 178; Times, Oct. 12 and 20, 1908; Warne's Vestiges, 17. Orig. pav. in Brit. Mus.

Woodcuts. Hypocausts. Arch. Review, IV. 303; Lanc. and Ches. Antiq. Soc. Trans. V. 334, VIII. 2; Pitt-Rivers, Lt.-Gen., Excavations in Cranborne Chase, I. 16, 29 (plans, etc.); Wilts. Arch. Soc. Mag. XXV. 284, 300.

Woodyates. Hypocausts. Lanc. and Ches. Antiq. Soc. Trans. VIII. 2; Pitt-Rivers, Lt.-Gen., Excavations in Bokerly and Wansdyke, 15, 67, 82 (plans, etc.).

Wynford Eagle. Buildings and pavement. Arch. Jour. XXII. 345; Arch. Review, IV. 303; B.A.A. Jour. XX. 273.

DURHAM

Billings. Billings, R. W. Illustrations of the Architectural Antiquities of the county of Durham, 1846.

Bruce's Rom. Wall. Bruce, J. Collingwood. The Roman Wall, 3rd ed. 1867.

Bruce's Handbook. Bruce, J. C. Handbook to the Roman Wall, 6th ed. 1909.

Durham and Northumb. Arch. Soc. Trans. Durham and Northumberland Architectural and Archaeological Society Transactions, I.—v. 1870—1907.

Hodgson. Hodgson, J. History of Northumberland, 3 vols., 1820—58.

Maclauchlan. Maclauchlan, H. Memoir on the Watling Street, 1852.

Newcastle S.A. Newcastle Society of Antiquaries.

   (*a*)   Archaeologia Æliana, I.—IV. (1816—54), N.S. I.—XXXV. (1857—1903), 3 S. I.—VI. (1904—1909).

   (*b*)   Proceedings, I.—X. (1883—1902), 3 S. I.—III. (1903—1909).

   (*c*)   Lapidarium Septentrionale, 1870.

Surtees. Surtees, R. History of the county of Durham, 4 vols., 1816—40.

Binchester (*Vinovium*). Station, buildings, etc. Antiquary, III. 83; Auckland Chronicle, Feb. 28, 1879; B.A.A. Jour. XLIII. 111 (plan), 177, 299 (plan), XLVI. 253 (plan); Britton and

Brayley, V. 217; Bruce's Rom. Wall, 353, and Handbook, 250; Builder, XXXIV. 77, 78 (plan), XXXVII. 289; Coll. Antiq. IV. 134; Hooppell, R. E., A Lecture on Vinovium, 1879, and Vinovia, a buried Roman City, 1891 (plans); Lewis, I. 239; Maclauchlan, 4, 6; Newcastle S.A. Arch. Æliana N.S. IX. 191, and Lapid. Septen. 371.

Chester-le-Street. Buildings. B.A.A. Jour. XXII. 87; Bruce's Rom. Wall, 310, and Handbook, 247; Newcastle S.A. Arch. Æliana, IV. 292, and Lapid. Septen. 279.

Ebchester. Buildings. Antiquary, XVIII. 75; Arch. Review, II. 51; Bruce's Rom. Wall, 346, and Handbook, 249; Phil. Trans. XXIII. 1129; Maclauchlan, 16; Surtees, II. 299.

Hylton. Bridge. Hooppell, R. E., On the evidences of a Roman bridge at Hylton, 1882; Newcastle Daily Journal, July 27, 1882.

Jarrow. Foundations. Bruce's Rom. Wall, 308; Hodgson, III. ii. 230; Lewis, II. 620; Newcastle S.A. Arch. Æliana, N.S. XXII. 30.

Lanchester. Station, buildings, etc. B.A.A. Jour. XXII. 87; Billings, 51; Britton and Brayley, V. 206; Bruce's Rom. Wall, 347, and Handbook, 249; Coll. Antiq. IV. 136; Durham and Northumb. Arch. Soc. Trans. IV. xlii, V. xlv; Maclauchlan, 13, 14; Newcastle S.A. Arch. Æliana, I. 118, and Proc. 3 S. II. 403, 406, 407; Surtees, II. 303, 304.

Piercebridge. Buildings. B.A.A. Jour. XLIII. 91; Britton and Brayley, V. 223; Maclauchlan, 2; Newcastle S.A. Proc. 3 S. I. 123.

Seaton Carew. Buildings. Arch. Instit. Newcastle vol. 1852, I. 52.

Shields, South. Station, buildings, etc. B.A.A. Jour. XXXIV. 233, 255, 373 (plan), XLII. 430; Britton and Brayley, V. 158; Bruce's Rom. Wall, 308, and Handbook, 245; Hodgson, III. ii. 228, 316; Hooppell, R. E., On the Discovery and Explorations of Roman Remains at South Shields, 1878 (plans, etc.); Lewis, IV. 79; Lond. S.A. Archaeologia, XLVI. 163 (plan); Newcastle S.A. Arch. Æliana, N.S. X. 223, 230 (plan), 3 S I. 94, III. 10, and Lapid. Septen. 273; Surtees, II. 101.

Stanley. Fort. Arch. Instit. Newcastle vol. 1852, I. 52.

Wearmouth. Building. Arch. Instit. Newcastle vol. 1852, I. 52.

ESSEX

Essex Arch. Soc. Trans. Essex Archaeological Society Transactions, I.—V.
1858—73, N.S. I.—XI. 1878—1910.
Essex Review, 1892—1910.
Morant's Colchester. Morant, P. History of Colchester, 1748.
Morant's Essex. Morant, P. History of Essex, 2 vols., 1768.
Muilman. Muilman, P. History of Essex, 6 vols., 1770—72.
Ogborne. Ogborne, E. History of Essex, 1814.
Salmon. Salmon, N. History of Essex, 1739.
Wright's Essex. Wright, T. History of Essex, 2 vols., 1842.

Alresford. Buildings and pavement. Antiquary, XI. 36; Athenaeum, Dec. 6, 1884; Essex Arch. Soc. Trans. N.S. III. 114, 130, 136 (plan), X. 87; Lond. S.A. Proc. 2 S. X. 178. Piece of original pavement in Colchester museum.

Ashdon. Buildings and kiln. Arch. Jour. X. 14, 16 (plan of building), 21, 22 (plan of kiln); Essex Arch. Soc. Trans. I. 195.

Bartlow. Buildings. Arch. Jour. X. 17, 18 (plan); Essex Arch. Soc. Trans. I. 195; Lond. S.A. Archaeologia, XXV. 6, XXVI. 462.

Billericay. Buildings (?). Essex Arch. Soc. Trans. II. 69.

Bradwell-near-the-Sea (*Othona*). Station, walls, etc. Arch. Jour. XXII. 64, XXIII. 60, LXIV. 201; Athenaeum, Oct. 22 and Nov. 12, 1864; Blome's Britannia, 97; Gent. Mag. 1865, ii. 403, and Lib. Rom. Brit. Rem. i. 67; Lond. S.A. Archaeologia, XLI. 439 (plan), and Proc. 2 S. III. 520; Reliquary and Illust. Arch. N.S. XIV. 258 (plan); Wright's Celt, Roman and Saxon, 448.

Brightlingsea. Buildings and pavement. Essex Arch. Soc. Trans. N.S. III. 137, X. 88; Lond. S.A. Proc. 2 S. XI. 195.

Chelmsford. Buildings. Arch. Jour. XVIII. 94; Athenaeum, Dec. 15, 1849; B.A.A. Jour. VI. 81; Essex Arch. Soc. Trans. I. 59 (plan), N.S. X. 117; Lond. S.A. Proc. 1 S. II. 28.

Chesterford, Great. Station, buildings, kilns and pavements. Arch. Jour. VI. 14, 18 (plan of building), XVII. 117, 158; B.A.A. Jour. III. 328, IV. 368 (plan of building), V. 54; Britton and Brayley, V. 381; Cambs. Antiq. Soc. Proc. X.

178 (kiln), and Trans. XX. 66; Essex Arch. Soc. Trans. I.
193, N.S. IX. 190; Gent. Mag. 1848, ii. 633, and Lib. Rom.
Brit. Rem. i. 72; King's Mun. Antiq. II. 55; Lewis, I. 569;
Lond. S.A. Archaeologia, IV. 84, 95, XXXII. 350; Morant, II.
553; Muilman, II. 328; Neville, Hon. R. C., Antiqua Explorata, 7, 9 (plan of station), and Sepulchra Exposita, 87
(plan of building and pavements); Salmon's Essex, 135,
and Herts. 261; Stukeley's Itin. Curios. I. 78 (plan), and
Letters II. 148; Wright's Essex, II. 131, and Celt, Roman
and Saxon, 204.

Chigwell. Pavement. Lond. S.A. Minute Book, XXIII. 270.

Chipping Ongar. Foundations. Britton and Brayley, V. 424;
Wright's Essex, II. 330.

Coggeshall. Foundations. Britton and Brayley, V. 341; Muilman, VI. 113; Dr Laver, F.S.A., notes foundations, etc., on
south side of church.

Colchester (*Camulodunum*). Walls, gates, etc. Antiquary, XII.
86, 97; Archaeologia Oxoniensis, 1892—95, 93, 175; Arch.
Instit. Winchester vol. 1845, under Porchester Castle, 16, 17;
B.A.A. Jour. II. 29, XXI. 169, L. 192; Blome's Britannia, 96;
Britton and Brayley, V. 286; Cutt's Colchester, caps. III.
and IV.; Essex Arch. Soc. Trans. I. 26; Lewis, I. 638; Lond.
S.A. Archaeologia, IV. 84, 95; Morant's Colchester, i. 5, and
Essex, I. i. 5; Muilman, VI. 254; Parish, J., Portfolio of
Antiquities, No. 1, Colchester, 1876; Scarth's Rom. Brit.
151; Wright's Celt, Roman and Saxon, 45, 52, 122, 159, 177,
188, and Essex, I. 268.

Angel Lane. Pavement. B.A.A. Jour. III. 318; Essex Arch.
Soc. Trans. N.S. X. 84, 89; Lond. S.A. Archaeologia, II. 287,
and Minute Book, XII. 204; Morgan, 150.

Berry Fields. Pavement. Morant's Colchester, iii. 21, and
Essex I. iii. 183; Wright's Essex, I. 295.

Botanic Garden. Pavement. Essex Arch. Soc. Trans. I. 36,
V. 159.

Castle Grounds. Buildings, drain and pavements. Antiquary,
XXVI. 187, XXVII. 24, XLII. 327; B.A.A. Jour. II. 37, N.S.
XII. 210, XIII. 71; Essex Arch. Soc. Trans. I. 55, 210, N.S.
IV. 299, IX. 122 (plan), X. 90, 323 (plan); Lond. S.A. Proc.

2 S. XIV. 242 ; Morant's Colchester, iii. 21, and Essex, I. iii. 183; Wright's Essex, I. 295.

Chantry Lands. Pavement. Essex Arch. Soc. Trans. V. 159.

Cherry Garden. Pavement. Morant's Colchester, iii. 21, and Essex, I. iii. 183.

Culver Street. Pavements. Antiquary, XV. 29 ; Essex Arch. Soc. Trans. N.S. III. 207, X. 88; Lond. S.A. Proc. 2 S. XI. 195. Piece of one pav. in town museum.

East Hill. Pavement. Essex Arch. Soc. Trans. N.S. X. 89; Lond. S.A. Archaeologia, XVI. 147.

Gardeners' Market. Pavement. Essex Arch. Soc. Trans. V. 155.

Head Street. Pavement. Essex Arch. Soc. Trans. N.S. III. 140; Lond. S.A. Proc. 2 S. VIII. 543 ; Morant's Colchester, iii. 21, and Essex, I. iii. 183 ; Wright's Essex, I. 295.

Herrick's Chapel. Pavement. Essex Arch. Soc. Trans. V. 159.

High Street. Pavements. Britton and Brayley, V. 293 ; Essex Arch. Soc. Trans. V. 154, 158, 160, N.S. X. 87, 89 ; Lond. S.A. Archaeologia, XVI. 147 ; Morant's Colchester, iii. 21, and Essex, I. iii. 183, 184; Morgan, 150 ; Stukeley's Letters, II. 162, 163 ; Wright's Essex, I. 295, 309.

Holy Trinity parish. Pavements. Britton and Brayley, V. 293 ; Morant's Colchester, iii. 21, and Essex, I. iii. 183 ; Wright's Essex, I. 295.

Hospital Garden. Pavement. Essex Arch. Soc. Trans. N.S. X. 89.

Lion Walk. Pavement. Essex Arch. Soc. Trans. V. 155, 157.

Long Wire Street. Pavement. Essex Arch. Soc. Trans. V. 157, N.S. X. 89.

Lordsland. Pavement. Essex Arch. Soc. Trans. V. 159, N.S. X. 89.

North Bridge. Wall. Gent. Mag. 1843, ii. 189, and Lib. Rom. Brit. Rem. i. 73.

North Hill. Buildings and pavements. Antiquary, XLII. 447; B.A.A. Jour. I. 54, 339, N.S. XII. 289; Essex Arch. Soc. Trans. IV. 53 (plan), V. 155, 156, 159, 161, N.S. X. 84, 85. Portions of pavements in town museum.

North Street. Pavement. Essex Arch. Soc. Trans. N.S. II. 189, III. 129, X. 87. Portion in town museum.

Osborne Street. Pavement. Antiquary, XXXIX. 65 ; Essex Arch. Soc. Trans. N.S. X. 88. Portion in town museum.

Papillon Road. Pavement. Antiquary, XXXI. 130.

Peoples' Hall. Pavement. Essex Arch. Soc. Trans. V. 158.

Queen Street. Pavement. Essex Arch. Soc. Trans. N.S. X. 89. Portion in town museum.

St Martin's Lane. Pavement. B.A.A. Jour. II. 366 ; Essex Arch. Soc. Trans. V. 160 ; Gent. Mag. 1794, ii. 801, and Lib. Rom. Brit. Rem. i. 72 ; Lond. S.A. Archaeologia, XVI. 147, Vet. Mon. III. pl. 39, and Topog. Colls., red portfolio (drawing).

St Mary-at-the-Wall. Buildings and pavements. B.A.A. Jour. XXI. 231 ; Britton and Brayley, V. 293 ; Essex Arch. Soc. Trans. V. 155, 156, 160 ; Morant's Colchester, iii. 21, and Essex, I. iii. 183 ; Wright's Essex, I. 295.

St Peter. Concrete floor. Essex Arch. Soc. Trans. V. 155.

Sheep's Head Field (near). Pavement. Essex Arch. Soc. Trans. V. 157.

Stockwell Street. Pavement. Essex Arch. Soc. Trans. V. 156, 159.

Terrace. Pavement. Essex Arch. Soc. Trans. V. 155.

No locality given. Buildings or pavements. B.A.A. Jour. I. 54, V. 85 ; Builder, LI. 682 ; Muilman, VI. 304.

Faulkbourn. Foundations. Lewis, II. 218 ; Wright's Essex, I. 226.

Hadstock. Buildings and pavement. Arch. Jour. VII. 389, VIII. 27 (plan), X. 64, XIV. 63 ; Athenaeum, Jan. 23, 1847 ; Cambs. Antiq. Soc. Trans. III. 23, XX. 35 ; Essex Arch. Soc. Trans. I. 193, 195, II. 62 ; Gent. Mag. 1850, ii. 418, and Lib. Eng. Topog. iv. 114 ; Lond. S.A. Archaeologia, XXXII. 352, and Proc. I S. I. 171 ; Neville, Hon. R. C., Antiqua Explorata, 36.

Harlow. Foundations and pavement. Essex Arch. Soc. Trans. I. 199 ; Lond. S.A. Archaeologia, XIX. 410, and Minute Book, XXXIV. 316, 317 ; Wright's Essex, II. 292.

Harwich. Pavement. Essex Arch. Soc. Trans. I. 198; Lewis, II. 427; Morant's Essex, I. 499.

Heydon. Foundations. B.A.A. Jour. III. 340, IV. 76; Cambs. Antiq. Soc. Trans. III. 64, XX. 102 (plan); Price's Rom. Antiq. 41.

Kelvedon. Building. Essex Arch. Soc. Trans. I. 198.

Latton. Foundations. Wright's Essex, I. 269.

Lexden (Stanway). Buildings and pavement. B.A.A. Jour. II. 45; Coll. Antiq. II. 41; Essex Arch. Soc. Trans. V. 92; Gent. Mag. 1842, ii. 526, and Lib. Rom. Brit. Rem. i. 73; Morgan, 150.

   Kilns. Arch. Jour. XXXIV. 302; Athenaeum, March 24, 1877; B.A.A. Jour. XXXIII. 221, 230, 231, 258, 267 (plan), 468; Builder, XXXV. 499; Coll. Antiq. VII. 1; Essex Arch. Soc. Trans. N.S. I. 192, V. 77; Lond. S.A. Proc. 2 S. IV. 433; Scarth's Rom. Brit. 151.

Leyton, see Wanstead.

Littlebury. Foundations. Morant's Essex, II. 594; Muilman, III. 67; Salmon, 133.

Mersea, West. Buildings and pavements. Antiquary, XXXIII. 231; Britton and Brayley, V. 324; Essex Arch. Soc. Trans. N.S. III. 132, VI. 284, VII. 112; Lond. S.A. Archaeologia, V. 230, XVI. 148, Proc. 2 S. XVI. 426 (plan), Minute Book, I. 96, and Topog. Colls., red portfolio (pavement found in 1767); Morant's Essex, I. 15, 424, 425; Muilman, V. 449; Salmon, 434. Piece of an orig. pav. in Colchester museum.

Pleshy. Traces of pavement. Gough, R., Hist. of Pleshy, 1803, 3; Wright, II. 255.

Ridgewell. Buildings and pavements. B.A.A. Jour. XIX. 279; Britton and Brayley, V. 374; Essex Arch. Soc. Trans. I. 197; Essex Review, II. 189; Lond. S.A. Archaeologia, XIV. 61, 62 (plan), XXXV. 62, and Minute Book, XXVIII. 342; Muilman, II. 194; Wright's Essex, I. 39, 605.

Rivenhall. Buildings and pavement. B.A.A. Jour. II. 281, 339; Essex Review, III. 145; Gent. Mag. 1847, i. 185, and Lib. Rom. Brit. Rem. i. 80.

St Osyth. Buildings and pavement. Essex Arch. Soc. Trans. N.S. X. 88.

Shoebury.   Camp, etc.   Arch. Jour. XLVII. 78 (plan).

  Kiln.   Essex Arch. Soc. Trans. N.S. IV. 202, VI. 13 (plan), 195;
    Lond. S.A. Proc. 2 S. XVI. 40 (plan).

Stanway, *see* Lexden.

Tollesbury.   Foundations (?).   B.A.A. Jour. XXXII. 419.

Tolleshunt Knights.   Pavement.   Essex Arch. Soc. Trans. I.
    199; Morant's Essex, I. 393.

Wakering.   Kiln.   Essex Review, V. 61.

Wanstead (Leyton).   Buildings and pavements.   Britton and
    Brayley, V. 467; Essex Arch. Soc. Trans. I. 199, N.S. X. 20;
    Gough's Camden, II. 348; Hammock, W. G., Hist. of Leyton-
    stone, 4; Kennedy, J., Hist. of Leyton, 2; King's Mun. Antiq.
    II. 170; Lewis, III. 78, IV. 452; Lond. S.A. Archaeologia, I.
    73, and Minute Book, II. 98; Lysons' Environs, IV. 158, 231;
    Morant's Essex, I. 22, 28; Muilman, IV. 226, 241; Ogborne,
    79; Stukeley's Letters, II. 145, 154.

Wenden.   Buildings.   Arch. Jour. X. 170, 357, XI. 77 (plan);
    Essex Arch. Soc. Trans. I. 193.

GLOUCESTERSHIRE

Atkyns.   Atkyns, Sir R.   The Ancient and Present state of Gloucestershire,
    1712.

Bath Field Club Proc.   Bath Natural History and Antiquarian Field Club
    Proceedings, I.—X. 1867—1905.

Bigland.   Bigland, R.   History of Gloucestershire, 2 vols., 1791—92.

Bristol and Glouc. Arch. Soc. Trans.   Bristol and Gloucestershire Archaeo-
    logical Society Transactions, I.—XXXI. 1876—1908.

Clifton Antiq. Club Proc.   Clifton Antiquarian Club Proceedings, I.—VI.
    1888—1908.

Cotts. Field Club Proc.   Cottswold Field Club Proceedings.

Fosbroke.   Fosbroke, T. D.   History of Gloucestershire, 2 vols., 1807.

Glouc. N. and Q.   Gloucestershire Notes and Queries, I.—VI. 1881—1906.

Lysons' Reliquiae.   Lysons, S.   Reliquiae Britannico Romanae, vol. II.
    Roman Antiquities discovered in Gloucestershire, 1817.

Lysons' Romans in Glouc.   Lysons, S.   The Romans in Gloucestershire.
    A lecture, 1860.

Lysons' Woodchester.   Lysons, S.   An account of Roman Antiquities dis-
    covered at Woodchester, 1797.

Rudder.   Rudder, S.   History of Gloucestershire, 1779.

Rudge. Rudge, T. History and Antiquities of Gloucester, 1811.

Scarth's Rom. Bath. Scarth, H. M. Aquae Solis, or Notices of Roman Bath, 1864.

Seyer. Seyer, S. Memoirs of Bristol, 2 vols., 1821—23.

Witts. Witts, G. B. Archaeological Handbook of the county of Gloucester, with map, 1883.

Beach, *see* Tracy Park.

Bibury. Buildings and pavement. Pointer, J., Account of a Roman pavement found at Stunsfield, Oxon., 1713, 37; Witts, 55.

Bisley (Lillyhorn). Buildings and pavement. Arch. Jour. II. 42 (plan), XX. 186; Athenaeum, Dec. 14, 1844, 1154; B.A.A. Jour. I. 44, II. 324 (plan); Bristol and Glouc. Arch. Soc. Trans. IV. 208, V. 11, 14, 38; Lewis, I. 257; Morgan, 79; Witts, 55 (plan on map).

(Custom Scrubs). Buildings. Bristol and Glouc. Arch. Soc. Trans. V. 39; Lewis, I. 257.

Bitton. Buildings and pavement. Arch. Instit. Bristol vol. 1851, lxvi; Bristol and Glouc. Arch. Soc. Trans. III. 28, 88; Cotts. Field Club Proc. VI. 231; Rudder, 294; Scarth's Rom. Bath, 125; Somerset Arch. Soc. Proc. V. ii. 59.

Bourton-on-the-Water. Buildings. Bristol and Glouc. Arch. Soc. Trans. VII. 16, 71, XX. 265, 349; Cotts. Field Club Proc. VI. 209; Rudder, 303; Witts, 56.

Brockworth, *see* Witcombe.

Brown's Hill, *see* Stroud.

Chedworth. Buildings and pavements. Arch. Cantiana, XV. 43; Arch. Jour. XXI. 391, XXII. 370, XLIV. 322 (plan), XLVII. 423; B.A.A. Jour. XXIV. 129, XXV. 177, 215 (plan), 400, XXVI. 251, XXIX. 126, XXXVIII. 303; Bath Field Club Proc. I. ii. 18 n, 68, iii. 88; Bristol and Glouc. Arch. Soc. Trans. II. 19, IV. 208, XIII. 99, XIV. 214, XX. 265, 266, 349, XXX. 13; Britton and Brayley, V. 667; Buckman, J., and Hall, R. W., Roman Villa at Chedworth, 1872 (plan); Builder, XXIII. 605, XXIV. 904, XXVI. 639; Clifton Antiq. Club Proc. I. 296, II. 57; Cotts. Field Club Proc. IV. 201, 233; Fosbroke, II. 519; Gent. Mag. 1865, ii. 302 and Lib. Rom. Brit. Rem. i. 81; Glouc. N. and Q. I. 215; Lewis, I. 547; Lond. S.A.

Archaeologia, LIX. 210 (plan); Morgan, 33, 69, 80 (plan); Rudder, 334; Scot. S.A. Proc. VI. 278; Somerset Arch. Soc. Proc. XXII. 38; Witts, 57 (plan on map).

Cherington. Buildings. Bristol and Glouc. Arch. Soc. Trans. XX. 265; Lond. S.A. Archaeologia, XVIII. 114 (plan), 117; Lysons' Romans in Glouc. 42; Morgan, 68; Witts, 58; Wright's Celt, Roman and Saxon, 227.

Cirencester (*Corinium*). Amphitheatre, buildings, pavements, walls, etc. (general). Arch. Jour. VI. 318, 321, VIII. 187, 415, IX. 91, XIV. 354, XVII. 333, 345; Atkyns, 350; B.A.A. Jour. II. 381, XIX. 100, XXV. 101, 212, XXXIII. 275, XXXVIII. 300, 303, XLVII. 93; Blome's Britannia, 102; Bristol and Glouc. Arch. Soc. Trans. II. 13, 14, III. 256, VIII. 185, 309, XVII. 13; Britton and Brayley, V. 592; Buckman, J., and Newmarch, C. H., Illustrations of the remains of Roman Art in Ciren-cester, 1850; Cambs. Antiq. Soc. Proc. I. 55; Church, A. H., The Corinium Museum, 10th ed. 1910; Dorset Field Club Proc. XXI. 172, 175; Fosbroke, II. 481; Gough's Camden, I. 287; Hoare's Anc. Wilts. II. (Rom. Aera) 97; Illust. Lond. News, Sept. 8 and Nov. 17, 1849; King's Mun. Antiq. II. 169; Leland's Itin. V. 65; Lewis, I. 598; Mag. Brit. 1738, II. 795; Morgan, 28, 72, 270, 274; Rudder, 345; Scarth's Rom. Brit. 141; Stukeley's Itin. Curios. I. 66; Witts, 60; Wright's Celt, Roman and Saxon, 161.

Basilica. Antiquary, XXXIV. 233; Bristol and Glouc. Arch. Soc. Trans. XXI. 70 (plan); Clifton Antiq. Club Proc. IV. 87; Lond. S.A. Proc. 2 S. XVII. 201 (plan); Reliquary and Illust. Arch. N.S. IV. 213.

Ashcroft. Buildings and pavement. Antiquary, XXXVIII. 377, XLV. 366.

Barton Farm. Pavement. B.A.A. Jour. II. 381, XXV. 103, XXXVIII. 303; Birmingham and Midland Instit. Trans. X. 126, XXIV. 74; Bristol and Glouc. Arch. Soc. Trans. II. 9, XXXIII. 67 (illustration); Buckman, 32; Gent. Mag. 1824, i. 454, and Lib. Rom. Brit. Rem. i. 94; Lond. S.A. Archaeo-logia, XXXI. 461, and Proc. 1 S. I. 18; Morgan, 33, 80; Wilts. Arch. Soc. Mag. XXVII. 7.

Cricklade Street. Pavement. Wilts. Arch. Soc. Mag. XIV. 192.

Dyer Street. Buildings and pavements. Antiquary, XXVI.
150; Arch. Jour. VI. 318, 321, 396; Athenaeum, Aug. 18,
1849; B.A.A. Jour. V. 360, VII. 64; Buckman, 28, 35 (plan),
62 (plan); Gent. Mag. 1849, ii. 357, 1850, i. 25, and Lib.
Rom. Brit. Rem. i. 87, 88; Illust. Lond. News, Sept. 8, 1849;
Lond. S.A. Vet. Mon. II. pl. 44, and Minute Book, XXII. 330;
Lysons' Reliquiae, II. pls. V, VII, XXXIII, and III. 10;
Reliquary, XIX. 97; Wright's Celt, Roman and Saxon, 197,
253. Orig. pavs. in town museum.

The Leauses. Buildings and pavements. Bristol and Glouc.
Arch. Soc. Trans. XVII. 63; Cheshire Arch. Soc. Jour.
I. 52; Lond. S.A. Archaeologia, VII. 407, XVIII. 124, and
Minute Book, I. 58, 98, XVII. 160, XVIII. 10, 106, XIX. 130,
XX. 11.

New Road. Buildings and pavement. B.A.A. Jour. XXV. 177;
Bristol and Glouc. Arch. Soc. Trans. II. 9, 14; Wilts. Arch.
Soc. Mag. XIV. 191.

Quern Lane. Pavement. Buckman, 32; Lond. S.A. Archaeologia, XXXI. 461, and Proc. 1 S. I. 18.

Watermoor. Foundations. Arch. Jour. VIII. 187.

Locality not given. Pavement. British Curiosities in Art and
Nature, 1721, 65; Lond. S.A. Proc. 2 S. XXI. 163.

Cold Harbour Farm, see Tracy Park.

Colesbourne (Combend). Buildings and pavement. Bigland, I.
409; Bristol and Glouc. Arch. Soc. Trans. IV. 208; Britton
and Brayley, V. 672; Fosbroke, II. 521; King's Mun. Antiq.
II. 174, 179; Lond. S.A. Archaeologia, IX. 319, XVIII. 112,
and Topog. Colls., red portfolio (plan, etc.); Lysons' Reliquiae, III. 7; Witts, 58; Wright's Celt, Roman and Saxon,
204.

Congrove, see Tracy Park.

Cromhall. Buildings and pavement. Arch. Jour. XVII. 332;
Bath Field Club Proc. IX. 52; Lond. S.A. Proc. 2 S. XXIII. 20
(plan); Lysons' Romans in Glouc. 42; Rudder, 397; Witts,
59 (plan on map); Wright's Celt, Roman and Saxon, 228.

Daglingworth. Buildings and pavement. Atkyns, 379; Lysons'
Rom. Antiq. at Woodchester, 19 n; Morgan, 68; Rudder,
400; Witts, 61; Wright's Celt, Roman and Saxon, 227.

Dodington. Buildings. Lysons' Romans in Glouc. 42 ; Witts, 61.

Dryhill, near Cheltenham. Buildings. Arch. Jour. XII. 10, XXXV. 72 ; Bath Field Club Proc. IX. 52 ; Bristol and Glouc. Arch. Soc. Trans. IV. 208, XX. 265 ; Gomond, W. H., Notes on Cheltenham, 1849 ; Witts, 60 (plan on map).

Eastington. Foundations. Lond. S.A. Proc. 2 S. III. 204.

Farmer's Field, *see* Tracy Park.

Frocester. Buildings. Morgan, 69 ; Wright's Celt, Roman and Saxon, 228.

Gloucester (*Glevum*). Gates, walls, etc. Antiquary, XXXIII. 231, 360 ; Assoc. Archit. Soc. Reports, XXII. ii. lxxxiii ; Bristol and Glouc. Arch. Soc. Trans. I. 34, 153 (plan), II. 210, VI. 345, XIII. 49, 96, 294 ; Builder, LXXIII. 334 ; Cotts. Field Club Proc. VI. 154 ; Gent. Mag. 1854, i. 487, and Lib. Rom. Brit. Rem. i. 91 ; Lysons' Romans in Glouc. 13 ; Reliquary and Illust. Arch. N.S. IV. 195 ; Rudge, 4 ; Witts, 62 ; Wright's Celt, Roman and Saxon, 161.

Cathedral. Pavement. Athenaeum, Dec. 28, 1867.

The Cross (near). Buildings and pavement. Gent. Mag. 1854, ii. 248, and Lib. Rom. Brit. Rem. ii. 580.

Eastgate Street. Buildings and pavements. Antiquary, XXVII. 69 ; Arch. Review, II. 254 ; Bigland, 8 ; Bristol and Glouc. Arch. Soc. Trans. I. 157 ; Gent. Mag. 1806, ii. 869, 1841, ii. 190, and Lib. Rom. Brit. Rem. i. 89 ; Glouc. N. and Q. VI. 184 (plan) ; Lond. S.A. Archaeologia, XVIII. 123, 443, Proc. 2 S. XII. 158, and Topog. Colls., brown portfolio (photos) ; Lysons' Reliquiae, III. 10 ; Rudge, 7. An orig. pav. in town museum.

Grey Friars. Pavement. Bristol and Glouc. Arch. Soc. Trans. I. 34.

Longsmith Street. Buildings and pavement. Gent. Mag. 1854, ii. 248, 1855, ii. 42, and Lib. Rom. Brit. Rem. i. 91, ii. 581.

Mitre Street. Pavement. Bristol and Glouc. Arch. Soc. Trans. XIII. 294 ; Gent. Mag. 1843, ii. 420, and Lib. Rom. Brit. Rem. i. 89 ; Morgan, 72.

New Guildhall. Pavement. B.A.A. Jour. XLVII. 97.

Northgate Street. Pavement. Bristol and Glouc. Arch. Soc.
Trans. XIII. 51; Rudge, 6.

Quay Street. Foundations and pavement. Antiquary, XXVII.
73; Gent. Mag. 1846, ii. 517, and Lib. Rom. Brit. Rem. i. 89.
Orig. pav. in town museum.

St Mary-le-Crypt. Pavement. Bigland, 8.

Tolsey (site of). Buildings. Bristol and Glouc. Arch. Soc.
Trans. XIX. 142, 154; Illust. Arch. I. 259 (plan).

Westgate. Buildings. B.A.A. Jour. IV. 58; Rudge, 6.

Locality not given. Pavement. Arch. Review, I. 282; B.A.A.
Jour. XI. 64.

Grammer's Rocks, see Tracy Park.

Hanham, see Bitton.

Haresfield. Buildings. Bristol and Glouc. Arch. Soc. Trans. IV.
208, XIX. 280; Cotts. Field Club Proc. VI. 211; Witts, 62.

Hucclecote. Buildings. Antiquary, XXXVII. 342.

Kingscote. Buildings and pavement. Lewis, II. 669; Lysons'
Woodchester, 19 n, and Romans in Glouc. 42; Morgan, 68;
Rudder, 512; Witts, 63; Wright's Celt, Roman and Saxon,
227.

Lasborough. Buildings. Lysons' Romans in Glouc. 42.

Lechlade. Buildings and pavement. Britton and Brayley, v.
629; Ireland, S., Picturesque Views on the river Thames,
31; Lewis, III. 44.

Lydney. Buildings, pavements and temple. Antiquarian Reper-
tory, 1st ed. 1775, I. 162 (plan), 2nd ed. 1808, II. 389 (plan);
Arch. Cantiana, XV. 136; Arch. Jour. XXVIII. 174, XXXVI.
419, XLVII. 345, 419, and Bristol vol. 1851, 61; Bath Field
Club Proc. I. ii. 17, IV. 369; Bathurst, W. H., Roman
Antiquities at Lydney Park, 1879 (Monmouth and Caerleon
Antiq. Assoc. XVII.); Bristol and Glouc. Arch. Soc. Trans.
VI. 40, 210 (plan), XIII. 99, XVIII. 10; Britton and Brayley,
V. 721; Builder, XXXVII. 425; Lond. S.A. Archaeologia,
V. 208, Proc. 2 S. v. 96, and Topog. Colls., brown portfolio
(plan); Rudder, 525; Scarth's Rom. Brit. 163; Somer-
set Arch. Soc. Proc. XII. 26; Witts, 63 (plan on map);
Woolhope Field Club Proc. 1874, 32, 37, 38.

Olveston, see Tockington.

L. 3

Painswick. Buildings. Bristol and Glouc. Arch. Soc. Trans.
XXVII. 156 (plan); Cotts. Field Club Proc. VI. 211; Witts,
64.

Rodmarton. Buildings and pavement. Britton and Brayley, V.
592; Lewis, III. 661; Lond. S.A. Archaeologia, XVIII. 113
(plan); Lysons' Reliquiae, II. pl. VIII (plan), III. 7, and
Romans in Glouc. 42; Morgan, 68, 80; Rudder, 631;
Witts, 64 (plan on map); Wright's Celt, Roman and Saxon,
227.

Sea Mills. Buildings and pavements. Clifton Antiq. Club
Proc. II. 159, III. 16, 80, 175; Seyer, I. 155 (plan).

Sedbury, *see* Tidenham.

Spoonley, *see* Winchcombe.

Stinchcombe (Stancombe Park). Buildings and pavement.
B.A.A. Jour. II. 349, and Worcester vol. 1851, 376; Bristol
and Glouc. Arch. Soc. Trans. I. 157, IV. 208, VIII. 158;
Sussex Arch. Colls. II. 314; Witts, 65.

Stroud (Brown's Hill). Buildings and pavement. Lysons' Woodchester, 19 n; Morgan, 69; Witts, 56.

Sudeley, *see* Winchcombe.

Swell, Nether. Buildings. Bristol and Glouc. Arch. Soc. Trans.
IV. 209, VII. 72 (plan), 76, XX. 349; Witts, 65.

Tidenham (Sedbury). Kiln. Arch. Jour. XVII. 190, 192.

Tockington. Buildings and pavement. Antiquary, XVI. 222,
XVII. 37; Arch. Instit. Bristol vol. 1851, 49, 50; Arch.
Review, II. 51; B.A.A. Jour. XLIV. 181, XLV. 192; Bath
Field Club Proc. VI. 355; Bristol and Glouc. Arch. Soc.
Trans. XII. 159 (plan), XIII. 196 (plan), XIV. 192; Builder,
LIII. 553, 699; Clifton Antiq. Club Proc. II. 160; Reliquary,
N.S. II. 26, 118; Seyer, I. 203.

Tracy Park (in and near). Buildings. Arch. Jour. XLVI. 334;
Athenaeum, Nov. 18, 1865; B.A.A. Jour. XXXIV. 248, XXXV.
208; Bath Field Club Proc. I. ii. 1; Lond. S.A. Proc. 2 S. II.
457; Rudder, 211; Scarth's Rom. Bath, 125; Somerset Arch.
Soc. Proc. XII. i. 25, XXIV. ii. 14.

Trewsbury. Buildings. Morgan, 68; Lysons' Romans in Glouc.
41; Wright's Celt, Roman and Saxon, 227.

Tytherington. Buildings and pavement. Arch. Instit. Bristol

vol. 1851, 49; Bristol and Glouc. Arch. Soc. Trans. XII. 323; Rudder, 766; Witts, 121.

Upton. Buildings. Scarth's Rom. Bath, 126.

Winchcombe (Spoonley). Buildings and pavement. Antiquary, V. 226; Arch. Jour. XLVII. 346; B.A.A. Jour. XXXVIII. 215; Bristol and Glouc. Arch. Soc. Trans. XIV. 208; Builder, XLII. 498; Dorset Field Club Proc. XXX. 4; Lond. S.A. Archaeologia, LII. 651 (plan), Proc. 2 S. XIII. 16, and Topog. Colls., brown portfolio (plan); Witts, 70 (plan on map).

(Wadfield). Buildings and pavement. B.A.A. Jour. N.S. I. 188, 242 (plan); Bristol and Glouc. Arch. Soc. Trans. IV. 27, 208; Dent, E., Annals of Winchcombe and Sudeley, 13 (plan); Witts, 66 (plan on map).

Witcomb, Great. Buildings and pavement. Arch. Jour. XII. 10; Bath Field Club Proc. V. 123; Bristol and Glouc. Arch. Soc. Trans. IV. 34, 207, XX. 265, 266, 319, XXVIII. 16, XXX. 246 (plan); Builder, XXXVII. 863; Cotts. Field Club Proc. V. 247; Knight's Old England, I. 54, fig. 178 (plan); Lewis, IV. 617; Lond. S.A. Archaeologia, XIX. 178 (plan), and Topog. Colls., red portfolio (plan); Witts, 66 (plan on map); Wright's Celt, Roman and Saxon, 253.

Withington. Buildings and pavement. B.A.A. Jour. XXXVIII. 300, 303; Bristol and Glouc. Arch. Soc. Trans. IV. 208, XX. 265, 349; Builder, XLII. 757, 758; Clifton Antiq. Club Proc. I. 295; Gent. Mag. 1811, ii. 80, and Lib. Rom. Brit. Rem. i. 95; Lewis, IV. 620; Lond. S.A. Archaeologia, XVIII. 118 (plan), and Minute Book, XXXIII. 239; Lysons' Reliquiae, II. pls. XVIII—XXI, III. 8; Morgan, 33, 78, 241, 273; Witts, 67 (plan on map); Wright's Celt, Roman and Saxon, 253. Four pieces of orig. pav. in British Museum.

Woodchester. Buildings and pavement. Arch. Cantiana, XV. 137; Arch. Jour. XLVII. 303, 365, 422; Atkyns, 848; B.A.A. Jour. II. 380, 382, XXXVI. 356, XXXVIII. 291, 292, 303, 304, 306; Bath Field Club Proc. I. ii. 17; Bristol and Glouc. Arch. Soc. Trans. IV. 209, V. 21, 34, 46, 142 (plan), VI. 3, 7, 28, XIII. 99, XX. 265; Britton and Brayley, V. 573; Builder, XLII. 757; Etchings of Views in Glouc. 1791, pl. XIX;

Fosbroke, I. 367; Glouc. N. and Q. IV. 225; Godwin's Arch.
Handbook, 56, 59; Gough's Camden, I. 283; Hearne's
Reliquiae, I. 226; Illust. Lond. News, XXI. 1852, 100;
King's Mun. Antiq. II. 185; Knight's Old England, I. 54,
fig. 177 (plan); Lewis, IV. 639; Lond. S.A. Minute Book, I.
269, XVIII. 8, 23, XXII. 331, XXV. 238, Vet. Mon. II. pl. 44,
and Topog. Colls., brown and red portfolios (drawings);
Lysons' Reliquiae, II. pls. XXII—XXVII, and Roman Anti-
quities discovered at Woodchester, and A Collection of
Gloucestershire Antiquities, 1803, I. 8, pl. XIX; Mag. Brit.
1738, II. 775; Morgan, 33, 67, 74, 241, 276; Rudder, 841;
Scarth's Rom. Brit. 162, 164; Witts, 68 (plan on map);
Wright's Celt, Roman and Saxon, 198, 227, 229 (plan), 251.
One orig. pav. in British Museum.

Wycomb. Buildings. Arch. Jour. XXI. 97, 263; Bristol and
Glouc. Arch. Soc. Trans. IV. 209, V. 188; Gent. Mag. 1863,
ii. 627, 1864, i. 86, ii. 85, and Lib. Rom. Brit. Rem. i. 97, 101;
Lond. S.A. Proc. 2 S. II. 302, 422, and Topog. Colls., red
portfolio (plan); Witts, 69.

HAMPSHIRE

Duthy. Duthy, J. Sketches of Hampshire, 1839.
Englefield. Englefield, Sir H. C. A Walk through Southampton, 1805.
Hants. Field Club Proc. Hampshire Field Club Proceedings, I.—v. 1885—
    1906.
Stevens. Stevens, J. History of St Mary Bourne, 1888.
V.C.H. Victoria History of the Counties of England. Hampshire, I. 1900.
Warner. Warner, R. History of Hampshire, 6 vols. in 2, 1795.
Wilkins. Wilkins, E. P. and Brion, J. and Sons. A concise Exposition of
    the Geology, Antiquities and Topography of the Isle of Wight, 1859.
Woodward. Woodward, B. B., Wilks, T. C. and Lockhart, C. History of
    Hampshire, 3 vols. 1858—69.

Abbot's Ann. Buildings and pavement. Arch. Jour. VII. 184,
XI. 392; Builder, XIII. 101, XLII. 757; Lewis, I. 2; Lond.
S.A. Archaeologia, XXXVI. 184; Morgan, 224, 241, 276;
Stevens, 58; V.C.H. I. 300; Wilts. Arch. Soc. Mag. XXI.
295; Woodward, III. 161. Three pieces of orig. pav. in
British Museum.

Alice Holt Woods. Kilns. Lond. S.A. Archaeologia, XXVIII.
452, and Proc. 2 S. XV. 178; V.C.H. I. 306.

Alton. Pavement. V.C.H. I. 306; Woodward, III. 308.

Andover (Castlefield and Finkley). Buildings and pavement.
Athenaeum, May 25, 1867; B.A.A. Jour. XXIII. 268 (plan),
295, 301, XXIV. 402, XXV. 67, XXVIII. 328, XXXIV. 256;
Hants. Field Club Proc. III. 177; Intellectual Observer, XI.
470, XII. 310; Newbury Field Club Trans. I. 135; Stevens,
60, 61; V.C.H. I. 302 (plan), 303 (plan); Wilts. Arch. Soc.
Mag. XXI. 296.

Appleshaw. Buildings. Antiquary, XXXIII. 103, 360, XXXIV.
70, XXXV. 40; V.C.H. I. 295.

Bighton, near Alresford. Buildings. Arch. Jour. I. 387; V.C.H.
I. 306.

Binsted, *see* Wick.

Bishopstoke. Buildings. Lond. S.A. Proc. 2 S. II. 329.

Bitterne (*Clausentum*). Foundations, pavements, walls and
bastions. Antiquary, VII. 79; B.A.A. Jour. IV. 382, N.S.
XII. 114, 115, and Winchester vol. 1845, 142, 161 (plan);
Britton and Brayley, VI. 122; Davis' Southampton, 2;
Englefield, 80, 107; Horsley's Rom. Brit. 441; Lewis, IV.
146; Lond. S.A. Proc. XIX. 56 (plan); Stukeley's Itin.
Curios. I. 193; V.C.H. I. 330; Warner, I. sec. ii. 179; Wood-
ward, II. 147; Wright's Arch. Album, 223.

Bossington (Horsebridge Mill). Piles of Bridge. Hoare's Anc.
Wilts. II. (Rom. Aera) 61.

Botley. Pavement and kiln(?). Arch. Review, IV. 68; B.A.A.
Jour. XLV. 200; Hants. N. and Q. VI. 47; V.C.H. I. 310.

Brading, I.W. Buildings and pavement. Antiquary, I. 279,
II. 35, 226, III. 3, IV. 182, V. 50, VIII. 228, XI. 59; Arch.
Cantiana, XV. 134; Arch. Jour. XXXVII. 344; Athenaeum,
May 22 and Oct. 9, 1880, Apr. 30, Aug. 27, and Oct. 15,
1881; B.A.A. Jour. XXXVI. 236, 240, 245, 363, XXXVII. 191,
XXXVIII. 291, 298, XXXIX. 361; Bath Field Club Proc. V.
i. 41; Builder, XXXVIII. 682, XXXIX. 26, 569, 573, 716, XL.
556, 780, XLV. 349; Coll. Antiq. VII. 236; Dorset Field Club
Proc. XXI. 167, 170, 174; Illust. Lond. News, Sept. 3, 1882;
Morgan, 25, 27, 32, 33, 41, 225, 234; Price, J. E. and Price,

F. G. Hilton, Remains of Roman Buildings at Morton, near Brading, 1881 (plans, etc.); R.I.B.A. Trans. 1880—81, 125; Reliquary, XXI. 50, 127; V.C.H. I. 313 (plan).

Bramdean. Buildings and pavement. Arch. Cantiana, XV. 133; B.A.A. Jour. XXXVIII. 303, 305; Builder, XIII. 100; Coll. Antiq. II. 54; Duthy, 32 and pl. XXI (plan); Gent. Mag. 1823, i. 631, 1824, ii. 100, and Lib. Rom. Brit. Rem. i. 109; Lewis, I. 328; Lond. S.A. Archaeologia, XXII. 52; Morgan, 33, 45, 218, 223; Smith, R., Illust. Rom. London, 59, 73; V.C.H. I. 307; Wright's Celt, Roman and Saxon, 253.

Brixton, I.W. Foundations. B.A.A. Jour. XII. 141, 159; V.C.H. I. 318; Wilkins, 58; Woodward, III. Supp. 22.

Candover, Chilton. Foundations. V.C.H. I. 306.

Carisbrooke, I.W. Buildings and pavement. Arch. Jour. XVI. 388, XVII. 63; B.A.A. Jour. XVI. 100, 312, XXXVIII. 303; Coll. Antiq. VI. 121 (plan); Gent. Mag. 1859, ii. 399, and Lib. Rom. Brit. Rem. i. 128; Liverpool Archit. and Arch. Soc. Proc. N.S. I. 13th Sess. 192; Morgan, 33, 239; Spickernell, W., Roman Villa, Carisbrooke, 1860 (plan); Times, Sept. 13, 1859; V.C.H. I. 316 (plan); Wilkins, 53, 89; Woodward, III. Supp. 19 (plan).

Clanville, *see* Weyhill.

Clatterford, I.W. Buildings. B.A.A. Jour. XII. 159; V.C.H. I. 317; Wilkins, 57; Woodward, III. Supp. 22.

Combly, I.W. Buildings. Gent. Mag. 1867, i. 791, and Lib. Rom. Brit. Rem. i. 131; Times, Sept. 23, 1910; V.C.H. I. 316; Woodward, III. Supp. 22.

Corhampton. Foundations. Arch. Jour. VI. 396; V.C.H. I. 309.

Crondall. Buildings and pavement. Arch. Jour. XVI. 298; B.A.A. Jour. XXXVIII. 303; Builder, XIII. 100; Gent. Mag. 1838, i. 192, and Lib. Rom. Brit. Rem. ii. 443; Lond. S.A. Archaeologia, XXII. 54, and Minute Book, XXXIV. 237; Morgan, 33, 222; Surrey Arch. Colls. IX. 350, 351; V.C.H. I. 305.

Dean, West, *see* Wiltshire.

Finkley, *see* Andover.

Froxfield. Buildings and pavement. Arch. Jour. XII. 199, 278;

Lond. S.A. Proc. 1 S. III. 191 ; Stukeley's Letters, II. 179 ;
V.C.H. I. 308.

Fullerton. Buildings and pavement. Athenaeum, Feb. 23,
1905.

Fyfield (Redenham). Buildings and pavement. Arch. Jour.
VII. 183 ; B.A.A. Jour. XXXVIII. 97 ; Hants. Field Club Proc.
III. 177 ; Lond. S.A. Archaeologia, XXII. 52 ; V.C.H. I. 294
(plan) ; Wilts. Arch. Soc. Mag. XXI. 295 ; Woodward, III.
160.

Grately. Building and pavement. Hants. Field Club Proc.
VI. 341 (plan).

Gurnard Bay, I.W. Buildings and pavement. B.A.A. Jour.
XXI. 228, XXII. 351 (plan) ; Intellectual Observer, VII. 230,
XI. 154 ; Morgan, 240 ; V.C.H. I. 317 ; Woodward, III.
Supp. 23.

Hayling Island. Buildings. Antiquary, XXXVII. 342 ; Arch.
Jour. LV. 290, LXIII. 117 (plan) ; Builder, LXXXI. 299 ; Ely,
Talfourd, Roman Hayling, 1st ed. 1904, 2nd ed. 1908 (plans,
etc.) ; V.C.H. I. 310.

Hurstbourne Priors. Buildings. B.A.A. Jour. XXIII. 280; Stevens,
25 ; V.C.H. I. 304.

Itchen Abbas. Buildings and pavement. Antiquary, VIII. 36 ;
B.A.A. Jour. XXXIII. 502, XXXIV. 233, 258, 504, XXXV. 109,
208 (plan), XXXVIII. 303 ; Builder, XXXVI. 482 ; Morgan,
33, 221 ; V.C.H. I. 307.

Kimpton (Great Shoddesden). Buildings. V.C.H. I. 295.

Meon, West. Buildings and pavement. Antiquary, XLI. 326,
XLII. 125, 283 ; Arch. Jour. LXII. 262 (plan), LXIV. 1 (plan) ;
Builder, XC. 329 ; Hants. Field Club Proc. V. 271 (plan) ;
V.C.H. I. 309.

Micheldever. Buildings. Arch. Jour. III. 160 ; B.A.A. Jour. II.
199 ; V.C.H. I. 307.

Morton, *see* Brading.

New Forest. Kilns. Arch. Jour. XXX. 319 ; Coll. Antiq. VI.
174 ; Lond. S.A. Archaeologia, XXXV. 91 (map, etc.), and
Proc. 1 S. II. 261, 285, IV. 167 ; V.C.H. I. 326.

Penton Mewsey (near). Buildings. V.C.H. I. 297.

Petersfield (Stroud). Buildings and pavement. Antiquary,

XLIV. 322, XLV. 375; Arch. Jour. LXV. 57 (plan), LXVI. 33 (plan).

Popham. Foundations. Arch. Jour. VI. 194; V.C.H. I. 306.

Porchester. Fort, walls, etc. Arch. Instit. Winchester vol. 1845 (plans, etc.); King's Mun. Antiq. II. 22, 26 (plan); Knight's Old England, I. 29, fig. 104 (plan); Royal Instit. Proc. XVI. 39; V.C.H. I. 328 (plan).

Redenham, *see* Fyfield.

Rowland's Castle. Buildings and pavement. Antiquary, XXXII. 53; V.C.H. I. 310.

St Mary Bourne. Buildings. B.A.A. Jour. XXXV. 93; Stevens, 59; V.C.H. I. 304.

Shoddesden, Great, *see* Kimpton.

Silchester (*Calleva Atrebatum*). The city, walls, buildings, excavations, etc. Antiquary, XII. 97, XXII. 170, 218, XXIV. 208, XXV. 49, 233, XXVI. 10, 24, 170, XXVII. 9, 137, 233, XXVIII. 97, 160, XXIX. 259, XXX. 41, 77, 207, XXXI. 161, 299, XXXII. 161, XXXIII. 16, 230, XXXIV. 232, XXXV. 248, 365, XXXVI. 335, XXXVII. 35, XXXVIII. 376, XXXIX. 225, 353; Archaeologia Oxoniensis, 1892—95, 33, 93, 177, 328; Arch. Jour. VIII. 227 (plan of site), XXII. 361, 374, XXIII. 331, XXX. 10, LI. 337 (plans), LIII. 319, also Oxford vol. 1850, xvi, xvii, 101 (plan of site), and Winchester vol. 1845, under Porchester Castle, 20, 27; Athenaeum, Sept. 8, 1866, Dec. 6, 1890, June 12, 1891, July 9 and 30, 1892, May 2, 1896, May 8 and 29, 1897, May 28, 1898, June 3, 1899, and June 23, 1900; B.A.A. Jour. XVI. 5, 90, 228, XX. 360, XLIII. 392, XLVII. 76, N.S. XIV. 211, and Winchester vol. 1845, 139; Bath Field Club Proc. I. i. 70, VII. 327; Berks. Quarterly Jour. II. 45, 50; Berks. Bucks. and Oxon. Arch. Jour. I. 94, III. 16, 63, V. 54, 63, VIII. 40, IX. 98, X. 50, XIII. 121; Bristol and Glouc. Arch. Soc. Trans. XXI. 294; Britton and Brayley, VI. 244; Builder, LX. 27, LXII. 40, LXIV. 186, LXVIII. 308, LXX. 378, LXXII. 507, LXXIV. 542, LXXVI. 544, LXXVII. 603, LXXVIII. 604, LXXX. 544, 581, LXXXII. 563, LXXXVI. 656, 685, XC. 671, XCIV. 742; Classical Review, XIII. 79; Coll. Antiq. VI. 266; Davis, F., The Romano-British City of Silchester (Andrews, W., Bygone Hampshire, 1898); Dorset Field

Club Proc. XVI. lxii, XVIII. xxix, XXI. 172; English Historical
Review, XIX. 625 ; Gent. Mag. 1833, i. 122, 1841, ii. 353, 1863,
ii. 490, 1865, ii. 297, 1866, ii. 467, 776, and Lib. Rom. Brit.
Rem. i. 114; Gough's Camden, I. 218; Graphic, Apr. 2, 1910;
Hants. Field Club Proc. II. 241, III. 177; Hoare's Anc.
Wilts. II. (Rom. Aera) 56 (plan); Horsley's Brit. Rom. 458;
Illust. Arch. I. 99, II. 22 ; Illust. Lond. News, Jan. 10, 1891 ;
King's Mun. Antiq. II. 154; Knight's Old England, I. 39;
Leicester Arch. Soc. Trans. III. 342 ; Lewis, IV. 109 ; Lond.
S.A. Archaeologia, XXVII. 414, XL. 403 (plans), XLVI. 329
(plans), 344 (plans), XLVIII. 231, 232, L. 263 (plans), LII. 733
(plans), LIII. 263 (plans), 539 (plans), LIV. 199 (plans), 439
(plans), LV. 215 (plans), 409 (plans), LVI. 103 (plans), 229
(plans), LVII. 87 (plans), 229 (plans), LVIII. 17 (plans),
413 (plans), LIX. 334 (plans), LX. 149 (plans), 431 (plans),
LXI. 199 (plans), 473 (plans), LXII. 317 (plans), and Proc.
2 S. III. 134, 494, VI. 55, XI. 78, 177, XIII. 85, 208, 209, XIV.
15, 18, 291, 292, XV. 152, 153, 360, 361, XVI. 73, 115, 357, 419,
XVII. 192, 433, XVIII. 173, 359, XIX. 133, 305, XX. 144, 338,
XXI. 212, 485, XXII. 321, 530, XXIII. 264; Mag. Brit. 1738,
II. 868 ; Morgan, 33, 143, 148 ; Newbury Field Club Trans.
III. 34; Oxford Archit. and Hist. Soc. Proc. N.S. V. 340, 363;
Phil. Trans. XLV. 603 ; Reliquary, N.S. IV. 246, VI. 178 ;
Scarth's Rom. Brit. 143 ; Shropshire Arch. Soc. Trans. 2 S.
XI. xi.; Strutt's Chronicle, I. 300; Stukeley's Itin. Curios.
I. 177, and Letters, II. 186; Sussex Arch. Colls. XXXI. 72 ;
V.C.H. I. 271 (plans), 350 (plans); Warner, I. sec. ii. 167 ;
Wilts. Arch. Soc. Mag. XXI. 292 ; Woodward, III. 193 ;
Wright's Arch. Album, 151, and Celt, Roman and Saxon,
122, 161, 189. Original pavements in Reading Museum
and at Stratfieldsaye House. Drawings, maps, plans, etc.
relating to the 1890—1909 excavations in the collections of
the Society of Antiquaries of London.

Sparsholt (Westwood). Buildings. Antiquary, XVIII. 32, XXXII.
53 ; Hants. Field Club Proc. III. 201 ; V.C.H. I. 312.

Stanstead Park, *see* Rowland's Castle.

Stroud, *see* Petersfield.

Thruxton. Buildings and pavement. Antiquary, XL. 282 ;

Arch. Jour. VII. 184, XXIV. 76, and Salisbury vol. 1849, 241;
B.A.A. Jour. XXXVIII. 303; Dorset Field Club Proc. XXX. 3;
Gent. Mag. 1823, i. 452, 559, ii. 230, and Lib. Rom. Brit.
Rem. i. 112; Hants. Field Club Proc. III. 177; Hoare's Mod.
S. Wilts. V. 210; Lond. S.A. Archaeologia, XXII. 49; Morgan,
33, 218, 221; Smith, Roach, Illust. Rom. Lond. 57; V.C.H.
I. 298; Wilts. Arch. Soc. Mag. XXI. 295, XXXIV. 150; Wood-
ward, III. 160; Wright's Celt, Roman and Saxon, 250, 253,
254. Orig. pav. in British Museum.

Twyford. Buildings. Antiquary, XVIII. 32; Arch. Review, II. 51;
Lond. S.A. Proc. 2 S. XIV. 11, and Topog. Colls., brown
portfolio (plan); V.C.H. I. 309.

Upham. Buildings. Arch. Jour. VI. 397; B.A.A. Jour. V. 376
(plan); Times, Dec. 17, 1849; V.C.H. I. 309.

Waltham, Bishop's. Pavement. V.C.H. I. 309.

Waltham, North. Buildings. Arch. Jour. VI. 193; V.C.H. I.
306.

Westwood, *see* Sparsholt.

Weyhill (Clanville). Buildings. Arch. Jour. VII. 184; Lond.
S.A. Archaeologia, LVI. 1 (plan), and Proc. 2 S. XVII. 5;
V.C.H. I. 295 (plan); Wilts. Arch. Soc. Mag. XXXIV. 149.

Whitchurch. Buildings. Newbury Field Club Trans. IV. 190.

Wick or Wyck (near Binsted). Buildings. Arch. Jour. I. 393;
Surrey Arch. Colls. IX. 351; V.C.H. I. 305.

Winchester (*Venta Belgarum*). City and walls. V.C.H. I. 285.

Barracks, formerly the King's House or Palace. Buildings
and pavement. Gent. Mag. 1838, ii. 371, and Lib. Rom.
Brit. Rem. i. 122; Hartshorne's Salop Antiq. 117 n; Phil.
Trans. XXV. 2229; V.C.H. I. 287; Wren, S., Parentalia, 325.

Brook Street, Upper. Pavement. B.A.A. Winchester vol.
1845, 463; V.C.H. I. 288.

Cathedral, south aisle of Nave. Pavement. Antiquary, N.S.
VII. 123, 162.

Cobbett's Road. Buildings. Antiquary, XXXVIII. 175.

Dome Alley. Pavement. B.A.A. Jour. XXXVI. 444; Builder,
XXXIX. 275; Reliquary, XXI. 128; V.C.H. I. 288.

Hall Court Wood. Kiln. Arch. Review, IV. 69.

Hammond Passage. Pavement. V.C.H. I. 287.

High Street. Foundations. V.C.H. I. 288.

Hyde Street. Buildings. Antiquary, XXXIII. 360; V.C.H. I. 289.

The Lawn. Water channel. Arch. Jour. VI. 397, 408.

Minster Lane and Street. Pavement. Arch. Jour. XXXV. 462; B.A.A. Jour. XXXV. 230; Lond. S.A. Proc. 2 S. VII. 487; V.C.H. I. 288. Orig. pav. in city museum.

Petersfield Road. Foundations. V.C.H. I. 288.

St Clement's Street. Pavement. V.C.H. I. 287.

St Giles' Hill. Pavement. Antiquary, XI. 84; V.C.H. I. 288.

St James' Street (near). Pavement. V.C.H. I. 286.

St Thomas' Street. Pavement. Antiquary, VII. 276; V.C.H. I. 287.

Wolvesey Castle. Pavement. B.A.A. Winchester vol. 1845, 146; V.C.H. I. 288.

Locality not given. Pavement. Antiquary, III. 132; B.A.A. Jour. XXXV. 110.

HEREFORDSHIRE

Arch. Survey. An Archaeological Survey of Herefordshire, by the Rev. J. O. Bevan, Jas. Davies, and F. Haverfield. Published by the Society of Antiquaries of London, 1896.

Duncumb-Cooke. Duncumb, Rev. J., and Cooke, W. H. History of Herefordshire, 4 vols., 1804—92.

V.C.H. Victoria History of the Counties of England. Herefordshire, I. 1908.

Woolhope Club Trans. Woolhope Naturalists' Field Club Transactions, 1872—1904.

Bishopstone. Buildings and pavement. Antiquary, XXVI. 246; Arch. Jour. XXXIV. 361; Arch. Survey, 4, 9; Duncumb-Cooke, IV. 6; Lond. S.A. Archaeologia, XXIII. 417, Minute Book, XXXVI. 54, and Topog. Colls., brown portfolio (pavement); Scarth's Rom. Brit. 166; V.C.H. I. 175, 191; Woolhope Club Trans. 1881—82, 257. Orig. pav. in Hereford Museum.

Bolitree, *see* Weston-under-Penyard.

Brinsop. Steened well. Antiquary, XXVI. 245 ; Arch. Survey, 9 ; V.C.H. I. 191 ; Woolhope Club Trans. 1886—89, 127.

Bury Hill, *see* Weston-under-Penyard.

Kenchester (*Magna*). Town, buildings, and pavements. Antiquary, XXV. 22, XXVI. 245, XXVIII. 209 ; Arch. Cambrensis, 3 S. II. 33 ; Arch. Jour. XIV. 83, XXXIV. 351 ; Arch. Survey, 4, 11 ; B.A.A. Jour. XXVII. 173 ; Blome's Britannia, 117, 118 ; British Curiosities in Art and Nature, 1721, 66 ; Britton and Brayley, VI. 583 ; Duncumb-Cooke, IV. 112 ; Gough's Camden, III. 73, 74 ; Horsley's Rom. Brit. 465 ; Lewis, II. 638 ; Lond. S.A. Archaeologia, XV. 391 ; Morgan, 72 ; Stukeley's Itin. Curios. I. 70 (plan), and Letters, II. 189 ; V.C.H. I. 175 (plan); Woolhope Club Trans. 1881—82, 241 (plan), 1893—94, 57 ; Wright's Celt, Roman and Saxon, 163, and Wanderings of an Antiquary, 35, 40, 41. An orig. pav. in Hereford Museum.

Putley. Buildings. Arch. Jour. XXXIV. 363 ; Arch. Survey, 6, 12 ; B.A.A. Jour. XXXII. 250; Duncumb-Cooke, III. 97 ; V.C.H. I. 193 ; Woolhope Club Trans. 1881—82, 258.

Stoke Prior. Kilns (?). Arch. Survey, 5, 12 ; V.C.H. I. 195.

Walterstone (Coed-y-Gravel near Old Castle). Buildings and pavement. Arch. Cambrensis, 2 S. II. 50 ; Arch. Jour. XXXIV. 368 ; Arch. Survey, 6, 13 ; King's Mun. Antiq. II. 174 ; Lond. S.A. Archaeologia, VI. 13 ; V.C.H. I. 196 ; Woolhope Club Trans. 1881—82, 258.

Wellington. Oven (?). Arch. Survey, 13.

Weston-under-Penyard. Buildings and pavement. Arch. Cambrensis, 2 S. V. 99 ; Arch. Jour. XXXIV. 358 ; Arch. Survey, 5, 13 ; Britton and Brayley, VI. 514 ; Duncumb-Cooke, III. 214 ; Fosbroke, T. D., Ariconensia, 1821, 36 ; V.C.H. I. 187 ; Woolhope Club Trans. 1881—82, 250 ; Wright's Wanderings of an Antiquary, 25.

Whitchurch. Buildings and pavement. Arch. Jour. XXXIV. 363 ; Arch. Survey, 13 ; Gent. Mag. 1831, i. 504, and Lib. Rom. Brit. Rem. i. 230; Lewis, IV. 537 ; Scarth's Rom. Brit. 166; V.C.H. I. 197 ; Woolhope Club Trans. 1881—82, 258 ; Wright's Wanderings of an Antiquary, 14.

HERTFORDSHIRE

Arch. Survey. An Archaeological Survey of Hertfordshire, by John Evans, printed in Archaeologia, LIII. (1892), 245—62.

Clutterbuck. Clutterbuck, R. History of Hertfordshire, 3 vols., 1815—27.

Cussans. Cussans, J. E. History of Hertfordshire, 3 vols., 1870—81.

East Herts. Arch. Soc. Trans. East Hertfordshire Archaeological Society Transactions, I.—III. 1901—08.

Norden's Herts. Norden, J. Speculum Britanniae, an historical description of Middlesex and Hertfordshire, 1723.

St Alban's Arch. Soc. Trans. St Alban's Architectural Society Transactions, 1885—1904.

Salmon. Salmon, N. History of Hertfordshire, 1728.

Boxmoor. Buildings and pavement. Arch. Jour. x. 4 ; Arch. Survey, 254 ; Lond. S.A. Archaeologia, XXXIV. 394, XXXV. 56, Proc. I S. II. 191, 295, and Topog. Colls., brown portfolio (plan).

Braughing. Buildings and pavement. Arch. Survey, 254 ; Clutterbuck, III. 149 ; East Herts. Arch. Soc. Trans. I. 173 ; Salmon, 227.

Coleshill. Traces of buildings. Salmon, 118.

Elstree (Brockley Hills). Foundations. Clutterbuck, I. 157 ; Norden's Herts. 23.

Hitchin. Kiln. Arch. Survey, 257 ; Cussans, II. (Hitchin) 6.

Langley, Abbot's. Buildings and pavement. Arch. Survey, 253 ; Cussans, III. (Cashio) 86.

Purwell Mill, *see* Wymondley, Great.

Radlett. Kiln. Antiquary, XXXV. 40 ; Lond. S.A. Proc. XVII. 261 (plans) ; St Alban's Arch. Soc. Trans. N.S. I. 176 (plans).

St Alban's (*Verulamium*). City, walls, etc. Antiquary, XII. 97 ; Arch. Jour. X. 357, and Winchester vol. 1845, under Porchester Castle, 17 ; Arch. Survey, 260 ; B.A.A. Jour. III. 331, XXVI. 45 (plan), 182, N.S. III. 134 ; Britton and Brayley, VII. 23 ; Clutterbuck, I. xvi, 5 (plan) ; Gent. Mag. 1851, i. 517, and Lib. Rom. Brit. Rem. ii. 395 ; Gough's Camden, II. 61 ; Knight's Old England, I. 46 ; Lewis, I. 22 ;

Lond. S.A. Archaeologia, II. 184, IV. 84, 95, Vet. Mon. I. pl. VIII (plan), and Topog. Colls., red portfolio (drawing); Norden's Herts. 24; St Alban's Arch. Soc. Trans. 1893—94, 49; Stukeley's Itin. Curios. I. 116 (plan); Wright's Celt, Roman and Saxon, 148, and Wanderings of an Antiquary, 45, 50, 55.

Theatre. Arch. Jour. V. 237; Arch. Survey, 260; B.A.A. Jour. III. 345, IV. 73, VI. 91, XXVI. 26, 45 (plan); Gent. Mag. 1848, ii. 143 (plan), and Lib. Rom. Brit. Rem. ii. 389; Lond. S.A. Archaeologia, XXXIII. 266; Lowe, R. Grove, Description of the Roman Theatre at Verulam, 1848.

Buildings and pavements. Antiquary, XXXV. 40; Arch. Jour. VI. 319, 406; Arch. Survey, 260; B.A.A. Jour. III. 337, 341, 345, V. 360, XXVI. 184; Blome's Britannia, 114; Lond. S.A. Proc. 2 S. XVII. 10, 367; Middsx. and Herts. N. and Q. III. 57; St Alban's Arch. Soc. Trans. N.S. I. 198, 205.

Destruction by the Abbots. Gesta Abbatum Monasterii S. Albani, Rolls Series, XXVIII. iv. 23, 24, 26, 27; Lond. S.A. Archaeologia, XXX. 441, XXXIII. 265.

Standon. Pavement. Arch. Survey, 261; Cussans, I. (Braughing) 164.

Stanstead Abbots. Pavement. Antiquary, XXIV. 212; Arch. Survey, 261.

Wymondley, Great (Purwell Mill). Buildings and pavement. Antiquary, XI. 37; Arch. Survey, 262; Builder, XLVII. 818; Herts. Nat. Hist. Soc. Trans. IV. 39 (plan), 43.

Youngsbury, near Ware. Buildings. Builder, XC. 702; East Herts. Arch. Soc. Trans. III. 229.

HUNTINGDONSHIRE

Alwalton, *see* Castor, Northants.

Chesterton, *see* Castor, Northants.

Earith. Kiln (?). Reliquary, XX. 245.

Ramsey. Pavement. Stukeley's Itin. Curios. I. 81.

Sibson, *see* Castor, Northants.

Stibbington, *see* Castor, Northants.

Water Newton, *see* Castor, Northants.

KENT

Arch. Cant. Archaeologia Cantiana, published by the Kent Archaeological
Society, I.—XXVIII. 1858—1909.
Arch. Survey. An Archaeological Survey of Kent, by George Payne,
printed in Archaeologia, LI. (1888), 447—68.
Gostling. Gostling, W. A walk in and about the city of Canterbury, 1825.
Hasted. Hasted, E. History of Kent, 4 vols., 1778—86.
Ireland. Ireland, W. H. History of Kent, 4 vols., 1828.
Somner. Somner, W. Antiquities of Canterbury, 1703.
Thorpe's Cust. Roff. Thorpe, J. Custumale Roffense, 1788.

Allington. Buildings. Arch. Cant. I. 156, 173, XV. 73; Arch.
Survey, 452; B.A.A. Jour. II. 88, IV. 67.

Aylesford (Eccles). Foundations. Arch. Survey, 452; B.A.A.
Jour. IV. 82; Wright's Wanderings of an Antiquary, 178.

(Kits Coty, near). Foundations. Arch. Jour. I. 264; Arch.
Survey, 452; Lond. S.A. Archaeologia, XXX. 536.

Badlesmere. Foundations. Arch. Survey, 453, from G. Payne's
Journal.

Barming. Buildings. Arch. Cant. I. 173, XIII. 169; Arch.
Survey, 453; Britton and Brayley, VIII. 1276; Coll. Antiq.
I. 190.

Borden. Foundations. Arch. Survey, 453; B.A.A. Jour. II.
346, IV. 68, VI. 448.

Boughton Monchelsea (Brushing Farm). Buildings. Arch.
Survey, 453; Liverpool Arch. Soc. Proc. N.S. I. 13th
Sess. 194; Lond. S.A. Archaeologia XXIX. 414 (plan), and
Topog. Colls., red portfolio (plan).

Boxted, see Newington.

Buckland, near Faversham. Buildings. Arch. Cant. I. 156, 173,
XV. 73; Arch. Survey, 454; Gent. Mag. 1866, ii. 758, and
Lib. Rom. Brit. Rem. i. 159; Reliquary, XIII. 144.

Burham. Buildings. Arch. Cant. XXIII. 10 (plan); B.A.A.
Jour. N.S. III. 31 (plan), 81; Lond. S.A. Proc. 2 S. XVIII. 38.

Mithraic Chamber. Antiquary, XXXI. 3; Lond. S.A. Proc.
XV. 184, XVI. 105, 108 (plan, etc.), and Topog. Colls., brown
portfolio (photos); Scot. S.A. Proc. XXIX. 202.

Canterbury (*Durovernum*). City, walls, gates, etc. Arch. Cant. XV. 338; Arch. Survey, 455; B.A.A. Jour. XII. 74, XVII. 59, XXXIII. 68, XXXV. 144; Britton and Brayley, VIII. 753; Coll. Antiq. VII. 203; Gostling, 6, 76; Gough's Camden, I. 345; Hasted, IV. 413, 415; Ireland, I. 117; King's Mun. Antiq. II. 215 n, 219; Lewis, I. 496; Lond. S.A. Archaeologia, XLIII. 151, and Proc. 2 S. I. 327; Somner, 4, 192; Stukeley's Itin. Curios. I. 122; Wright's Celt, Roman and Saxon, 146.

Burgate Street. Pavements. Arch. Cant. XV. 127; B.A.A. Jour. XXXIII. 79, XLVII. 189; Gent. Mag. 1868, i. 666, and Lib. Rom. Brit. Rem. i. 144; Lond. S.A. Proc. 2 S. V. 128, and Topog. Colls., brown portfolio (photo); Morgan, 154.

Dane John (near). Pavement. Antiquary, VIII. 266.

Fountain Inn. Pavement. Arch. Cant. XV. 127.

High Street. Pavements. Arch. Cant. XV. 127; Gent. Mag. 1805, i. 17 (plan), 1861, i. 78, and Lib. Rom. Brit. Rem. i. 141; Lond. S.A. Minute Book, VIII. 130, 131, and Topog. Colls., red portfolio (drawing); Morgan, 153.

Jewry Lane. Pavement. Arch. Cant. IV. 38, XV. 127; B.A.A. Jour. XII. 74; Gostling, 66; Hasted, IV. 411; Morgan, 154.

St Alphege (parish of). Pavement. Arch. Cant. IV. 38; Hasted, IV. 411; Somner, 192.

St Margaret (parish of). Pavement. Arch. Cant. IV. 37, XV. 127; B.A.A. Jour. XII. 74; Somner, 192.

St Martin (parish of). Pavement. Arch. Cant. IV. 38, XV. 127.

Whitefriars. Pavement. Arch. Cant. XVII. 36.

Chatham (Luton). Foundations. Arch. Cant. IX. 174; Arch. Survey, 455; Britton and Brayley, VIII. 671; Gough's Camden, I. 338, 339; Hasted, II. 74; Ireland, IV. 352; Lond. S.A. Proc. 2 S. XIV. 31, and Minute Book, XVIII. 245; Morgan, 147.

Chilham. Foundations. Arch. Cant. VII. lii, liii; Arch. Survey, 455; Gough's Camden, I. 352, 353; Hasted, III. 126; Ireland, II. 523; Lewis, I. 580.

Crayford. Foundations. Arch. Cant. XVIII. 313; Arch. Survey, 455.

Cuxton. Foundations. Arch. Cant. XXV. lxvii.

Darenth. Buildings. Antiquary, XXXI. 2, 33, 37 ; Arch. Cant. XXII. 49 (plan); B.A.A. Jour. N.S. I. 88 ; Builder, LXVII. 441, 447, 469, XC. 731 ; Dunkin, J., Hist. of Dartford, xxvi n; Lond. S.A. Archaeologia, LIX. 218 (plan) ; Reliquary and Illust. Arch. N.S. I. 45.

Dartford. Building and pavement. Arch. Cant. XVIII. 312, 313.

Dover (*Portus Dubris*). Fort and pharos. Antiquary, XIX. 122 ; Arch. Cant. XX. 128 ; Arch. Jour. XIX. 86, XXXIII. 117, LIII. 364, and Winchester vol. 1845, under Porchester Castle, 12 (plan), 13 ; Arch. Survey, 456; B.A.A. Jour. XXXIX. 415, and Canterbury vol. 1845, 298 ; Batcheller, W., Hist. of Dover, 1828, 15 ; Britton and Brayley, VIII. 1030 ; Coll. Antiq. IV. 214 ; Gent. Mag. 1811, ii. 217, 1852, i. 354, 1855, ii. 504, and Lib. Rom. Brit. Rem. i. 145 ; Gough's Camden, I. 360 ; Hasted, IV. 58 ; Ireland, II. 5 ; King's Mun. Antiq. II. 157, 159, 215, 218 ; Knight's Old England, I. 27, figs. 89, 91 ; Lond. S.A. Archaeologia, V. 331, X. 14, XLI. 436, XLV. 333; Lyon, J., Hist. of Dover, 23 ; Newcastle S.A. Arch. Æliana, N.S. VI. 183 ; Scarth's Rom. Brit. 156 ; Stukeley's Itin. Curios. I. 128 ; Wright's Celt, Roman and Saxon, 191, and Wanderings of an Antiquary, 110.

Buildings. Arch. Cant. XX. 120, 131, 295 ; Arch. Jour. XXXVIII. 432 ; Gent. Mag. 1852, i. 355 ; Lond. S.A. Archaeologia, V. 325, and Minute Book, XV. 403 ; Lyon, J., Hist. of Dover, 9 ; Wright's Wanderings of an Antiquary, 111.

Ewell, *see* Faversham.

Farleigh, East. Buildings. Arch. Cant. I. 173 ; Arch. Survey, 457 ; B.A.A. Jour. II. 75 ; Lewis, II. 210.

Faversham. Buildings. Arch. Cant. IX. lxxi, lxxii ; Arch. Survey, 457 ; Reliquary, XIII. 142, 144.

Folkestone. Buildings. Arch. Cant. X. 173; Arch. Survey, 457; Lond. S.A. Proc. 2 S. V. 479.

Frindsbury. Buildings. Arch. Cant. XVII. 189, XVIII. 189 ; Arch. Survey, 457 ; Lond. S.A. Proc. 2 S. XII. 162.

Greenwich Park. Buildings. Antiquary, XXXVIII. 108, 376 ; Arch. Jour. LIX. 210 ; Builder, LXXXII. 327.

Halstow, Lower. Foundations. Arch. Survey, 459; Gent. Mag. 1857, i. 232, and Lib. Rom. Brit. Rem. i. 161.

Hartlip. Buildings. Arch. Cant. I. 146, IX. lxxvi, XV. 107; Arch. Jour. XLVI. 334; Arch. Survey, 459; Athenaeum, June 9, 1849; B.A.A. Jour. I. 314, IV. 398 (plan), V. 88, 370, XXXIV. 249, 256; Coll. Antiq. II. 1 (plan); Godwin's Arch. Handbook, 59; Hasted, II. 540 (plan); Ireland, IV. 9; Wright's Celt, Roman and Saxon, 199, 200.

Holwood Hill, *see* Keston.

Horton Kirby. Buildings. Arch. Survey, 459; Gent. Mag. 1866, i. 817, and Lib. Rom. Brit. Rem. i. 146.

Hythe. Foundations. Lond. S.A. Archaeologia, XL. 366.

Ickham. Buildings. Arch. Cant. XIV. 139, XV. 355; Arch. Survey, 459; Gent. Mag. 1863, i. 354, and Lib. Rom. Brit. Rem. i. 146.

Keston. Buildings. Antiquary, XXIX. 56; Arch. Cant. XIII. 5; Arch. Survey, 459, 460; Athenaeum, Sept. 23, Oct. 28, Nov. 18, 1893; Cambs. Antiq. Soc. Proc. V. 257; Dunkin, J., Hist. of Bromley, 45, and of Dartford, 95; Gent. Mag. 1828, ii. 255, 1829, i. 401, and Lib. Rom. Brit. Rem. i. 147; Godwin's Arch. Handbook, 37; Illust. Lond. News, XXV. (1854), 416 (plan); Ireland, IV. 490; Lond. S.A. Archaeologia, XXII. 336 (plan), XXXVI. 120 (plan), Proc. 1 S. III. 127, and Topog. Colls., red portfolio (drawings and plans).

Loose (Joy Wood, Lockham). Walled cemetery. Arch. Cant. XV. 75, 81 (plan); Arch. Survey, 460.

Luddenham. Buildings. Arch. Cant. IX. lxxii; Arch. Survey, 460; Reliquary, XIII. 143.

Lullingstone. Pavement. Arch. Survey, 460; Britton and Brayley, VIII. 1343; Lewis, III. 185; Thorpe's Cust. Roff. 128.

Luton, *see* Chatham.

Lyminge. Buildings. Arch. Cant. IX. lxxxvii, 206, X. ci; Arch. Survey, 460; B.A.A. Jour. XL. 233; Coll. Antiq. V. 185, 198 (plan); Gent. Mag. 1860, ii. 479, 1866, i. 38, and Lib. Rom. Brit. Rem. i. 150; Lond. S.A. Proc. 2 S. X. 169.

Lymne or Lympne (*Portus Lemanis*). Fort, walls, buildings, excavations, etc. Antiquary, XII. 97, XXX. 208; Arch.

Cambrensis, 3 S. III. 311 ; Arch. Cant. XVIII. 41 ; Arch.
Jour. XXXIII. 114, LIII. 364 (plan), and Winchester vol. 1845,
under Porchester Castle, 11 ; Arch. Survey, 460 ; Britton
and Brayley, VIII. 1136 ; Coll. Antiq. II. Appendix ; Gent.
Mag. 1850, i. 631, and Lib. Rom. Brit. Rem. i. 152 ; Godwin's
Arch. Handbook, 36 ; Gough's Camden, I. 321, 365 ; Illust.
Lond. News, Oct. 5, 1850 ; Ireland, II. 246 ; Leland's Itin.
VII. 141 ; Lond. S.A. Archaeologia, XL. 361, 377, XLI. 435,
Proc. 1 S. II. 89, and Topog. Colls., red portfolio (drawings);
Price, J. E., Roman Pavement in Bucklersbury, 37 (plan of
building with hypocaust) ; Royal Instit. Proc. XVI. 40, 41 ;
Scarth's Rom. Brit. 156 ; Smith, C. Roach, Antiquities of
Richborough, Reculver, and Lymne, 1850, 233 (plans, etc.);
Stukeley's Itin. Curios. I. 132 ; Sussex Arch. Colls. VI. 103 ;
Times, Sept. 9, 1850 ; Wright's Celt, Roman and Saxon,
173, 174, 175, 179, 191, and Wanderings of an Antiquary,
123.

Maidstone. Buildings and pavement. Arch. Cant. I. 166, 171,
173, X. 163 (plan), XV. 71 ; Arch. Jour. I. 68, XXXIII. 196 ;
Arch. Survey, 461 ; B.A.A. Jour. II. 86 (plan); Morgan, 150.

Milton-next-Sittingbourne. Foundations. Arch. Cant. XII. 428 ;
Arch. Survey, 461 ; B.A.A. Jour. XXXIII. 265.

Newington (Boxted). Buildings and pavement. Arch. Cant.
XV. 104 (plan), 129 ; Arch. Survey, 462 ; Lond. S.A. Proc.
2 S. IX. 162, 357 ; Morgan, 147, 154. Fragment of orig. pav.
in Town Museum.

Northfleet. Buildings. Antiquary, XLV. 326 ; Builder, XCVII.
222.

Ospringe. Buildings. Arch. Cant. IX. lxxii ; Britton and
Brayley, VIII. 722 ; Hasted, II. 800 ; Ireland, II. 663 ;
Reliquary, XIII. 144.

Plaxtol. Buildings. Arch. Cant. II. 1 (plan); Arch. Survey,
462 ; Coll. Antiq. IV. 217 ; Gent. Mag. 1857, ii. 201, and Lib.
Rom. Brit. Rem. ii. 594 ; Lond. S.A. Proc. 2 S. XXIII. 109.

Reculver (*Regulbium*). Fort, walls, etc. Arch. Cant. XII. 1, XV.
54 ; Arch. Jour. XXXIII. 114, LIII. 352 (plan), 380 ; Arch.
Survey, 463 ; B.A.A. Jour. IX. 393 ; Boys, W., Hist. of
Sandwich, 837 ; Britton and Brayley, VIII. 935 ; Coll. Antiq.

VI. 222, VII. 163 ; Gough's Camden, I. 343 ; Hasted, III. 634; Ireland, I. 424 ; Knight's Old England, I. 34, 35, fig. 103 ; Lewis, III. 624 ; Lond. S.A. Archaeologia, XXI. 504, XLI. 431, Proc. 2 S. I. 369, and Topog. Colls., red portfolio (plan); Smith, C. Roach, Antiquities of Richborough, Reculver, and Lymne, 1850, 175 (plans, etc.).

Richborough (*Rutupiae*).   Fort, walls, buildings, excavations, etc.   Antiquary, XII. 97, XXVII. 207, XXXVI. 334; Arch. Cant. VIII. I (plan), XVI. lx, XVIII. 8 (plan), XXIV. 201 (plan), 267 (plan) ; Arch. Jour. XXXII. 506, XXXIII. 118, LIII. 204, 356 (plan), and Winchester vol. 1845, under Porchester Castle, 9, 11 ; Arch. Survey, 464; B.A.A. Jour. XXVI. 171, XXXIX. 416, XL. 105, 235, 260 (plan), N.S. VII. 334, VIII. 103 (plan), 209, and Canterbury vol. 1845, 272 ; Battely, J., Antiquitatis Rutupinae, 1745 ; Birmingham and Midland Instit. Proc. VI. 26; Boys, W., Hist. of Sandwich, 835, 865 (plan); Britton and Brayley, VIII. 943 ; Coll. Antiq. VII. 164; Godwin's Arch. Handbook, 36 ; Gostling, 356 ; Gough's Camden, I. 316, 355; Hasted, III. 686 ; Ireland, I. 573 ; King's Mun. Antiq. II. 2, 6 (plan), 276 ; Knight's Old England, I. 30, 31, figs. 98, 99, 100; Lewis, I. 78; Lond. S.A. Archaeologia, XLI. 434, Proc. 1 S. II. 28, and Topog. Colls., red portfolio (drawings) ; Mag. Brit. 1738, II. 1164 ; Newcastle S.A. Arch. Æliana, II. 369 ; Planché, J. R., A corner of Kent, 1864, cap. i ; Royal Instit. Proc. XVI. 39 ; Scarth's Rom. Brit. 154; Smith, C. Roach, Antiquities of Richborough, Reculver, and Lymne, 1850, 1 (plans, etc.); Stukeley's Itin. Curios. I. 124, and Letters, II. 224 ; Wright's Arch. Album, 13, Celt, Roman and Saxon, 146, 172, 177, 179, 188, and Wanderings of an Antiquary, 88, 94, 95.

Rochester (*Durobrivae*).   City, walls, etc.   Antiquary, XXIX. 244 ; Arch. Cant. II. 65, XVIII. 194, XXI. 1 (plan), 17 (plan), XXII. lviii, XXIV. 6, 7, 12, 15 ; Arch. Survey, 464; B.A.A. Jour. IV. 30; Builder, LXVI. 432; Chatham Observer, Apr. 28, 1894; Gough's Camden, I. 337; Hasted, II. 2; Lond. S.A. Proc. 2 S. XV. 76; Reliquary, N.S. VIII. 183; Stukeley's Itin. Curios. I. 120.

Foundations.   Arch. Cant. XXII. lxi.

Saltwood. Foundations. Arch. Survey, 465, Mr Mackeson's note.

Snodland. Foundations. Arch. Jour. I. 164, 262; Arch. Survey, 465; Wright's Wanderings of an Antiquary, 189.

Southfleet (Springhead). Buildings. Antiquary, XVI. 127; Arch. Cant. XI. xlii, XXIII. 8; Arch. Jour. XXII. 63; Arch. Survey, 465; B.A.A. Winchester vol. 1845, 235; Lond. S.A. Archaeologia, XIV. 221, 223 (plan), and Minute Book, XXVIII. 453.

Stone, near Faversham. Foundations. Arch. Cant. IX. lxxix; Arch. Survey, 465; B.A.A. Jour. XXXI. 253, 257; Hasted, II. 800.

Strood. Pavement. Arch. Survey, 466; Coll. Antiq. I. 32.

Stutfall Castle, see Lymne.

Sutton Valence. Walled cemetery. Arch. Cant. XXV. 198; Arch. Survey, 466; Lond. S.A. Archaeologia, XXIX. 421.

Swanscombe. Kiln. Arch. Cant. XXVII. lxxiii.

Teston. Buildings. Arch. Survey, 467; B.A.A. Jour. XXVIII. 282, 397, XXIX. 45 (plan).

Teynham, see Buckland.

Thurnham. Buildings. Arch. Survey, 467; Lond. S.A. Archaeologia, XXX. 536.

Upchurch. Foundations. Arch. Survey, 467; Gent. Mag. 1857, i. 232, and Lib. Rom. Brit. Rem. i. 160.

Remains of potteries. Arch. Survey, 467; B.A.A. Jour. II. 133; Coll. Antiq. VI. 173; Gent. Mag. 1857, i. 232, and Lib. Rom. Brit. Rem. i. 160; Lond. S.A. Archaeologia, XXIX. 223, and Proc. 2 S. VII. 291.

Wingham. Buildings and pavement. Antiquary, IV. 237; Arch. Cant. XIV. 134 (plan), XV. 351; Arch. Survey, 468; B.A.A. Jour. XXXVII. 427, 449, XXXVIII. 291; Builder, XLI. 591; Morgan, 146, 151; Reliquary, XXIII. 64.

Worth. Buildings. Arch. Survey, 468; Boys, W., Hist. of Sandwich, 869 (plan).

Wouldham, see Burham.

LANCASHIRE

Arch. Survey. An Archaeological Survey of Lancashire, by William Harrison. Published by the Society of Antiquaries of London, 1896.

Baines. Baines, E. History of Lancashire, edited by J. Harland. 2 vols. 1868—70.

Lanc. and Ches. Antiq. Soc. Trans. Lancashire and Cheshire Antiquarian Society Transactions, I.—XXI. 1884—1903.

Lanc. and Ches. Hist. Soc. Trans. Lancashire and Cheshire Historic Society Transactions, I.—XXV. 1849—1909.

Leigh. Leigh, C. History of Lancashire, etc. 1700.

Rauthmell. Rauthmell, R. Antiquitates Bremetonacenses, or the Roman Antiquities of Overborough, 1st ed. 1746, 2nd ed. 1824.

Watkin. Watkin, W. T. Roman Lancashire, 1883.

Whitaker's Manchester. Whitaker, John. History of Manchester, 2 vols. 1773.

Whitaker's Richmond. Whitaker, T. D. History of Richmondshire, 2 vols. 1823.

Whitaker's Whalley. Whitaker, T. D. History of Whalley, 1872—76.

Dalton-in-Furness. Foundations. Builder, XXXVII. 1059.

Dalton-near-Warton (The Quamps). Foundations. Arch. Survey, 10; Gent. Mag. 1776, 310, and Lib. Rom. Brit. Rem. ii. 343.

Hornby. Tile pavement. Arch. Survey, 14; Baines, II. 613; Lanc. and Ches. Hist. Soc. Trans. 3 S. VIII. 82; Watkin, 84, 218; Whitaker's Richmond, II. 250.

Kirkham. Foundations and tile pavement. Arch. Survey, 14; Fishwick, H., History of Kirkham, 5, 6; Lanc. and Ches. Hist. Soc. Trans. III. 60; Watkin, 206.

Lancaster. Fort, walls, foundations, etc. Arch. Survey, 15; Baines, II. 550; Britton and Brayley, IX. 51; Gough's Camden, III. 393; Lanc. and Ches. Hist. Soc. Trans. 3 S. IV. 95; Leigh, iii. 10; Leland's Itin. I. 95; Lond. S.A. Archaeologia, v. 98, and Minute Book, XIV. 408, 410; Simpson, R., Hist. of Lancaster, 1852, cap. V; Stukeley's Itin. Curios. II. 38; Watkin, 164; Whitaker's Richmond, II. 211.

Lydiat. Buildings. Lanc. and Ches. Hist. and Genealogical Notes, III. pt. 8, pars. 342, 348, and pt. 9, par. 351.

Manchester (*Mancunium*). Fort, walls, buildings, etc. Antiquary, XXXIV. 133; Arch. Jour. XLIV. 54; Arch. Survey, 16; B.A.A.

Jour. N.S. I. 214, XIII. 72, 197; Baines, I. 267; Britton and Brayley, IX. 251; Bruton, F. A., The Roman fort at Manchester, 1909; Earwaker, J. D., Local Gleanings relating to Lanc. and Ches. II. 169; Gough's Camden, III. 385; Lanc. and Ches. Antiq. Soc. Trans. VI. 189, XVI. 137, 182, XVII. 87 (plan), 178 (plan), 208 (plan); Leigh, iii. 13; Leland's Itin. v. 94; Lewis, III. 229; Lond. S.A. Archaeologia, IV. 76; Phil. Trans. XLII. 216; Stukeley's Itin. Curios. II. 28; Times, Jan. 14, 1907; Watkin, 92; Whitaker's Manchester, I. cap. ii.

Overborough. Buildings and pavement. Arch. Survey, 17, 18; Baines, II. 620; Britton and Brayley, IX. 101; Gough's Camden, III. 379; Lanc. and Ches. Hist. Soc. Trans. 3 S. XII. 4; Rauthmell; Watkin, 84.

Ribchester (*Bremetennacum*). Fort, walls, gates, buildings, excavations, etc. Antiquary, XXXV. 70, XXXVI. 8, XLII. 404; Arch. Survey, 20; Athenaeum, May 12, 1900; B.A.A. Jour. VI. 229, N.S. XIII. 124, XIV. 213; Baines, II. 104; Britton and Brayley, IX. 150; Garstang, J., Roman Ribchester, being the report of excavations made in 1908; Godwin's Arch. Handbook, 37; Gough's Camden, III. 391; Horsley, Brit. Rom. 302; Lanc. and Ches. Antiq. Soc. Trans. VII. 231, XVI. 216, XVII. 105, 141; Lanc. and Ches. Hist. Soc. Trans. 4 S. XVII. 189 (plan), 208 (plan); Leigh, iii. 1; Leland's Itin. IV. i. 22; Lewis, III. 634; Smith, T. C., and Shortt, J., Hist. of Ribchester, 1890, cap. i; Stukeley's Itin. Curios. II. 36; Watkin, 125; Whitaker's Manchester, I. 182, 185; Richmond, II. 458, and Whalley, I. 17—40, II. 373.

Walton-le-Dale, near Preston. Foundations. Arch. Survey, 24; Baines, II. 90; Lanc. and Ches. Hist. Soc. Trans. VIII. 127, X. 352; Watkin, 202.

Warrington, *see* Wilderspool, Cheshire.

Wennington. Abutments of bridge. Arch. Survey, 25; Rauthmell, 2nd ed., 135; Watkin, 81.

Worsthorne. Foundations. Arch. Survey, 26; Watkin, 210; Whitaker's Whalley, II. 223.

Wyersdale. Abutment of bridge. Arch. Survey, 26; Lanc. and Ches. Antiq. Soc. Trans. X. 252.

LEICESTERSHIRE

Burton. Burton, W. Description of Leicestershire, 1622.

Leic. Arch. Soc. Trans. Leicestershire Architectural and Archaeological Society Transactions, I.—IX. 1866—1905.

Nichols. Nichols, J. History of Leicestershire, 4 vols. in 8, 1795—1811.

Thompson. Thompson, J. History of Leicester, 1849.

Throsby's Leic. Throsby, J. History and Antiquities of the Town of Leicester, 1791.

Throsby's Views. Throsby, J. Select Views in Leicestershire, 2 vols. 1790—92.

V.C.H. Victoria History of the Counties of England. Leicestershire, I. 1907.

Broughton, Nether. Foundations and pavement. Nichols, II. i. 121 ; Stukeley's Itin. Curios. I. 107 ; V.C.H. I. 215.

Burrough-on-the-Hill. Foundations. Britton and Brayley, IX. 431; Gough's Camden, II. 318; Leland's Itin. V. 105; Lond. S.A. Archaeologia, IV. 76; Nichols, II. ii. 524; Stukeley's Itin. Curios. I. 108 ; V.C.H. I. 211.

Croft (Langham Bridges). Bridge. Country Life, March 21, 1908; Throsby's Views, II. 519; V.C.H. I. 211.

High Cross (*Venonae*). Foundations. Bib. Topog. Brit. VII. 287 ; Burton, 72; Dugdale's Warw. 2nd ed. I. 71 ; Gough's Camden, II. 297, 303; Horsley, Brit. Rom. 385, 420; Lond. S.A. Proc. 2 S. V. 284 ; Nichols, I. i. cli, IV. i. 125 ; Stukeley's Itin. Curios. I. 110, and Letters, III. 442 ; V.C.H. Leicestershire, I. 213, and Warwickshire, I. 232.

Leicester (*Ratae*). Town, walls, gates, etc. Antiquary, XII. 97 ; Arch. Jour. XLVI. 46; B.A.A. Jour. N.S. VII. 270; Bib. Topog. Brit. VII. 593 ; Britton and Brayley, IX. 330; Burton, 160; Gough's Camden, II. 313; Leic. Arch. Soc. Trans. I. 169, 215, II. 20, IV. 55, V. 219; Lewis, III. 56, 59 ; Nichols, I. i. 4; Stukeley's Itin. Curios. I. 108 (plan); Thompson, 3, 443 ; Throsby's Leic.; V.C.H. I. 181 (plan); Wright's Celt, Roman and Saxon, 151, 189.

Jewry wall or Westgate. Arch. Jour. XLVI. 47, and Winchester, vol. 1845, under Porchester Castle, 18 ; B.A.A. Jour. VI. 393; Britton and Brayley, IX. 335 ; Gough's

Camden, II. 313; King's Mun. Antiq. II. 215; Leic. Arch. Soc. Trans. I. 298, 305, II. 20, 202, 354, III. 5, IV. 53, 79, VI. 312, VIII. 42; Leic. Lit. and Phil. Soc. Report, Jan. 13, 1851; Lond. S. A. Archaeologia, XXVI. 28, Proc. 2 S. XV. 286; Nichols, I. i. 5, ii. 355, 617; Reliquary, XXIV. 174; Stukeley's Itin. Curios. I. 109; Throsby's Leic. 388; V.C.H. I. 184, 186 (plan).

Bath Lane. Foundations. Arch. Jour. XLVI. 62; Leic. Arch. Soc. Trans. II. 22, v. 41; V.C.H. I. 206.

Blackfriars Street. Pavements. Arch. Jour. XLVI. 62; Assoc. Archit. Soc. Reports, XVIII. lix; Britton and Brayley, IX. 333; Gough's Camden, II. 314; Leic. Arch. Soc. Trans. VI. 175, 208; Lond. S.A. Minute Book, VII. 163, VIII. 170, X. 196, and Topog. Colls., red portfolio (drawing); Nichols, I. i. 11; Thompson, 445; V.C.H. I. 194, 206, 207.

Dannet's Hall (Cherry Orchard). Buildings and pavement. Antiquary, XXX. 216; Arch. Jour. XLVI. 47, 53; Assoc. Archit. Soc. Reports, IX. lxix, cxvii; B.A.A. Jour. VII. 439; Britton and Brayley, IX. 333; Builder, IX. 743; Gent. Mag. 1786, ii. 825, and Lib. Rom. Brit. Rem. i. 168; Gough's Camden, II. 314; King's Mun. Antiq. II. 174; Leic. Arch. Soc. Trans. III. 280, 334, 387; Leic. Lit. and Phil. Soc. Reports, June, 1852, 15, 17; Lond. and Middsx. Arch. Soc. Trans. III. 406; Lond. S.A. Proc. 1 S. II. 205, 2 S. IV. 183; Nichols, I. i. 12; Thompson, 445; V.C.H. I. 196, 197 (plan). Portions of orig. pav. in Town Museum.

Eastgate. Sewer. Arch. Jour. XLVI. 61; Thompson, 447; V.C.H. I. 205.

Gardiner's factory. Foundations. Gent. Mag. 1806, ii. 870, and Lib. Rom. Brit. Rem. i. 169.

Goal. Pavement. Arch. Jour. XLVI. 62; Britton and Brayley, IX. 332; Throsby's Leic. 383; V.C.H. I. 205.

Grey Friars. Pavement. Nichols, I. ii. 619; Throsby's Leic. 396; V.C.H. I. 190, 206.

High Street and Silver Street. Buildings and pavement. Assoc. Archit. Soc. Reports, XX. lx, XXVI. 461; Leic. Arch. Soc. Trans. II. 23, 24; V.C.H. I. 206.

High Cross Street. Buildings and Pavements. Antiquary,

XXXVII. 100, XXXVIII. 108; Arch. Jour. XIV. 280, XLIV. 53,
XLVI. 49, 61, 62, 63; Assoc. Archit. Soc. Reports, XXVI. 459;
Bib. Topog. Brit. VII. 596; Builder, LXXX. 195; Fowler,
No. 11; Gough's Camden, II. 314; Lanc. and Ches. Antiq.
Soc. Trans. III. 264; Leic. Arch. Soc. Trans. I. 215, II. 23,
IX. 169; Leic. and Rutland N. and Q. III. 136; Lond. S.A.
Proc. 2 S. XIX. 246, Minute Book, XVIII. 271, 295, and
Topog. Colls., red portfolio (drawing of pavement); Morgan,
35, 113, 121, 276; Nichols, I. i. 9, 11, ii. 356; Phil. Trans.
XXVII. 324; Pointer's Stunsfield, 34; Reliquary, XIII. 224,
XXIV. 174; Stukeley's Itin. Curios. I. 109; Thompson, 445,
447; Throsby's Leic. 19, 20, 383; V.C.H. I. 190, 205,
206, 207. Octagonal panel and other pieces in Town
Museum.

Jewry Wall Street (now Great Central Station). Pavements.
Antiquary, XXXIII. 17; Arch. Jour. XLVI. 62; Assoc. Archit.
Soc. Reports, XV. civ, XVIII. lix, XXIV. xcix, XXV. xxxvii,
lxxviii; B.A.A. Jour. N.S. VII. 159; Builder, LXXI. 363,
LXXV. 64; Gent. Mag. 1830, ii. 355, 1841, ii. 190, and Lib.
Rom. Brit. Rem. i. 169, 170; King's Mun. Antiq. II. 172; Leic.
Arch. Soc. Trans. II. 22, V. 296, IX. 152; Lond. S.A. Proc.
2 S. VII. 280, XV. 287, and Topog. Colls., brown portfolio
(print); Morgan, 113; Reliquary, XXVI. 56; Thompson,
445; V.C.H. I. 194, 205. One pavement *in situ* under the
station. Portions of another in the Museum of Archaeology,
Cambridge.

St Martin's Church. Foundations and pavement. Arch.
Jour. I. 390, XLVI. 50, 59, 62; Assoc. Archit. Soc. Reports,
VI. 274; B.A.A. Jour. XIX. 113; Gent. Mag. 1861, ii. 141,
and Lib. Rom. Brit. Rem. ii. 593; Leic. Arch. Soc. Trans.
II. 90, 151, IV. 273; Nichols, I. i. 8, 12; V.C.H. I. 189, 205.

St Nicholas Street. Foundations and pavements. Antiquary,
XXXIV. 234, XXXV. 41; Arch. Jour. XLVI. 48, 49, 62; Assoc.
Archit. Soc. Reports, IX. lxix, XX. lx, XXIX. xcix, XXV.
xxxvii; Athenaeum, Oct. 1, 1898; B.A.A. Jour. N.S. IV. 289,
VII. 158; Gent. Mag. 1863, ii. 358, and Lib. Rom. Brit. Rem.
i. 169; Leic. Arch. Soc. Trans. II. 207, 301, III. 334, V. 41 n,
VII. 17, 207, VIII. 375, IX. 6; Nichols, I. i. 12; Reliquary

and Illust. Arch. N.S. v. 26; Thompson, 445; V.C.H. I. 187, 188, 205, 206.

Sarah Street. Foundations and pavement. Antiquary, XII. 228, Arch. Jour. XLVI. 62; Builder, XLIX. 114, 520; Leic. Arch. Soc. Trans. II. 22, V. 41, VI. 210, IX. 174; V.C.H. I. 195, 206.

Silver Street. Pavement, etc. Arch. Jour. XLVI. 62; Assoc. Archit. Soc. Reports, XIII. cii, XX. lix; Leic. Arch. Soc. Trans. IV. 106, 194, V. 49, 55, VII. 207; V.C.H. I. 190, 206, 207.

Southgate Street. Pavement, etc. Arch. Jour. XLVI. 62; Leic. Arch. Soc. Trans. II. 22, 175; V.C.H. I. 190, 205.

Talbot Lane. Foundations and sewer. Arch. Jour. XLVI. 62; Leic. Arch. Soc. Trans. VIII. 40 (plan); Nichols, I. ii. 618; Thompson, 447; Throsby's Leic. 2, 388; V.C.H. I. 198, 205.

Town Hall Lane. Pavement. Assoc. Archit. Soc. Reports, XXVI. 462; Builder, LXXXIV. 316; V.C.H. I. 189, 207.

Vauxhall. Pavement. Arch. Jour. XLVI. 62; Gough's Camden, II. 314; Nichols, I. i. 11; Throsby's Leic. 19; V.C.H. I. 196, 205.

Vine Street. Pavement. Arch. Jour. XLVI. 63; Thompson, 445; V.C.H. I. 196, 207. A portion in the Town Museum.

White Lion Inn. Pavement. Arch. Jour. XLVI. 62; Nichols, I. i. 11; V.C.H. I. 205.

Medbourne. Buildings and pavement. Arch. Jour. XIX. 182, LXVIII. 218; Assoc. Archit. Soc. Reports, XIV. lxii; Gent. Mag. 1795, i. 274, 1801, ii. 1182, and Lib. Rom. Brit. Rem. i. 170; Gough's Camden, II. 301; Leic. Arch. Soc. Trans. I. 209, V. 69, 70, 92, 171; Leic. and Rutland N. and Q. II. 209; Lewis, III. 271; Lond. S.A. Proc. 2 S. VII. 196, 315, and Topog. Colls., brown portfolio (lithograph of pavement); Nichols, II. ii. 717; Stukeley's Itin. Curios. I. 109 n; V.C.H. I. 214.

Mountsorrel. Sepulchral chamber. Leic. Arch. Soc. Trans. V. 344; V.C.H. I. 215.

Rothley. Buildings and pavement. Antiquary, XXXVII. 66, XXXVIII. 108; Assoc. Archit. Soc. Reports, XXVI. 458;

Britton and Brayley, IX. 406; Leic. Arch. Soc. Trans. IX.
157, 169; Lond. S.A. Archaeologia, IX. 370, Proc. 2 S. XIX.
245, and Minute Book, XXII. 434; Nichols, III. ii. 956;
Reliquary, XIII. 18; Reliquary and Illust. Arch N.S. III.
113; V.C.H. I. 216 (plan).

Sapcote. Pavement. Nichols, IV. ii. 898; Throsby's Views, II.
231; V.C.H. I. 217.

Wanlip. Pavement. Britton and Brayley, IX. 408; Lewis, IV.
452; Lond. S.A. Minute Book, I. 58; Reliquary, XIII. 18;
V.C.H. I. 218.

Wymondham. Buildings and pavement. Assoc. Archit. Soc.
Reports, VIII. lxiii; Gent. Mag. 1797, i. 75, and Lib. Rom.
Brit. Rem. i. 175; Lond. S.A. Minute Book, XXXIII. 15;
Nichols, II. ii. 889; V.C.H. I. 219.

LINCOLNSHIRE

Allen.   Allen, T. History of the County of Lincoln, 2 vols. 1834.
Andrew's Winterton. Andrew, W. History of Winterton, 1836.
Howlett. Howlett, B. Selection of views in the County of Lincoln, 1805
    (not paged).
Lincs. N. and Q. Lincolnshire Notes and Queries, I.—VII. 1888—1904.
Trollope. Trollope, E. Sleaford, 1872.

Ancaster (*Causennae*). Buildings and Pavement. Allen, II. 267,
268; Arch. Jour. XXVII. 1 (plan); Arch. Review, III. 178;
Assoc. Archit. Soc. Reports, VII. 53; Britton and Brayley,
IX. 761; Coll. Antiq. V. 149; Gough's Camden, II. 335, 358;
Holinshed, R., Chronicles of England, 1587, I. 217; Horsley's
Brit. Rom. 432; Leland's Itin. I. 29; Lewis, I. 57; Mag.
Brit. 1738, II. 1428; Stukeley's Itin. Curios. I. 86; Trollope,
471, 474.

Kiln. Arch. Jour. XXVII. 11; Trollope, 480.

Appleby. Foundations. Andrew's Winterton, 47.

Blyborough. Pavement. Lewis, I. 275; Trollope, 57.

Boston. Foundations (?). Lewis, I. 296; Marrat, W., Hist. of
Lincs. 1814, I. 3; Stukeley's Letters, II. 257.

Bottesford. Hypocaust. Arch. Review, III. 179.

Bourne. Pavement. Arch. Jour. XXII. 336; Lewis, I. 303.

Caistor. Foundations. Allen, II. 225; Arch. Review, III. 179; Assoc. Archit. Soc. Reports, VI. 150; Britton and Brayley, IX. 687; Gough's Camden, II. 386; Stukeley's Itin. Curios. I. 101.

Claxby. Pavement. Allen, II. 208; Lewis, I. 606.

Denton. Buildings and pavement. Allen, II. 315; Arch. Review, III. 179; Britton and Brayley, IX. 773; Fowler, Nos. 9 and 10; Gough's Camden, II. 359, and Brit. Topog. I. 533; Howlett; Lewis, II. 29; Lond. S.A. Archaeologia, XXII. 26, 28, and Minute Book, XXXIII. 15; Morgan, 139; Phil. Trans. XXXV. 428; Stukeley's Letters, I. 203, II. 261; Trollope, 45; Turnor, E., Hist. of Grantham, 1806, 126.

Gedney Hill. Foundations (?). Arch. Review, III. 180; Gough's Camden, II. 342.

Haceby. Buildings and pavement. Allen, II. 284; Arch. Review, III. 180; Fowler, Appendix 2, No. 22; Gent. Mag. 1818, i. 634, ii. 38, and Lib. Rom. Brit. Rem. i. 176; Lond. S.A. Archaeologia, XXII. 26, 28; Morgan, 139.

Hibaldstow. Foundations. Allen, II. 217; Arch. Review, III. 180; Britton and Brayley, IX. 679; Gough's Camden, II. 376; Lewis, II. 501; Phil. Trans. XXII. 561; Stukeley's Letters, II. 251; Trollope, 57.

Horkstow. Buildings and pavement. Allen, II. 235; Andrew's Winterton, 32; Arch. Jour. X. 71; Arch. Review, III. 180; Assoc. Archit. Soc. Reports, XIX. lxi, XXVIII. 44; B.A.A. Jour. XXXVIII. 99; Brown, R., History of Barton-on-Humber, I. 3; East Riding (Yorks.) Antiq. Soc. Trans. XIV. 82; Fowler, No. 2; Lond. S.A. Minute Book, XXVI. 499; Lysons' Reliquiae, I. i. 1, and pls. I—VII; Morgan, 33, 129, 136; Trollope, 61; Wright's Celt, Roman and Saxon, 253.

Horncastle. Walls. Allen, II. 90; Antiquary, XLIV. 402; Arch. Review, III. 180; Gough's Camden, II. 378; Stukeley's Itin. Curios. I. 30 (plan); Weir, G., Hist. of Horncastle, 1820, 5.

Lincoln (*Lindum*). The city, walls, gates, etc. Allen, I. 101; Antiquary, XII. 97, XIX. 33, XXIV. 21; Arch. Jour. XVII. 4, XXXVIII. 125, XL. 106, XLI. 313, XLIV. 53, XLV. 485, XLVIII. 186, LXVI. 343 (plan), 353, Lincoln, vol. 1848, lx (plan), and

Norwich, vol. 1847, 129, 131; Arch. Review, III. 137, 177, 180; Assoc. Archit. Soc. Reports, XXII. 56; B.A.A. Jour. I. 258, VIII. 257, XXXV. 308 (plan), XLVI. 8, 55, XLVII. 186, 188; Britton and Brayley, IX. 593; Builder, LXXIV. 215; Gent. Mag. 1771, 200, 1836, i. 583, and Lib. Rom. Brit. Rem. i. 177, ii. 395; Godwin's Arch. Handbook, 37; Gough's Camden, II. 361 (plan); Knight's Old England, I. 46; Lewis, III. 86; Lincoln, History of, 1816, 25, 26, 27, 124, 125; Lincoln, A Survey of the Antiquities of the city of, 1840—48, 17, 35, 43, 44; Lincs. N. and Q. I. 144; Lond. S.A. Archaeologia, IV. 81, XII. 179; Scarth's Rom. Brit. 152; Stukeley's Itin. Curios. I. 88 (plan), and Letters, II. 315, 317; Wright's Celt, Roman and Saxon, 177.

Bailgate. Basilica, forum, mint, wall, etc. Allen, I. 103; Antiquary, XXXIII. 99, 231; Arch. Jour. XXXV. 100, XXXVI. 281, XL. 317, XLIX. 131 (plan), 203, and Winchester vol. 1845, under Porchester Castle, 15; Arch. Review, III. 181; Assoc. Archit. Soc. Reports, XXI. 3 (plan), XXII. 57; Athenaeum, May 18, 1878, June 14, 1884, April 18, 1891; B.A.A. Jour. XXXIV. 269, XXXV. 315; Britton and Brayley, IX. 595; Builder, XXXVII. 328, LX. 319, LXXII. 304; Gough's Brit. Topog. I. 522; Howlett; Lincoln, Hist. of, 1816, 125, 140, 141; Lincoln, A Survey of the Antiquities of the city of, 1840—48, 16; Lond. S.A. Archaeologia, LIII. 233 (plan), LVI. 371 (plan), Proc. 2 S. VII. 435 (plan), XIII. 341, XVII. 5, and Topog. Colls., brown portfolio (plans); Reliquary, N.S. I. 107.

Castle. Buildings and pavement. Gent. Mag. 1786, ii. 540, and Lib. Rom. Brit. Rem. i. 177.

Cathedral cloisters. Pavement, 1793. Allen, I. 106, 107; Britton and Brayley, IX. 601; Fowler No. 4; Lincoln, Hist. of, 1816, 131; Lond. S.A. Minute Book, XXV. 118, and Topog. Colls., red portfolio (coloured drawing).

Eastgate. Foundations and shaft. Arch. Jour. XIX. 169, XLI. 317 (plan).

Exchequergate. Buildings and pavement. Allen, I. 104; Arch. Jour. XXXVI. 277; Assoc. Archit. Soc. Reports, XXII. 59; Britton and Brayley, IX. 597; Fowler, No. 4; Gough's

Camden, II. 366, and Brit. Topog. I. 522; Knight's Old England, I. 51, fig. 41; Lanc. and Ches. Antiq. Soc. Trans. III. 264; Lincoln, Hist. of, 1816, 127; Lincoln, A Survey of the Antiquities of the city of, 1840—48, 25; Liverpool Arch. Soc. Trans. N.S. I. Session 13, 190; Lond. S.A. Archaeologia, IV. 83, Minute Book, III. 230, and Vet. Mon. I. pl. LVII; Phil. Trans. XLI. 855; Stukeley's Letters, II. 279, 315.

Greetwell Fields. Buildings and pavement. Antiquary, X. 228, XXVIII. 162; Arch. Jour. XLI. 321, XLVIII. 187, XLIX. 258 (plan), 408; Assoc. Archit. Soc. Reports, XXI. 48 (plan), XXII. 61, 68; Builder, LXI. 134; Hull Museum Publications, No. 16 (Sept. 1903); Reliquary, N.S. VII. 185. Orig. pav. in Hull Museum.

High Street. Bases of pillars, causeway and pavement. Athenaeum, Aug. 9, 1845; B.A.A. Jour. I. 259, XLVI. 74, 221.

King's Arms. Buildings and pavement. Lincoln, Hist. of, 1816, 128.

Monson Street. Pavement. Arch. Jour. XVII. 16.

New Road. Pilaster. Arch. Jour. XLII. 261.

Localities not given. Pavement. B.A.A. Jour. II. 186; Dorset Field Club Proc. XXI. 170, 172; Gent. Mag. 1794, i. 274, and Lib. Rom. Brit. Rem. i. 177; Linc. N. and Q. III. 179; Morgan, 138.

Marton. Pavement. Trollope, 54.

Nettleham. Reservoir. Britton and Brayley, IX. 600; Lincoln, Hist. of, 1816, 130; Stukeley's Letters, II. 255 n.

Paunton, Great and Little. Buildings and pavement. Allen, II. 316; Arch. Review, III. 183; British Curiosities in Art and Nature, 1721, 100; Britton and Brayley, IX. 778; Gough's Camden, II. 335, 358; Howlett; Lond. S.A. Archaeologia, XXII. 26, 29; Mag. Brit. 1738, II. 1420; Stukeley's Itin. Curios. I. 85; Trollope, 45.

Roxby. Pavement. Allen, II. 222; Andrew's Winterton, 32, 55; Arch. Review, III. 183; Assoc. Archit. Soc. Reports, XIX. lxi, lxiii; Britton and Brayley, IX. 679; Fowler, No. 3; Gough's Camden, II. 376, 388; Lond. S.A. Proc. 2 S. VI. 114, and Vet. Mon. II. pl. IX; Lysons' Reliquiae, I. i. 1;

Morgan, 129, 139; Phil. Trans. XXII. 565; Prynne's Diary,
Surtees Soc. LIV. 212; Stukeley's Letters, II. 253, 291;
Trollope, 59.

Sandton, near Thornholme.   Kiln (?).   Arch. Review, III. 183;
Gough's Camden, II. 376; Phil. Trans. XXII. 564, and Royal
Soc. Archives, classified papers, XVI. 47; Stukeley's Letters,
II. 252.

Saxby.   Buildings.   Allen, II. 35; Arch. Review, III. 183.

Scampton.   Buildings and pavement.   Allen, II. 58; Arch.
Review, III. 183; Britton and Brayley, IX. 658; Fowler,
No. 8; Howlett; Illingworth, C., Account of Scampton,
1808, 3 (plans, etc.); Lewis, IV. 28; Morgan, 139; Trollope,
52.

Scawby, see Weston.

Stainby or Steanby.   Buildings and pavement.   Gent. Mag.
1819, i. 422, and Lib. Rom. Brit. Rem. i. 180; Lewis, IV.
172; Lond. S.A. Archaeologia, XXII. 26, 29.

Stamford.   Foundations and pavement.   Arch. Review, III. 183;
Gent. Mag. 1839, ii. 527, and Lib. Rom. Brit. Rem. i. 180;
Lond. and Middsx. Arch. Soc. Trans. III. 500; Lond. S.A.
Minute Book, XVI. 401; Nevinson C., Hist. of Stamford,
1879, 23; Reliquary, X. 16; Trollope, 42 n.

Stoke, North.   Buildings and pavement.   Godwin's Arch. Handbook, 59; Lond. S.A. Archaeologia, XXII. 26, 30 (plan);
Stukeley's Letters, II. 323.

Stoke Rochford.   Building.   Allen, II. 317; Lond. S.A. Archaeologia, XXIII. 385.

Sturton-by-Stow.   Pavement.   Fowler, App. 2, Nos. 10 and 11;
Morgan, 139.

Torksey.   Foundations.   Arch. Review, III. 184; Britton and
Brayley, IX. 660; Howlett; Stukeley's Letters, II. 274.

Walesby.   Buildings.   Arch. Review, III. 184; Assoc. Archit.
Soc. Reports, VI. 135; Gent. Mag. 1861, i. 683, and Lib.
Rom. Brit. Rem. i. 180; Illust. Lond. News, XXXVIII. (1861),
482; Reliquary, II. 49, 52 (plan).

Weston, near Scawby.   Buildings and pavement.   Lewis, IV. 31;
Trollope, 57.

Winteringham.   Pavement.   Allen, II. 222; Andrew's Winterton,

86; Arch. Review, III. 184; Stukeley's Itin. Curios. I. 95; Trollope, 62.

Winterton. Buildings and pavement. Allen, II. 223; Andrew's Winterton, 32; Arch. Jour. X. 71; Arch. Review, III. 184; Britton and Brayley, IX. 678; Fowler, Nos. 1 and 5; Gough's Camden, II. 388, and Brit. Topog. I. 529; King's Mun. Antiq. II. 168, 178; Lewis, IV. 611; Lond. S.A. Minute Book, VI. 75; Lysons' Reliquiae, I. i. 1; Morgan, 33, 129, 135, 139; Phil. Trans. XXII. 565; Stukeley's Letters, II. 290, 293, 344; Trollope, 59, 60; Wright's Celt, Roman and Saxon, 253.

Kiln (?) Lond. S.A. Proc. 2 S. IV. 190; Reliquary, IX. 145; Trollope, 60.

LONDON

Allen's Lond. Allen, Thomas. The History and Antiquities of London, Westminster and Southwark, 1837.

Archer. Archer, J. W. Vestiges of Old London, 1851.

Cunningham Lond. Cunningham, P. London Past and Present, edited by H. B. Wheatley, 1891.

Guildhall Mus. Guildhall Museum Catalogue, 2nd ed. 1908.

Harrison's Lond. Harrison, Walter. History, Description and Survey of the Cities of London and Westminster, 1775.

Herbert's Hist. of St Michael. Herbert, William. History and Antiquities of St Michael, Crooked Lane, 1831.

Hughson's Lond. Hughson, David. History of London, 1806.

Kelsey's Descr. of Sewers. Kelsey, Richard, surveyor, and William Santle, inspector. "A Description of the sewers of the City of London and liberties hereof" (MS. Guildhall), 1840.

Knight's Lond. Knight, Charles. London, 1841.

Lethaby's Lond. Lethaby, W. R. London before the Conquest, 1902.

Loftie's Lond. Loftie, W. J. A History of London, 2nd ed. 1884.

Lond. and Middsx. Arch. Soc. Trans. London and Middlesex Archaeological Society Transactions, 1856—1911.

Lond. and Middsx. Arch. Soc. Proc. London and Middlesex Archaeological Society Proceedings, 1860—3, 1870—4.

Lond. Topog. Record. London Topographical Record I—VI. 1901—9.

Maitland's Lond. Maitland, William, The History and Survey of London, 1756.

Malcolm's Lond. Malcolm, J. P., Londinium Redivivum, 1802—7.

Newton's Lond. Newton, William, London in the Olden Times, 1855.

L.

Price's Bastion. Price, J. E. On a Bastion of London Wall, or Excavations in Camomile Street, Bishopsgate, 1880.

Price's Bucklersbury. Price, J. E. A Description of the Roman Tessellated Pavement found in Bucklersbury, 1870.

Price's Roman Antiq. Price, J. E. Roman Antiquities illustrated by remains recently discovered on the site of the National Safe Deposit Company's Premises, Mansion House, London, 1873.

Seymour's Lond. Seymour, Robert. Survey of London and Westminster, 1734—5.

Smith, C. Roach, Rom. Lond. Smith, C. Roach. Illustrations of Roman London, 1859.

Smith, J. T. Lond. Topog. Smith, J. T. Ancient Topography of London, 1815.

Smith, J. T. Streets of Lond. Smith, J. T. The Streets of London, 1849.

Stow's Lond. Stow, John. Survey of London, Strype's edition, 1720.

Timbs' Lond. Timbs, John. Curiosities of London, new edit. 1868.

Tite's Cat. Roy. Exch. Tite, W. Descriptive Catalogue of the Antiquities found at the New Royal Exchange, London, 1848.

V. C. H. Lond. Victoria Histories of the Counties of England, London, I. 1909.

Wilkinson's Lond. Wilkinson, R. Londina Illustrata, 1819.

Woodward's Bishopsgate. Woodward, J. An Account of some Roman Urns and other Antiquities lately digg'd up near Bishopsgate, 1713.

Woodward's Lond. Woodward, J. Remarks upon the Ancient and Present state of London, 3rd ed. 1723.

City Wall and Gates

Aldermanbury Postern. Wall with blind arches, 1857. Arch. Review, I. 274; Smith, C. Roach, Rom. Lond. 17 (illus.); V.C.H. Lond. I. 62, 86.

Aldersgate. Wall. Arch. Jour. L. 233; Builder, LIV. 314, 316, 335 (section and illus.); Lewis, III. 163; Lond. S.A. Proc. XII. 380, 396; Lond. Topog. Record, III. 72.

Aldgate. Old Ald-gate. Builder, LXXX. 196.

Aldgate. Tower of Wall, 1753. Lond. Topog. Record, IV. 9; Timbs' Lond. 713.

Aldgate. Corner of Jewry Street, 1861. Gent. Mag. 1861, i. 646, and Lib. Rom. Brit. Rem. i. 221; Lond. S.A. Topog. Coll., red portfolio (drawing by D. A. Cobbett).

1905. Antiquary, XLI. 244, XLII. 2; The Sphere, June 10, 1905 (illus.).

America Square (Minories, Vine Street, Fenchurch Street, G.E.R. Station). 1908. Antiquary, III. 62—5 (plan); Arch. Jour. XXXVII. 452, XL. 299; B.A.A. Jour. XXXVI. 463, XXXVII. 209; Builder, XCV. 266; Knight's Lond. I. 163—4, and Old England, I. 50; Lewis, III. 164; Lond. S.A. Archaeologia, XL. 299, LII. 613, and Proc. 2 S. XXII. 475; Lond. Topog. Record, IV. 9; Maitland's Lond. I. 31; Times, Dec. 7, 1880; V.C.H. Lond. I. 52, 87, 131.

Angel Street and Butcher Hall Lane. Wall, 1842. Gent. Mag. 1843, i. 21, 22; V.C.H. Lond. 87.

Bethlehem Hospital. Hughson's Lond. I. 37; Smith, J. T., Lond. Topog. 28, 32 (engravings).

Bevis Marks, Aldgate, see Goring Street and Houndsditch.

Bishopsgate Street and Wormwood Street. Wall and bastion. Harrison's Lond. 10; Knight's Lond. I. 160, and Old England, I. 47; Price's Bastion; Stow's Lond. I. 10; V.C.H. Lond. I. 56; Woodward's Lond. 15, 48.

Blackfriars. 1843. Lond. and Middsx. Arch. Soc. Trans. N.S. I. 353; Lond. S.A. Proc. I. 7.

Bloomfield Street, Broker Row. Antiquary, XI. 180.

Broad Street, New, at Allhallows Church. Wall and bastion, 1905. Arch. Jour. LX. 176; Lond. S.A. Archaeologia, LX. 197, 214, and Proc. 2 S. XXI. 163, 228, 441; Smith, J. T., Rom. Lond. 28; V.C.H. Lond. I. 58, 92.

Bull and Mouth Street, and see Aldersgate. 1841. Arch. Review, I. 282; Athenaeum, April 28, 1888, 540; B.A.A. Jour. XLVII. 98; Builder, LIV. 314 (illus.); Knight's Lond. I. 165; Lond. S.A. Archaeologia, XXX. 522 (section), LII. 609—16 (plan); V.C.H. Lond. I. 63, 122.

Bush Lane. Gale's Iter. Brit. (1709), 89; Lond. S.A. Archaeologia, XXIX. 156, 404, XXXIII. 118.

Camomile Street. Wall and bastion. B.A.A. Jour. XXXII. 490 (plan); Britton and Brayley, X. i. 83; Lond. S.A. Proc. 2 S. III. 16; Malcolm's Lond. I. 350; Price's Bastion; V.C.H. Lond. I. 55, 56.

Castle Street. Wall and bastion. Builder, XLVII. 311; Illust. Lond. News, XLVII. (August 19, 1865), 157; V.C.H. Lond. I. 63.

Christ's Hospital. Wall and bastion, 1842. B.A.A. Jour. N.S.
xv. 119; Builder, XCII. 672, XCIV. 110; Lond. S.A. Proc.,
2 S. XXII. 277; V.C.H. Lond. I. 64, 106.

Coopers Row, Crutched Friars. 1864. Antiquary, XII. 97;
Lond. and Middsx. Arch. Soc. Trans. III. 52 (illus.); Lond.
S.A. Archaeologia, XL. 297 (illus.), and Proc. 2 S. II. 419;
V.C.H. Lond. I. 99.

Cripplegate, St Giles' Church Yard. Wall and bastion. Anti-
quary, XII. 97, XXXVI. 335; Arch. Review, I. 276; Archer,
(pls. IV—VI); Builder, LXXIX. 182; Gent. Mag. 1843, i. 607—8,
Lib. Rom. Brit. Rem. i. 219; Lethaby's Lond. 79; Lewis, III.
163; Lond. and Middsx. Arch. Soc. Trans. I. 338, III. 223,
N.S. I. 356 (photo and drawing); Lond. Topog. Record,
IV. 9, V. 101; Smith, C. Roach, Rom. Lond. 17; Smith, J. T.
Rom. Lond. 36; V.C.H. Lond. I. 62, 99.

Crutched Friars. Wall, 1905. Antiquary, XLI. 206; Builder,
LXXXVIII. 533; Daily Graphic, May 9, 1905 (with sketch);
V.C.H. Lond. I. 52.

Duke Place. Wall. B.A.A. Jour. XXXVII. 209.

Duke Street. Wall and bastions. B.A.A. Jour. XLIII. 203;
Maitland's Lond. I. 31; Price's Bastion, 17 (illus.); Smith, C.
Roach, Rom. Lond. 16 (illus.); V.C.H. Lond. I. 53 (plan),
see also Houndsditch.

Falcon Square. Wall. Lewis, III. 163.

Fenchurch Street. Wall and bastion. Athenaeum, Feb. 26, 1881,
304—5; Builder, XXXIX. 741.

Fore Street, back of. Wall. Lewis, III. 163.

Giltspur Street. Wall and bastion. Lond. S.A. Proc. 2 S. XXII.
476.

Goring Street, formerly Bevis Marks. Wall and bastion, 1884.
Antiquary, X. 134; V.C.H. Lond. I. 55.

Houndsditch. Wall and bastion. Arch. Jour. XXXVIII. 289;
B.A.A. Jour. XXXVII. 86, XXXVIII. 132; Lond. S.A. Archaeologia, LX. 187 (plan and illus.), and Proc. 2 S. XX. 300, XXI.
229; Lond. Topog. Record, IV. 9; Maitland's Lond. I. 31;
Smith, C. Roach, Rom. Lond. 16 (illus.); V.C.H. Lond. I.
54, 55, 105.

Jewry Street. Wall, 1861. B.A.A. Jour. XXXVI. 163, XLIII. 203;

Builder, LXXXIX. 521 ; Gent. Mag. 1861, i. 646, and Lib.
Rom. Brit. Rem. i. 221; Lond. S.A. Archaeologia, LX. 191,
193 (plan), and Proc. 2 S. XXI. 229; The Sphere, XXI.
240 ; V.C.H. Lond. I. 52, 106.

Lambeth Hill, *see* Thames Street, upper.

London Wall. Wall, 1817, 1882, 1905. Arch. Jour. LX. 137;
Antiquary, XI. 180, XII. 97, XVII. 243 ; B.A.A. Jour. XXXVIII.
424 ; Builder, LVII. 236; Gent. Mag. 1817, i. 196; Kelsey's
Descr. of Sewers, 138 ; Knight's Lond. I. 164—5; Lewis, III.
163 ; Lond. S.A. Archaeologia, LX. 169—212 (illus.), 237,
and Proc. II. 307, 351, III. 16; Smith, C. Roach, Rom. Lond.
15 ; Tite's Cat. Roy. Exch. xxxi; V.C.H. Lond. I. 59, 60,
90, 112.

Ludgate. Wall and Barbican Tower, 1792. Timbs' Lond. 715;
V.C.H. Lond. I. 69, 114.
1892. Antiquary, XXV. 51; Archer (plate III); Athenaeum,
March 10, 1855, 297 ; B.A.A. Jour. XLV. 200 ; Builder, XLII.
468 ; Gent. Mag. 1806, ii. 792; Lib. Rom. Brit. Rem. i. 213;
Knight's Lond. I. 165 ; Lewis, III. 163 ; Lond. S.A. Proc.
2 S. XXII. 278.

Mincing Lane. Wall. Loftie's Lond. I. 32.

Monkwell Street (Windsor Court). Wall and bastion. Arch.
Review, I. 360; V.C.H. Lond. I. 63, 115.

Monument Yard. Wall, 1880. Antiquary, II. 222; V.C.H. Lond.
I. 71, 116.

Moorgate Street. Wall. Arch. Jour. LX. 176; B.A.A. Jour.
XXXVIII. 424 ; Lond. S.A. Proc. 2 S. III. 16, XX. 299; Smith,
J. T., Rom. Lond. 28 ; V.C.H. Lond. I. 61.

Newgate. Wall and gate, 1857 and 1900, 3 and 4. Antiquary,
XII. 97 (woodcut), XXXVI. 314; Archer (plate VIII); Arch. Jour.
XXXII. 327, 477 ; B.A.A. Jour. XXXI. 76, 80, 108, XXXII. 385,
388; Builder, LXXIX. 443 (illus.), LXXXIV. 546, XCIV. 202;
Gent. Mag. 1836, i. 135—6, 1857, ii. 449; Lond. and Middsx.
Arch. Soc. Trans. I. 195, V. 403, N.S. I. 351 (illus.); Lethaby's
Lond. 76 ; Lewis, III. 163; Lond. S.A. Archaeologia, LIX.
125—140 (plan and illus.), and Proc. 2 S. XXII. 278; Lond.
Topog. Record, III. 72; Price's Rom. Antiq. 49; V.C.H.
Lond. I. 35, 49, 65 (plan, fig. 21), 66, 68, 117, 118.

Playhouse Yard, Blackfriars. Wall. Arch. Jour. XXXIX. 426;
    Gent. Mag. 1843, i. 635; Lethaby's Lond. 76; Lond. and
    Middsx. Arch. Soc. Trans. N.S. I. 353; Lond. S.A. Proc. I. 7;
    Smith, C. Roach, Coll. Antiq. I. 125, 127; V.C.H. Lond. I.
    69, 118, 133.
Printing House Square. Wall, 1849. B.A.A. Jour. V. 155;
    Timbs' Lond. 56, 713; V.C.H. Lond. I. 69, 119.
St Martin le Grand. Wall. Arch. Review, I. 282; Athenaeum,
    April 28, 1888, 540, Feb. 7, 1891, 192; Lond. S.A. Archaeo-
    logia, LII. 609, and Topog. Coll., brown portfolio (3 photos).
St Peter's Hill, Upper Thames Street. Wall. Lond. S.A.
    Archaeologia, XL. 48; V.C.H. Lond. I. 125.
Suffolk Lane. Wall. Lond. S.A. Archaeologia, XL. 48; V.C.H.
    Lond. I. 71, 126.
Thames Street, Lower. Wall, 1813. Laing, David, Descrip. of
    New Custom House, 5—6; Lond. S.A. Archaeologia, XL.
    48; Timbs' Lond. 713; Tite's Cat. Roy. Exch. xxiii;
    V.C.H. Lond. I. 35, 71.
Thames Street, Upper, at Lambeth Hill. Wall. Antiquary, XII.
    100; Knight's Old England, I. 50; Lond. S.A. Archaeo-
    logia, XXIX. 150—1; Smith, C. Roach, Rom. Lond. 18;
    V.C.H. Lond. I. 70, 107.
Thames Street, Upper, opposite Queen Street. Wall, 1839—40.
    Lond. S.A. Archaeologia, XXIX. 151; Smith, J. T., Streets
    of Lond. 380; Timbs' Lond. 717; V.C.H. Lond. I. 70;
    Wright's Arch. Album, 136.
Throgmorton Avenue, opposite Carpenters' Hall. Wall. Lond.
    S.A. Proc. 2 S. XX. 300.
Tower Hill. Wall. Antiquary, XII. 97; Archer, 4 (pl. II);
    Arch. Review, I. 359; B.A.A. Jour. VIII. 240 (illus.), XXXVIII.
    447; Cunningham's Lond. II. 435; Gent. Mag. 1843, i. 607,
    Lib. Rom. Brit. Rem. i. 219; Illust. Lond. News, 1821, XXI.
    208, and Sept. 11, 1852; Lewis, III. 163; Lond. Topog.
    Record, III. 72; Price, J. E., Rom. Antiq. 47; Smith,
    C. Roach, Coll. Antiq. III. 255; and Rom. Lond. 14, 15
    (pl. I), 27 (pl. III), 28; V.C.H. Lond. I. 50, 51, 130, 131.
Tower of London. Wall. Antiquary, XII. 98—9 (illus.); B.A.A.
    Jour. VII. 241, XXXVI. 464, XXXVII. 209, 280, XXXVIII. 127,

447, XLI. 210; Gent. Mag. 1835, i. 491; Hübner, VII. 23; Lethaby's Lond. 74; Lond. S.A. Archaeologia, V. 291, LX. 239, and Proc. 2 S. XX. 299; Lond. Topog. Record, IV. 7; Maitland's Lond. I. 148; V.C.H. Lond. I. 49, 130.

Trinity Place. Wall. V.C.H. Lond. I. 50; Wilkinson's Lond. 7.

Trinity Square. Wall. Arch. Review, I. 359 n. 25; Athenaeum, Feb. 25, 1843, 191, Nov. 11, 1843, 1009—10, Nov. 18, 1843, 1030; B.A.A. Jour. XXXVIII. 447; Builder, X. 562; Knight's Lond. I. 163.

Vine Street and Vine Yard, *see* America Square.

Warwick Square. Wall. Antiquary, XII. 97; Lethaby's Lond. 76; V.C.H. Lond. I. 68.

Water Lane, *see* Playhouse Yard.

BUILDINGS AND PAVEMENTS

Aldersgate Street. Buildings. Lewis, III. 164.

Bank Buildings. Wall, 1841. Archaeologist, 221; Lond. S.A. Archaeologia, XXIX. 273.
　Pavement, 1895. Lond. S.A. Proc. 2 S. XVI. 36; V.C.H. Lond. I. 87.

Bank of England, *see* Lothbury.

Bartholomew Lane. Pavement, 1841. Lond. S.A. Archaeologia, XXIX. 155; Smith, C. Roach, Rom. Lond. 58; Tite's Cat. Roy. Exch. xxxi; V.C.H. Lond. I. 87.

Basinghall Street, near. Kiln. B.A.A. Jour. XLIV. 357.

Birchin Lane. Walls and pavement, 1785. Allen's Lond. I. 28; Knight's Lond. I. 293; Lond. S.A. Archaeologia, VIII. 119, and Minute Book, XXI. 92; Price's Bucklersbury, 18; Timbs' Lond. 531, 715; V.C.H. Lond. I. 80, 81 (plan), 88.
　Wall, 1846. B.A.A. Jour. II. 205; V.C.H. Lond. I. 89.
　Pavement, 1857. Arch. Review, I. 274; Guildhall Mus. No. 28, and Catalogue, 72; Lond. and Middsx. Arch. Soc. Proc. 1861, 33; V.C.H. Lond. I. 89.

Bishopsgate Church. Vaulted arch, 1725. Allen's Lond. I. 25; Britton and Brayley, X. i. 90; Gough's Camden, II. 93.

Bishopsgate, St Helen's, Great. Pavement. Guildhall Mus. No. 7, and Catalogue 71.

Bishopsgate, St Helen's, Little. Pavement, 1712. Maitland's
    Lond. 12 ; Timbs' Lond. 713.
  Pavement, 1733. Arch. Jour. XXXIII. 269; Gent. Mag. 1733,
    436; V.C.H. Lond. I. 122.
Bishopsgate Street Within. Pavement, 1839. Lond. S.A. Archaeo-
    logia, XXIX. 155; Morgan, 182; Smith, C. Roach, Rom.
    Lond. 54—5 (plate VIII, fig. 1); V.C.H. Lond. I. 89.
  Pavement, 1873. Illust. Lond. News, July 19, and Aug. 2,
    1873 ; V.C.H. Lond. I. 80, 89.
Bishopsgate Street Within, opposite Crosby Hall. Pavement,
    1875. B.A.A. Jour. XXXIII. 106 ; V.C.H. Lond. I. 89.
Bishopsgate Street Within, nearly opposite Crosby Hall.
    Pavement, 1907—8. Lond. S.A. Proc. 2 S. XXII. 278.
Bread Street. Chalk wall. V.C.H. Lond. I. 92.
Bread Street Hill. Foundations. Illust. Lond. News, July 20,
    1844 ; V.C.H. Lond. I. 92.
Broad Street, Old, site of Winchester House. Pavement, 1792.
    Gent. Mag. 1807, i. 416, and Lib. Rom. Brit. Rem. i. 188 ;
    Knight's Lond. I. 290; Lond. S.A. Archaeologia, XXXIX.
    493 ; Morgan, 179; Smith, C. Roach, Rom. Lond. 56;
    Timbs' Lond. 716; Wright's Arch. Album, 134.
Broad Street, Old, site of Old Excise Office. Pavement,
    1854 and 1893. Arch. Jour. XI. 184, LXVIII. 220 ; Athen-
    aeum, Feb. 18, 1854, 221, 284; B.A.A. Jour. X. 112;
    Britton and Brayley, X. i. 95 ; Builder, XII. 108 ;
    Guildhall Mus. Nos. 8—9, Catalogue 72 ; Illust. Lond.
    News, April 1, 1854 (illus.); Lond. S.A. Archaeologia,
    XXXVI. 203—13 (illus. and map), XXXIX. 496, 498, Proc.
    III. 15, 114, and Topog. Colls., red portfolio (coloured
    drawing); Lond. and Middsx. Arch. Soc. Trans. I. 31 ; Lond.
    Topog. Record, III. 69; Morgan, 187; Price's Bucklersbury,
    23 ; R.I.B.A. Trans. 3 S. XII. 137 ; Smith, C. Roach, Coll.
    Antiq. III. 257, and Rom. Lond. 54 (pl. VII); Timbs' Lond.
    713; Times, Feb. 8, 1854; V.C.H. Lond. I. 92.
Bucklersbury. Pavement, 1869. Arch. Jour. LX. 171 ; Arch.
    Review, I. 275; B.A.A. Jour. XXXVIII. 99; Builder, XXVII.
    392, 424; Guildhall Mus. No. 1, Catalogue 71 (pl. LV);
    Lond. Topog. Record, III. 69, 71; Morgan, 195 ; Price's

Bucklersbury, 26 (plan and illus.); R.I.B.A. Trans. 3 S. XII. 137; V.C.H. Lond. I. 76 (fig. 26), 93 (fig. 40).

Tile wall on piles, 1869. Builder, LVII. 236 (illus.); Lond. S.A. Proc. 2 S. V. 11.

Budge Row. Wall. B.A.A. Jour. IX. 84; V.C.H. Lond. I. 93.

Bush Lane, Scot's Yard. Pavement, 1666. Harrison's Lond. 7; Knight's Lond. I. 290; Leland's Coll. I. lx; Lond. S.A. Archaeologia, XXIX. 156, XXXIX. 492, XL. 67, and Minute Book, VIII. 25; Lond. Topog. Record, III. 69; Maitland's Lond. I. 17; Morgan, 176; Price's Bucklersbury, 17; Seymour's Lond. II. 868—9; Stow's Lond. II. 1 App. 23; Timbs' Lond. 716; V.C.H. Lond. I. 75, 93; Wright, Arch. Album, 134.

Pavement, walls, etc. 1841. Gent. Mag. 1842, i. 268, Lib. Rom. Brit. Rem. ii. 484; Lond. and Middsx. Arch. Soc. Trans. III. 213; Lond. S.A. Archaeologia, XXIX. 156, 404, XL. 67, and Minute Book, XXXVIII. 152; V.C.H. Lond. I. 94.

Walls. Lond. and Middsx. Arch. Soc. Trans. III. 213; V.C.H. Lond. I. 75, 94.

Bush Lane, Little. Pavement and wall. B.A.A. Jour. II. 341; V.C.H. Lond. I. 94.

Camomile Street. Pavement, 1707. Allen's Lond. I. 24—5; Arch. Jour. XXXIV. 131; Britton and Brayley, X. i. 84; Gent. Mag. 1807, i. 415, and Lib. Rom. Brit. Rem. i. 185; Gough's Camden, II. 92; Knight's Lond. I. 158; Leland's Itin. VIII. (Woodward's letter to Sir C. Wren), 15; Lond. S.A. Archaeologia, XXXIX. 492, LII. 613; Lond. Topog. Record, III. 69; Maitland's Lond. I. 12; Malcolm's Lond. I. 350; Morgan, 177; Price's Bucklersbury, 17; R.I.B.A. Trans. 3 S. XII. 137; Stow's Lond. II. 1 App. 23; Timbs' Lond. 713; V.C.H. Lond. I. 12, 25, 81, 94; Woodward's Bishopsgate, 7, and Lond. 12.

Cannon Street, Basing Lane. Walls, 1845. B.A.A. Jour. I. 254; V.C.H. Lond. I. 95.

Pavement, 1852. Illust. Lond. News, April 17, 1852 (illus.); Timbs' Lond. 714.

Cannon Street, near Bush Lane. Pavement, 1852. Arch. Jour. IX. 297; Chaffers, W., Marks and Monograms on Pottery

Antiquary, XXIV. 212; Lond. S.A. Archaeologia, LX. 223, Proc. 2 S. XIV. 6—7, XXI. 229, and Topog. Colls., brown portfolio (plan and photograph); V.C.H. Lond. I. 99.

Crooked Lane, St Michael. Pavement, 1831. Gent. Mag. 1834, i. 157; Guildhall Mus. No. 6, Catalogue 72; Herbert's Hist. of St Michael, 19; Lond. S.A. Archaeologia, XXIV. 190; V.C.H. Lond. I. 123.

Crosby Square. Pavement, 1836. B.A.A. Jour. XXXIII. 106; Gent. Mag. 1836, i. 369, and Lib. Rom. Brit. Rem. i. 193; Knight's Lond. I. 290, and Old England, I. 50; Lond. S.A. Archaeologia, XXVII. 397 (plan), XXXIX. 496, 501, and Minute Book, XXXVII. 67; Morgan, 182; Smith, C. Roach, Rom. Lond. 57; Timbs' Lond. 713, 716; V.C.H. Lond. I. 99; Wright's Arch. Album, 134.

Crutched Friars. Pavement, 1787. Allen's Lond. I. 29; Knight's Lond. I. 290, and Old England, I. 50; Lond. S.A. Minute Book, XXII. 281, and original piece at Burlington House; Morgan, 179; Timbs' Lond. 716; V.C.H. Lond. I. 99; Wright's Arch. Album, 134.

Cullum Street, see Fenchurch Street.

Custom House. Wall. Tite's Cat. Roy. Exch. xxiii; V.C.H. Lond. I. 71.

Dowgate Hill. Building and pavement. Allen's Lond. III. 508; Archer's Vestiges of Lond. 11; Loftie's Lond. I. 33; Timbs' Lond. I. 714; V.C.H. Lond. I. 100; Wren's Parentalia, 265.

East Cheap. Building and pavement, 1831—6. Gent. Mag. 1833, i. 69—70, ii. 422, 1836, i. 135—37, and Lib. Rom. Brit. Rem. 191, 206; Herbert's Hist. of St Michael, 20; Knight's Lond. 290; Lond. S.A. Archaeologia, XXIV. 192, XXV. 602, and Minute Book, XXXVI. 337; Timbs' Lond. 716; V.C.H. Lond. I. 35, 37—38 (fig. 11), 100; Wright's Arch. Album, 134.

East Cheap, Little. Foundations. Lond. S.A. Archaeologia, XXIX. 154; V.C.H. Lond. I. 100.

Fenchurch Street, N. end of Mincing Lane. Walls and Pavement, 1833. Gent. Mag. 1834, i. 156, and Lib. Rom. Brit. Rem. i. 207; Knight's Lond. I. 290; Lond. S.A. Archaeologia, XXIX. 153; Morgan, 185; V.C.H. Lond. I. 101.

Fenchurch Street, opposite Cullum Street. Pavement, 1859.
B.A.A. Jour. XXIV. 76, 77 ; Brit. Mus. (orig. fragment pre-
served); Lond. and Middsx. Arch. Soc. Trans. I. 313; Lond.
S.A. Proc. 2 S. XVII. 322 ; Lond. Topog. Record, III. 69 ;
Morgan, 157, 191 ; Price's Bucklersbury, 24 (illus.); Smith,
C. Roach, Rom. Lond. 58 (illus.), and Retrospections, II.
200 ; V.C.H. Lond. I. 101.

Finch Lane.   Pavement, 1844—5.   B.A.A. Jour. I. 64, II. 206 ;
V.C.H. Lond. I. 102.

Finsbury.   Kiln.   B.A.A. Jour. XLIV. 357.

Fish Street Hill, Old.   Walls, 1845.   Arch. Jour. II. 72 ; B.A.A.
Jour. I. 45 (illus.); V.C.H. Lond. I. 102.

Fleet Street.   Arch and Wall, 1886.   B.A.A. Jour. XLII. 81 (illus.).

Foster Lane.   Pavement.   Lond. Topog. Record, III. 68; R.I.B.A.
Trans. 3 S. XII. 137.

Friday Street, site of St Matthew's church.   Pavement, 1844.
B.A.A. Jour. XLII. 435, XLIII. 198; Lond. and Middsx. Arch.
Soc. Trans. III. 339; Reliquary, N.S. I. 108; V.C.H. Lond.
I. 102.

Friday and Knightrider Streets, between.   Wall, 1906.   Lond.
S.A. Archaeologia, XL. 49, LX. 219, 221, and Proc. 2 S. XXI.
229 ; V.C.H. Lond. I. 76, 102.

Gracechurch Street, Halfmoon passage and Corbet Court.   Wall,
1834.   Kelsey's Descr. of Sewers, 100; Lond. S.A. Archaeologia, LX. 236; Tite's Cat. Roy. Exch. xii ; V.C.H. Lond.
I. 99, 103.

Gracechurch Street, opposite St Benet's Place.   Walls and
Pavement, 1841.   B.A.A. Jour. XXIV. 76—78 ; Lond. S.A.
Archaeologia, XXIX. 154, LX. 226 ; Price's Rom. Antiq. 24 ;
Tite's Cat. Roy. Exch. xii ; V.C.H. Lond. I. 80, 103.

Gracechurch Street, Spread Eagle Yard.   Pavement, 1866—8.
B.A.A. Jour. XXIV. 76, 77 ; V.C.H. Lond. I. 103.

Gracechurch Street, Crypt of St Benet's Church.   Wall, 1872.
B.A.A. Jour. XXVIII. 179 ; V.C.H. Lond. I. 103.

Gracechurch Street, corner of Leadenhall Avenue.   Wall, 1906.
Lond. S.A. Archaeologia, LX. 225 ; V.C.H. Lond. I. 103.

Gresham Street, formerly Maiden Lane, Lad Lane, and Cateaton
Street, *see also* Huggin Lane and Wood Street.   Pavement,

1843. B.A.A. Jour. I. 248, III. 335 ; Gent. Mag. 1843, i. 21, 190, and Lib. Rom. Brit. Rem. i. 197 ; Lond. S.A. Proc. II. 184 ; V.C.H. Lond. I. 103—4.

Gresham Street (Maiden Lane). Pavements, 1844. B.A.A. Jour. III. 336 ; Lond. S.A. Proc. II. 184.

Gresham Street (Lad Lane). Pavement, 1848. B.A.A. Jour. III. 335 ; Lond. S.A. Proc. II. 126.

Guildhall. Pavement, 1861. B.A.A. Jour. XVII. 325 ; V.C.H. Lond. I. 104.

Holborn, opposite St Andrew's Church. Pavement, 1681. Allen's Lond. I. 23 ; Gent. Mag. 1807, i. 415—17, 1833, i. 549, and Lib. Rom. Brit. Rem. i. 188 ; Grew's Catalogue of rarities belonging to the Royal Society, 1681, 380; Knight's Lond. I. 290; Lond. S.A. Archaeologia, XXXIX. 491 ; Morgan, 176 ; Stow's Lond. II. 1 App. 23 ; Timbs' Lond. 716 ; V.C.H. Lond. I. 104; Wright's Arch. Album, 134.

Honey Lane. Pavements. Arch. Rev. I. 278 ; Lond. and Middsx. Arch. Soc. Proc. Jan. 1862, 68 ; V.C.H. Lond. I. 105.

Huggin Lane, Wood Street, *see* Gresham Street. Pavement, 1851. Lond. S.A. Proc. II. 184 ; V.C.H. Lond. I. 105.

King William Street, St Clement Church. Walls and Pavement, 1834. Gent. Mag. 1835, i. 82; Knight's Lond. I. 290; Lond. S.A. Archaeologia, XXVII. 140 ; Morgan, 181 ; Timbs' Lond. 715, 716 ; V.C.H. Lond. I. 106.

King's Arms Yard, Moorgate Street. Pavement. Gent. Mag. 1843, i. 520, and Lib. Rom. Brit. Rem. i. 199; V.C.H. Lond. I. 106.

Knightrider Street, Great. Walls. Lond. S.A. Archaeologia, XL. 49, LX. 219 (plans) ; V.C.H. Lond. I. 69, 76, 107.

Knightrider Street, Little. Sewer arch. B.A.A. Jour. I. 253 (illus.) ; V.C.H. Lond. I. 76, 77 (fig. 27), 107.

Lad Lane, *see* Gresham Street.

Lambeth Hill. Pavement. B.A.A. Jour. XXXV. 215 ; V.C.H. Lond. I. 107.

Laurence Pountney Lane. Walls and pavement, 1846. Arch Review, I. 278 ; B.A.A. Jour. II. 340, 345 ; V.C.H. Lond. I. 35, 107.

Leadenhall Market. Building and pavement, 1880. Arch.

Review, I. 278; Athenaeum, Jan. 8, 1881, 63, Feb. 19, 1881, 271; B.A.A. Jour. XXXVII. 84, 90, 209, XXXVIII. 95; Guildhall Mus. No. 110, Catalogue 74; Lond. S.A. Archaeologia, XLVIII. 225, and Proc. 2 S. VIII. 524, 528; V.C.H. Lond. I. 74, 107.

Foundations and pavements, 1888. Antiquary, XVII. 175; Arch. Review, I. 278, n 13*; Builder, LVII. 236; Guildhall Mus. Nos. 10—15 (?), Catalogue 72; V.C.H. Lond. I. 107.

Walls, 1906. Lond. S.A. Archaeologia, LX. 225; V.C.H. Lond. I. 107.

Leadenhall Street, end of Lime Street. Pavement, wall, hearth and arched gate, 1576. Allen's Lond. I. 292; Newton's Lond. 24; Timbs' Lond. 715.

Leadenhall Street, under East India House. Pavement, 1803. Allen's Lond. I. 29, 30; Bayley's Lond. and Middsx. I. 95; B.A.A. Jour. II. 91—2, XIX. 64; Brit. Mus. orig. pavement; Britton and Brayley, X. i. 95; Dorset Field Club Proc. XXIII. 113; Gent. Mag. 1804, i. 83, 1806, II. 892, 1807, i. 415, and Lib. Rom. Brit. Rem. i. 185, 212; Hughson's Lond. I. 34; Kelsey's Descr. of Sewers, 53; Knight's Old England, I. 50 (fig. 161); Lond. S.A. Archaeologia, XXXIX. 492, 500, LX. 235, Minute Book, XXX. 182, 253 (coloured engraving inserted), 318, and Topog. Coll., red portfolio; Lond. Topog. Record, III. 69; Morgan, 157, 166, 179, 241 (plate); Newton's Lond. 24; R.I.B.A. Trans. 3 S. XII. 137; Smith, C. Roach, Rom. Lond. 57 (pl. XII); Timbs' Lond. 319, 715; Tite's Cat. Roy. Exch. xiii; V.C.H. Lond. I. 12, 79, 107 (fig. 45); Wright's Arch. Album, 134, and Celt, Roman and Saxon, 250.

Leadenhall Street, site of King's Head Inn, close to site of East India House. Walls, 1846. B.A.A. Jour. II. 340; Lond. S.A. Archaeologia, XXXIX. 494; V.C.H. Lond. I. 108.

Leadenhall Street, site of E. India House. Pavement, 1863. Arch. Jour. XX. 177; B.A.A. Jour. XIX. 63, 307; Brit. Mus. portion of orig. pavement; Illust. Lond. News, March 12, 1864, 267; Lond. S.A. Archaeologia, XXXIX. 500 (pl. XXI), 502, and Proc. 2 S. II. 360, III. 93; Morgan, 192, 193; Timbs' Lond. 715; V.C.H. Lond. I. 108.

Leadenhall Street, site of Rochester Buildings. Pavement, 1882. Arch. Jour. XL. 108; B.A.A. Jour. XXXIX. 393; V.C.H. Lond. I. 108.

Lombard Street, St Mary Woolnoth. Pavement, 1716. Britton and Brayley, X. i. 91; Hughson's Lond. I. 33; Maitland's Lond. II. 1145; Stow's Lond. II. 1 App. 24; V.C.H. Lond. I. 123.

Pavement, 1730. Allen's Lond. I. 25; Britton and Brayley, X. i. 91; Malcolm's Lond. III. 518; Price's Rom. Antiq. 26.

Pavements and Walls, 1785—6. Allen's Lond. I. 27; Britton and Brayley, X. i. 93; Gent. Mag. 1785, ii. 845, 1807, i. 415, and Lib. Rom. Brit. Rem. i. 186, ii. 593; Knight's Lond. I. 293; Lond. S.A. Archaeologia, VIII. 116 (plates and plans), 127, XXXIX. 492, XL. 69, and Minute Book, XXI. 92, 169; Malcolm's Lond. III. 519—521; Morgan, 177; Timbs' Lond. 715; V.C.H. Lond. I. 79, 80, 81 (plan and fig. 30), 109.

Pavement, 1839. Lond. Topog. Record, III. 68; R.I.B.A. Trans. 3 S. XII. 137; Smith, C. Roach, Rom. Lond. 59; V.C.H. Lond. I. 109.

Pavement, 1868. B.A.A. Jour. XXIV. 294; Lond. Topog. Record, III. 69; V.C.H. Lond. I. 109.

Lombard Street, at Plough Court. Wall, 1873. Lond. and Middsx. Arch. Soc. Proc. 1873, 119; Price's Rom. Antiq. 26; V.C.H. Lond. I. 109.

London Wall, opp. Finsbury Circus. Arched sewer or culvert, 1837. Kelsey's Descr. of Sewers, 138; Lond. S.A. Archaeologia, XXIX. 152, LX. 237; Timbs' Lond. 714; Tite's Cat. Roy. Exch. xxxi; V.C.H. Lond. I. 111.

Long Lane, Smithfield. Pavement. Britton and Brayley, X. i. 95; Gent. Mag. 1807, i. 417, and Lib. Rom. Brit. Rem. i. 188; Knight's Lond. I. 290; Timbs' Lond. 716; Wright's Arch. Album, 134.

Lothbury, Bank of England. Wall, 1732. Lond. S.A. Minute Book, II. 14.

Pavement, 1805. Allen's Lond. I. 31; Brit. Mus. orig. pavement; Britton and Brayley, X. i. 95, 97; Builder, XLII. 759; Gent. Mag. 1807, i. 415, and Lib. Rom. Brit. Rem. 187; Knight's Old England, I. 50; Lond. and Middsx. Arch. Soc. Trans. III. 219; Lond. S.A. Archaeologia, XXXIX. 495,

Minute Book, XXXI. 63, and Topog. Coll., red portfolio; Lond. Topog. Record, III. 69; Morgan, I. 81, 241; R.I.B.A. Trans. 3 S. XII. 137; Smith, C. Roach, Rom. Lond. 56 (pl. XI); Timbs' Lond. 715; Tite's Cat. Roy. Exch. xiv; V.C.H. Lond. I. 87; Wright's Arch. Album, 135.

Lothbury, Bank Buildings. Pavement, 1895. Lond. S.A. Proc. 2 S. XVI. 36; V.C.H. Lond. I. 87.

Lothbury, Founder's Court. Pavement, 1834. Kelsey's Descr. of Sewers, 112; Knight's Lond. I. 290; Lond. S.A. Archaeologia, XXVII. 141, 147, LX. 236; Lond. Topog. Record, III. 69, 70; Morgan, 181; R.I.B.A. Trans. 3 S. XII. 137; Smith, C. Roach, Rom. Lond. 57; Timbs' Lond. 716; V.C.H. Lond. I. 112; Wright's Arch. Album, 134.

Pavement, 1892. Lond. S.A. Proc. 2 S. XIV. 25; V.C.H. Lond. I. 113.

Ludgate Square (formerly Holiday Yard, Creed Lane). Bath and aqueduct. Leland, Coll. I. lxvi; Stow's Lond. II. 1 App. 24; V.C.H. Lond. I. 114.

Maiden Lane, *see* Gresham Street.

Mansion House. Pavement, 1870. Arch. Jour. XXVIII. 164; Price's Rom. Antiq. 54; V.C.H. Lond. I. 114.

Mark Lane. Pavement, 1871. B.A.A. Jour. XXVII. 387; Lond. and Middsx. Arch. Soc. Proc. 1871, 59; V.C.H. Lond. I. 114.

Miles Lane. Wall, 1831. Gent. Mag. 1833, i. 69, 1842, i. 268, and Lib. Rom. Brit. Rem. i. 206, ii. 484.

Mincing Lane, opp. Clothworkers' Hall. Hypocaust, 1824. Kelsey's Descr. of Sewers, 83; Lond. S.A. Archaeologia, LX. 235; V.C.H. Lond. I. 115.

Building, pavement, 1850. B.A.A. Jour. VI. 442; Lond. and Middsx. Arch. Soc. Proc. 1862, 91; V.C.H. Lond. I. 115.

Monument. Bath or tank, 1833. Gent. Mag. 1834, i. 95, and Lib. Rom. Brit. Rem. i. 214; V.C.H. Lond. I. 35, 115—6.

Monument Street, *see* Pudding Lane.

Moorgate Street, *see* King's Arms Yard.

Nicholas Lane. Building, 1795[1], 1847[2], 1850[3]. B.A.A. Jour. II. 341; Gent. Mag. 1850, ii. 114; Hübner, VII. 22, 23; Lond. S.A. Archaeologia, VIII. 129[1]; Smith, C. Roach, Coll. Antiq. I. 146[2], and Rom. Lond. 29[3]; V.C.H. Lond. I. 117[2].

Newgate. Pavement, 1857. Lond. and Middsx. Arch. Soc. Trans. I. 195; V.C.H. Lond. I. 81, 117.

Northumberland Alley. Foundations and pavement, 1787. Allen's Lond. I. 29; Britton and Brayley, x. i. 95; Gent. Mag. 1807, i. 416, and Lib. Rom. Brit. Rem. i. 188; Knight's Lond. I. 290; Lond. S.A. Archaeologia, XXXIX. 501, and Minute Book, XXII. 281, piece of orig. pavement in Coll. Soc. Antiq.; Timbs' Lond. 716; V.C.H. Lond. I. 117; Wright's Arch. Album, 134.

Old Jewry, St Olave. Pavement and Wall, 1888. V.C.H. Lond. I. 124.

Paternoster Row. Wall, 1834—6. Knight's Lond. I. 166; Lond. S.A. Archaeologia, XXVII. 150; V.C.H. Lond. I. 118.
  Pavement, 1839—41. Lond. and Middsx. Arch. Soc. Trans. III. 500; Lond. S.A. Archaeologia, XXIX. 155; Morgan, 184; Price's Bucklersbury, 22; Smith, C. Roach, Rom. Lond. 57; V.C.H. Lond. I. 79, 118.
  Pavement, 1843. Gent. Mag. 1843, ii. 81, and Lib. Rom. Brit. Rem. i. 200; V.C.H. Lond. I. 22, 33, 118.
  Pavement, 1855, and destroyed. Lond. and Middsx. Arch. Soc. Trans. I. 31.
  Hypocaust, 1884. B.A.A. Jour. XL. 210.

Paternoster Square. Pavement, 1883—4. B.A.A. Jour. XL. 123; Builder, XLV. 267; V.C.H. Lond. I. 118.

Poultry, St Mildred's Court. Pavement, 1867. Lond. and Middsx. Arch. Soc. Trans. III. 195, 217; Lond. Topog. Record, III. 71; Morgan, 193; Price's Bucklersbury, 25; V.C.H. Lond. I. 119.

Poultry, *see also* Bucklersbury.

Princes Street, Lothbury, and Bartholomew Lane, area between. Pavements. Kelsey's Descr. of Sewers, 258; Lond. S.A. Archaeologia, LX. 237; V.C.H. Lond. I. 87.

Pudding Lane. Wall and hypocaust, 1841. Lond. S.A. Archaeologia, XXIX. 154 (plate); V.C.H. Lond. I. 119.
  Pavement, 1887. Academy, Aug. 13, 1887, 109, Sept. 3, 155; Arch. Jour. XLV. 184; Lond. S.A. Proc. 2 S. XII. 128, and Topog. Coll. (original drawing by Henry Hodge); Reliquary, N.S. I. 234.

Queen Street, Cheapside, near Well Court. Walls and Pavement, 1841. Lond. S.A. Archaeologia, XXIX. 155, and Proc. II. 93; V.C.H. Lond. I. 120.

Queen Street, Cheapside. Wall and pavement, 1842. Gent. Mag. 1843, i. 21, and Lib. Rom. Brit. Rem. i. 196; Lond. and Middsx. Arch. Soc. Trans. III. 500; Lond. S.A. Archaeologia, XXX. 543; Smith, C. Roach, Rom. Lond. 71; Timbs' Lond. 717; V.C.H. Lond. I. 11, 119, 120.

Queen Street, Great St Thomas Apostle. Pavement, 1847. B.A.A. Jour. II. 350; V.C.H. Lond. I. 125.

Queen Street, Little St Thomas Apostle. Walls, 1848. B.A.A. Jour. X. 195; V.C.H. Lond. I. 125—6.

Royal Exchange. Buildings and pavements, 1841. Archaeologist, I. 220; B.A.A. Jour. VII. 82; Lewis, III. 164; Lond. S.A. Archaeologia, XXIX. 267, XXXV. 60, XXXIX. 497; Smith, C. Roach, Retrospections, I. 129, and Rom. Lond. 12; Tite's Cat. Roy. Exch. xxxix (plan and sections); Timbs' Lond. 716; V.C.H. Lond. I. 121; Wright's Arch. Album, 131.

St Bartholomew's Hospital. Column and brick. Athenaeum, Dec. 22, 1877, 824.

St Dunstan's Hill. Pavement, 1824. Herbert's Hist. of St Michael, 19; Kelsey's Descr. of Sewers, 80; Knight's Lond. I. 159, 290; Lond. S.A. Archaeologia, LX. 235; Timbs' Lond. 713, 716; V.C.H. Lond. I. 11, 122; Wright's Arch. Album, 134.

Wall, 1863. B.A.A. Jour. XIX. 63; V.C.H. Lond. I. 122.

St Martin's Lane. Brick arch, 1772. Timbs' Lond. 716.

St Martins le Grand. Vaulting, 1819. Timbs' Lond. 716; V.C.H. Lond. I. 122.

St Mary Axe. Pavement, 1849. B.A.A. Jour. V. 90; V.C.H. Lond. I. 123.

St Paul's Cathedral. Potter's kiln, 1677. Essex. Arch. Soc. Trans. N.S. VI. 15; Gough's Brit. Top. I. 719, and Camden, II. 93; Lond. S.A. Proc. 2 S. XVI. 42; Lond. Topog. Record, III. 74; Smith, C. Roach, Coll. Antiq. VI. 174, 185, and Rom. Lond. 79; Stow, Lond. II. 1 App. 23; Tite's Cat. Roy. Exch. xx, xxxvi; V.C.H. Lond. I. 124, figs. 55, 56; Wren's Parentalia, 286.

St Paul's Churchyard. Pavement and hypocaust, 1841. Archaeo-
logist, 221 ; Gent. Mag. 1841, ii. 264, and Lib. Rom. Brit.
Rem. i. 216—17 ; Lond. S.A. Archaeologia, XXIX. 272 ;
Morgan, 185 ; V.C.H. Lond. I. 33, 125.

Seething Lane. Pavement, 1839—41. Lond. S.A. Archaeologia,
XXIX. 154 ; V.C.H. Lond. I. 126.

Sherborne Lane. Wall and pavement, 1785—6. Allen's Lond.
I. 27 ; Lond. S.A. Archaeologia, VIII. 116—32, XXXIX. 492 ;
Morgan, 177 ; Price's Bucklersbury, 18, and Rom. Antiq.
25 ; Timbs' Lond. 531, 715. *See also* Birchin Lane.

Suffolk Lane. Walls, 1848—9. B.A.A. Jour. IV. 388 ; Lond.
S.A. Archaeologia, XXXIII. 120, and Proc. II. 19, III. 194;
V.C.H. Lond. I. 126.

Thames Street, Lower, at foot of Fish Street Hill. Masonry,
1834. Kelsey's Descr. of Sewers, 90 ; Lond. S.A. Archaeologia, LX. 235 ; V.C.H. Lond. I. 128 ; Wright's Arch. Album,
132, and Celt, Roman and Saxon, 188.

Thames Street, Lower, in Old Fish Street Hill. Foundations,
1845. Arch. Jour. II. 72.

Thames Street, Lower. Foundations, pavement and hypocaust,
1848 and 1859. Arch. Jour. V. 25 ; Athenaeum, Feb. 5,
1848, 144, 167 ; B.A.A. Jour. IV. (plan and illus.) 38, 75,
XXIV. 295 (plate); Builder, XVII. 389, XLI. 509 ; Gent. Mag.
1848, i. 293—4, and Lib. Rom. Brit. Rem. i. 217 ; Illust.
Lond. News, Feb. 5, 1848 (illus.) ; Lond. and Middsx. Arch.
Soc. Proc. 1860, 9 ; Lond. S.A. Archaeologia, XXXVI. 209,
XXXIX. 502, Proc. I. 236, 239, 251, and Topog. Coll., red
portfolio; Morgan, 157, 167, 186 ; Newton's Lond. 18 ;
Timbs' Lond. 713, 717 ; V.C.H. Lond. I. 35, 74, 75 (plan),
128.

Thames Street, Upper, corner of Suffolk Lane. Walls and
foundation tiles, 1865. Timbs' Lond. 717.

Thames Street, Upper, opposite Vintner's Hall. Pavement.
Lond. and Middsx. Arch. Soc. Trans. III. 410 ; V.C.H.
Lond. I. 128.

Threadneedle Street, foundations of French Protestant Church.
Pavement, 1841. Athenaeum, April 17, 1841, 310 ; Brit.
Mus., two original pieces ; Builder, XLII. 757—9 ; Knight's

Lond. I. 290; Lewis, III. 164; Lond. and Middsx. Arch.
Soc. Trans. I. 31; Lond. S.A. Archaeologia, XXIX. 400,
XXXIX. 496, and Minute Book, XXXVIII. 149; Lond.
Topog. Record, III. 69; Morgan, 183, 184; Price's
Bucklersbury, 21; R.I.B.A. Trans. 3 S. XII. 137; Smith,
C. Roach, Rom. Lond. 55 (plates IX and X); Timbs'
Lond. 717; V.C.H. Lond. I. 129; Wright's Arch. Album,
135.

Threadneedle Street, near Merchant Taylors' Hall. Pavement,
1844. Lond. Topog. Record, III. 69; Morgan, 184; V.C.H.
Lond. I. 129.

Tank or bath, 1895. Arch. Jour. LII. 198; Lond. S.A.
Archaeologia, LX. 218, and Proc. 2 S. XXI. 229; V.C.H.
Lond. I. 129.

Tower Hill. Portions of buildings, 1852. B.A.A. Jour. VIII.
240 (illus.); Morgan, 168; Timbs' Lond. 717.

Tower of London. Masonry and hypocaust, 1899. B.A.A. Jour.
N.S. V. 351, VI. 26; V.C.H. Lond. I. 130.

Tower Street. Foundations on piles. Wright's Arch. Album,
132.

Trinity Lane. Walls and remains of fresco paintings, 1845.
B.A.A. Jour. I. 254; V.C.H. Lond. I. 131.

Trinity Square. Building and pavement. Arch Review, I. 359;
B.A.A. Jour. XXXVIII. 447; V.C.H. Lond. I. 51, 131.

Wallbrook. Pavement. Maidstone, Kent. Original tesserae
in the Town Museum.

Warwick Square. Buildings. Lond. S.A. Archaeologia, XLVIII.
221, 225—6; V.C.H. Lond. I. 76, 133.

Wood Street, St Michael's Church. Pavements, 1843. Gent.
Mag. 1843, i. 190—1, and Lib. Rom. Brit. Rem. i. 198;
Lond. S.A. Proc. II. 184; Morgan, 185; Price's Bucklers-
bury, 23; V.C.H. Lond. I. 134.

Wood Street. *See also* Huggin Lane and Gresham Street.

SOUTHWARK

Lindsay's Southwark. Lindsay, Ralph. Etymology of Southwark, 3rd ed. 1839.

Taylor's St Mary Overy. Taylor, W. Annals of St Mary Overy (St Saviour's, Southwark), 1833.

Bankside, *see* Park Street.

Deverell Street. Hypocaust, 1825. Gent. Mag. 1825, ii. 633, and Lib. Rom. Brit. Rem. ii. 320; V.C.H. Lond. I. 137.

High Street. Buildings and pavement prior to 1831. Lond. S.A. Archaeologia, XXIV. 198; V.C.H. Lond. I. 35, 82.

High Street, King's Head Yard. Pavement, 1880—1. B.A.A. Jour. XXXVI. 234, XXXVII. 211; V.C.H. Lond. I. 138.

Kent Road, Bricklayer's Arms. Building. Lond. S.A. Archaeologia, XLVIII. 231.

Park Street, Winchester House. Pavement, 1658. Allen's Lond. I. 35—6; Dugdale, W.,' The History of Imbanking and Draining, 2nd ed. 1772, 65; Gent. Mag. 1815, i. 225 note; Knight's Lond. I. 290; Taylor's St Mary Overy, 9; Timbs' Lond. 716; V.C.H. Lond. I. 139.

Park Street, site of Globe Theatre. Pavement, 1892—3. B.A.A. Jour. XLVIII. 344, XLIX. 151; V.C.H. Lond. I. 140.

St George's Fields. Pavement, 1810. Allen's Lond. I. 36, 37; Britton and Brayley, X. i. 75; Gent. Mag. 1825, i. 149; Pointer's Brit. Rom. 40; V.C.H. Lond. I. 140.

St Saviour's. Pavement and Walls, 1818—22, 33—39. Allen's Lond. I. 37; Brayley's Surrey, I. 22; Gent. Mag. 1825, ii. 633, 1832, i. 399, 1833, i. 255, 1840, i. 192, and Lib. Rom. Brit. Rem. ii. 320, 321, 327; Lindsay's Southwark, 6; Lond. S.A. Archaeologia, XXIV. 198, XXIX. 148; Price's Rom. Antiq. 17 note; Taylor's St Mary Overy, 15; Timbs' Lond. 716; V.C.H. Lond. I. 140.

St Thomas' Hospital. Pavements, walls, 1840. Gent. Mag. 1840, i. 191, 192, and Lib. Rom. Brit. Rem. ii. 327; Lindsay's Southwark, 5; Lond. S.A. Archaeologia, XXIX. 148 (pl. XVIII); V.C.H. Lond. I. 140.

St Thomas' Street, corner of High Street. Pavement, 1819.
Price's Rom. Antiq. 17 note; V.C.H. Lond. I. 141.

Southwark Park, *see* Park Street.

Southwark Street. Pavements, 1862, 1866. B.A.A. Jour. XXII.
447; Lond. and Middsx. Arch. Soc. Proc. 1862, 84; V.C.H.
Lond. I. 141.

Union Street, Court Yard of St Saviour's Schools. Pavement,
1820. Lindsay's Southwark, 5; V.C.H. Lond. I. 142.

WESTMINSTER

College Street. Concrete flooring, 1883. Arch. Jour. XLII. 274;
V.C.H. Lond. I. 135.

St Martins in the Fields. Brick arch, 1722. Allen's Lond. I.
25; Britton and Brayley, X. i. 91 ; Gough's Camden, II. 93 ;
V.C.H. Lond. I. 136.

Strand Lane. Bath. Assoc. Archit. Soc. Reports, XX. xxxiii;
B.A.A. Jour. XLIX. 240, 305 ; Builder, XXX. 983 ; Diprose,
John, Some account of the Parish of St Clement Danes,
1868, 265; Godwin's Arch. Handbook, 59; Knight's Lond.
II. 165 ; Loftie's Lond. II. 70, 433 ; Middsx. and Herts N.
and Q. I. 72 ; Morgan, 167 ; Newton's Lond. 103 ; Scot.
S.A. Proc. XXIV. 150; Timbs' Lond. 37, 716; V.C.H. Lond.
82, 136.

Westminster Abbey. Building, hypocaust, 1882. Antiquary,
VI. 37; Arch. Jour. XLII. 274, 300; Loftie's Lond. I. 30 note,
II. 70 ; V.C.H. Lond. I. 29, 136.

MONMOUTHSHIRE

Arch. Cambrensis. Archaeologia Cambrensis of the Cambrian Archaeological Association, I.—LIV. 1846—1911.

Coxe. Coxe, W. Tour in Monmouthshire, 1801.

Mon. and Caerleon Antiq. Assoc. Monmouthshire and Caerleon Antiquarian
Association.

Wyndham. Wyndham, H. P. A Tour through Monmouthshire and Wales,
2nd ed. 1781.

Abergavenny. Foundations. B.A.A. Jour. I. 254, XXIV. 112;
Britton and Brayley, XI. 91; Gough's Camden, III. 114;
Horsley's Brit. Rom. 319; Lond. S.A. Archaeologia, v.
34.

Caerleon (*Isca Silurum*). Town, walls, gates, excavations,
buildings and pavements. Antiquary, XXIX. 116, 166, 202,
XLV. 241, 285, 335; Arch. Cambrensis, 1 S. IV. 73, 4 S. VIII.
161; Arch. Jour. XXIII. 74, XXXII. 330, XXXIV. 461, XLIV.
54, and Winchester vol. 1845, under Porchester Castle, 19;
B.A.A. Jour. IV. 257, VII. 61, X. 204, XXIV. 113, XLIII. 392,
XLIX. 206, 219, N.S. XV. 114; Blome's Britannia, 166;
Britton and Brayley, XI. 124; Builder, XCV. 245; Clifton
Antiq. Club Proc. II. 169; Coll. Antiq. VI. 258; Coxe, 80;
Gent. Mag. 1835, i. 599, 1866, i. 471, ii. 42, and Lib. Rom.
Brit. Rem. i. 222, 225, 229; Godwin's Arch. Handbook, 37;
Grose's Antiq. of England and Wales, V.; Gough's Camden,
III. 108, 117; Hoare's Giraldus Cambrensis, I. 103; Horsley's
Brit. Rom. 320; Lee, J. E., Roman Antiquities at Caerleon,
1845, Isca Silurum, 1862, and Supplement, 1868; Lewis,
I. 453; Lond. S.A. Archaeologia, II. 5, V. 62, 66, VI. 10, and
Proc. 2 S. III. 259, VII. 219; Mon. and Caerleon Antiq.
Assoc. XIII. 5, XVIII. 18, XIX. 57; Morgan, O., Notice of
Tessellated Pavement at Caerleon, 1866; Morgan, T.,
Romano-British Mosaic Pavements, 93; Pointer's Stunsfield,
35; Scarth's Rom. Brit. 150; Wright's Celt, Roman and
Saxon, 162; Wyndham, 13.

Caerwent (*Venta Silurum*). Town, walls, gates, excavations,
buildings and pavement. Antiquary, XIV. 228, XXVIII.
192, XXIX. 56, 168, 170, 245, XXXV. 365, XXXVI. 336, XXXVII.
342, XXXIX. 230, 348, XLV. 2; Arch. Cambrensis, 6 S.
IX. 114, 161; Arch. Jour. XII. 275, XIII. 91, XXIII. 67,
XXXVIII. 429, Bristol vol. 1851, 41, and Winchester vol.
1845, under Porchester Castle, 19; Athenaeum, Nov. 18,
1899; B.A.A. Jour. IV. 248, X. 209, XIII. 77, XLIII. 392,
XLIX. 216, N.S. XIII. 196, XIV. 211; Bath Field Club Proc.
I. i. 66, X. 258, 365; Bristol and Glouc. Arch. Soc. Trans.
XXVI. 77; Britton and Brayley, XI. 169; Builder, LXXVIII.
40, LXXXII. 238, LXXXIV. 467, LXXXV. 255, LXXXVII. 235;

Clifton Antiq. Club Proc. III. 41 (plans), IV. 236, V. 99, 158, 253; Coll. Antiq. IV. 212; Coxe, 24; Dorset Field Club Proc. XXI. 168, 171, 175; Godwin's Arch. Handbook, 36; Gough's Camden, III. 112; Horsley's Brit. Rom. 469; King's Mun. Antiq. II. 170; Lee, J. E., Isca Silurum, 47, 94; Lewis, I. 454; Lond. S.A. Archaeologia, V. 48, 55, 58, VI. 7, VII. 410, XXXVI. 418 (plans), LVII. 295 (plans), LVIII. 119 (plans), 391 (plans), LIX. 87 (plans), 289 (plans), LX. 111 (plans), 451 (plans), LXI. 565 (plans), LXII. 1 (plans), Proc. 1 S. III. 188, 231, 2 S. VIII. 542, XI. 195, XV. 142, XVII. 337, XVIII. 237, XIX. 35, 255, XX. 35, 319, XXI. 207, 475, XXII. 294, 357, XXIII. 216, Minute Book, IX. 62, 64, XVI. 12, 31, 191, and Topog. Colls., red portfolio (drawing of pav. found in 1777 and etching of wall); Mon. and Caerleon Antiq. Assoc. XVIII. 22; Morgan, 91, 92, 103; Pointer's Stunsfield, 35; Seyer's Memoirs of Bristol, I. 131; Wright's Celt, Roman and Saxon, 169, 173, 189; Wyndham, 7.

Chepstow. Potteries. Arch. Jour. XIV. 276.

Oldcastle, *see* Walterstone, Herefordshire.

Usk. Foundations. Arch. Jour. XXXV. 20, 26; Britton and Brayley, XI. 144; Coxe, 124; Cymmrodorion Soc. Trans. 1908—9, 129.

NORFOLK

Blomefield. Blomefield, F. and Parkin, C. History of Norfolk, 11 vols. 1805—10.

Norf. Arch. Norfolk Archaeology. Original papers of the Norfolk and Norwich Archaeological Society, I.—XVI. 1847—1907.

Spelman. Spelman, Sir Henry. Icenia (in the English Works of), 1723.

V.C.H. Victoria History of the Counties of England. Norfolk, I. 1901.

Ashill. Foundations and shaft. Arch. Jour. XXXII. 108, XLVI. 333, 334, 352; B.A.A. Jour. XXXI. 469; Coll. Antiq. VII. 110; Norf. Arch. VIII. 224; V.C.H. I. 295.

Brampton. Kiln. Blomefield, VI. 430; Browne, Sir Thomas, Posthumous Works, 1712, concerning some urnes found in Brampton Field in 1667; Gough's Camden, II. 193 (under Oxnead); V.C.H. I. 314.

Brancaster (*Branodunum*). Fort, walls, etc. Arch. Jour. XLVI. 345, 353, and Norwich vol. 1847, 9 (plan); Blomefield, X. 298; Britton and Brayley, XI. 306; Coll. Antiq. VII. 159; Gough's Camden, II. 179, 197; Lewis, I. 334; Lond. S.A. Archaeologia, XII. 134, XXIII. 361, XLI. 428; Spelman, 147; V.C.H. I. 304 (plan).

Brundall. Foundations. Arch. Jour. XLVI. 354, 355; V.C.H. I. 297.

Caister-by-Norwich (*Venta Icenorum*). Town, walls, etc. Arch. Jour. XLVI. 342, 355, and Norwich vol. 1847, I. 178; B.A.A. Jour. XIV. 123; Blomefield, V. 422; Britton and Brayley, XI. 186; Gent. Mag. 1807, ii. 913, and Lib. Rom. Brit. Rem. ii. 496; Gough's Camden, II. 176, 188; King's Mun. Antiq. II. 49, 74, 146; Lewis, I. 455; Lond. S.A. Archaeologia, XII. 135, 137 (plan), XXIII. 365, and Minute Book, XXXIII. 723; Phil. Trans. XLVI. 200; Stukeley's Letters, III. 30; V.C.H. I. 288, 289 (plan).

Buildings. Arch. Jour. IV. 72 (plan), VI. 180, XVII. 159, XLVI. 356; B.A.A. Jour. XIV. 82, 123, 200; V.C.H. I. 291 (plan).

Kiln. Arch. Jour. XLVI. 343, 355; Godwin's Arch. Handbook, 61; Lond. S.A. Archaeologia, XXII. 412; Norf. Arch. VI. 155; V.C.H. I. 291, 292 (plan).

Caister-by-Yarmouth. Fort, foundations, etc. Arch. Jour. XLVI. 342, 347, 357; B.A.A. Jour. XXXVI. 89; Britton and Brayley, XI. 348; Gent. Mag. 1837, ii. 518, and Lib. Rom. Brit. Rem. i. 230; Gough's Camden, II. 194; Ives, J., Garianonum, 1803; Norf. Arch. IX. 361; Spelman, 155; V.C.H. I. 293.

Kiln. Arch. Jour. XLVI. 357; B.A.A. Jour. XXI. 346; XXXVI. 89, 206; Norf. Arch. IV. 352; V.C.H. I. 294.

Elmham, North. Foundations (?). Arch. Jour. XLVI. 360; Blomefield, IX. 491.

Fring. Pavement (?). Arch. Jour. XLVI. 332, 360; Gough's Camden, II. 201; Lond. S.A. Archaeologia, XXIII. 370; V.C.H. I. 297.

Gayton Thorpe. Buildings and pavement. Norf. Arch. XVI. 226.

Grimston. Buildings. Antiquary, XLII. 443; Builder, XCI. 549; Norf. Arch. XVI. 219 (plan).

Hedenham. Kiln. Arch. Jour. XLVI. 361; Lond. S.A. Proc. I S. IV. 201; Norf. Arch. VI. 149 (plan); V.C.H. I. 318.

Kirby Cane. Kiln (?). Arch. Jour. XLVI. 362; Norf. Arch. IV. 314; V.C.H. I. 318.

Methwold. Buildings. Arch. Jour. XLVI. 332, 362; B.A.A. Jour. XXXVIII. 110 (plan); Builder, XLII. 301; Norf. Arch. IX. 366; V.C.H. I. 297.

Reedham. Circular foundation. Arch. Jour. XLVI. 363, LVII. 127; V.C.H. I. 298.

Saham Tony. Kiln (?). Arch. Jour. XLVI. 363; Norf. Arch. VII. 349; V.C.H. I. 320.

Stalham. Pavement. Lewis, IV. 177.

Weybourne. Kiln. Arch. Jour. XLVI. 366; Norf. Arch. V. 254 (plan), VI. 155; V.C.H. I. 322.

NORTHAMPTONSHIRE

Artis. Artis, E. T. The Durobrivae of Antoninus, 1828.

Baker. Baker, G. History of the County of Northampton, 2 vols., 1822—41.

Bridges. Bridges, J. History of the County of Northampton, 2 vols., 1762—91.

Gibson. Gibson, K. History of Castor, 2nd ed., 1819.

Morton. Morton, J. History of Northamptonshire, 1712.

V.C.H. Victoria History of the Counties of England. Northamptonshire, I. 1902.

Wetton. Wetton, G. N. Guide to Northampton, 1849.

Whellan. Whellan, W. History of Northamptonshire, 2nd ed., 1874.

Apethorpe. Buildings and pavement. Assoc. Archit. Soc. Reports, V. 97 (plan); Coll. Antiq. VI. 250; Lond. S.A. Archaeologia, XLIII. 119; Times, Sept. 9, 1859; V.C.H. I. 191 (plan).

Ashley. Pavement. Nichols' Leic. I. cliv; V.C.H. I. 193; Whellan, 781.

Ashton. Foundations (?). Assoc. Archit. Soc. Reports, IX. 156; V.C.H. I. 189.

Bedford Purlieus, see Castor.

Borough Hill, *see* Daventry.

Brixworth. Foundations. Lond. S.A. Archaeologia, XLIII. 119; V.C.H. I. 194.

Castor (*Durobrivae*) including Alwalton, Hunts.; Bedford Purlieus; Chesterton, Hunts.; Mill Hill or Field; Sibson, Hunts.; Stibbington, Hunts.; Sutton Field; Thornhaugh; Wansford; Water Newton, Hunts.; and Yarwell. Buildings and pavements. Antiquary, II. 34, XXII. 208; Arch. Jour. XXX. 127; Artis, pls. I, XIII, XXIII (maps), III, IV, VII, XII, XVIII, XIX, XXI (pavements), VI, VIII, XI, XVI, XX, XXII, XXXIV, XXXV (plans of buildings); Assoc. Archit. Soc. Reports, V. 98; B.A.A. Jour. XXXIV. 513, XXXV. 325, XLIV. 114, N.S. V. 53, 55, 71, 147; Blome's Britannia, 176; Bib. Topog. Brit. III. 91; Builder, LXXXIII. 586; Gent. Mag. 1821, i. 460, 1822, i. 483, 1826, ii. 355, and Lib. Rom. Brit. Rem. i. 140, 238; Gibson's Castor; Gough's Camden, II. 269, 286; Morgan, 114, 124, 125, 126; Morton, 509, 510; Stukeley's Itin. Curios. I. 82, and Letters, II. 214, III. 56, 59, 60; V.C.H. I. 166 (plans, etc.), 189.

Kilns. Arch. Jour. I. 280, XXX. 127; Artis, pls. XXV, XXVI, XXVII, XXXIX, XL; B.A.A. Jour. I. 1, II. 164, and Canterbury vol. 1845, 332, 334; Coll. Antiq. VI. 173, 179; Godwin's Arch. Handbook, 60; Lond. S.A. Proc. 1 S. I. 60; Norf. Arch. VI. 156; Trollope's Sleaford, 35; V.C.H. I. 174, 175, 206; Wright's Celt, Roman and Saxon, 263.

Chipping Warden. Buildings. B.A.A. Jour. V. 83, 168 (plan); Baker, I. 531; Bridges, I. 111; Gough's Camden, II. 272; Morton, 526; V.C.H. I. 200 (plan).

Corby. Buildings and kiln. Antiquary, XXXVIII. 377.

Cotterstock. Buildings and pavement. Artis, pls. LIX, LX; B.A.A. Jour. XXXVIII. 303; Daily Gazetteer, April 1, 1737; Fowler, No. 17; Gent. Mag. 1737, 254; Gibson, 172; Gough's Camden, II. 286, and Brit. Topog. II. 48; King's Mun. Antiq. II. 168; Lond. S.A. Minute Book, II. 233, III. 16, 130, XXV. 126, and Vet. Mon. I. 48; Morgan, 33, 121; Northampton Mercury, March 23, 1737; Stukeley's Letters, III. 33, 38, 39, 49, 52, 67; V.C.H. I. 192 (plan). Portion of a pavement preserved at Dean Park.

Daventry (Borough Hill). Buildings and pavement. Assoc. Archit.' Soc. Reports, II. 426; B.A.A. Jour. I. 245; Baker, I. 339, 345 (plan); Britton and Brayley, XI. 59; Coll. Antiq. I. 113, III. 208; Lewis, II. 16; Lond. S.A. Archaeologia, XXXV. 383 (plan), and Proc. 1 S. II. 312; Morgan, 122; North Oxford Arch. Soc. Trans. III. 117; V.C.H. I. 195 (plan).

Drayton, *see* Lowick.

Duston. Foundations. Assoc. Archit. Soc. Reports, VI. 222; B.A.A. Jour. XX. 273; Lond. S.A. Proc. 2 S. XXII. 252; V.C.H. I. 197.

Gayton. Buildings. B.A.A. Jour. I. 214; Lond. S.A. Archaeologia, XXX. 125 (plan); V.C.H. I. 198; Wetton, 166.

Harpole. Buildings and pavement. B.A.A. Jour. II. 364, V. 375, VI. 81, 126, X. 93; Lond. S.A. Archaeologia, XXXV. 395, XLIII. 119; Morgan, 122; V.C.H. I. 197; Wetton, 148; Whellan, 316.

Helpstone. Pavement. Artis, pl. XXIV; Britton and Brayley, XI. 228; Gibson, 62; Morgan, 126; V.C.H. I. 189.

Heyford, Nether. Buildings and pavement. Baker, I. 190; Bridges, I. 519; Gough's Camden, II. 277; King's Mun. Antiq. II. 174; Lond. S.A. Archaeologia, XXXV. 395; Morgan, 115, 122; Morton, 527; V.C.H. I. 196.

Higham Ferrers. Baths (?). Cole, J., History of Higham Ferrers, 1838, 2, 102; V.C.H. I. 218 ("probably an error"); Whellan, 917.

Irchester. Town, buildings, and pavement. Arch. Jour. XXXVI. 99, XXXIX. 78; Assoc. Archit. Soc. Reports, XIII. 88, XV. 49 (plan); Bridges, II. 181; Britton and Brayley, XI. 186; Builder, XXXVI. 1125; Gibson, 172; Gough's Camden, II. 282; Lond. S.A. Proc. 2 S. IX. 85, and Minute Book, I. 86; Morton, 517; V.C.H. I. 178 (plan).

Kettering. Foundations. Assoc. Archit. Soc. Reports, XXVII. 382.

Longthorpe. Buildings and pavement. Gough's Camden, II. 287; Lond. S.A. Archaeologia, XXXV. 392; Stukeley's Itin. Curios. I. 84; V.C.H. I. 175, 189.

Lowick. Pavement. Britton and Brayley, XI. 198 ; Gough's
Brit. Topog. II. 48 ; V.C.H. I. 194.

Mill Cotton, *see* Raunds.

Mill Hill or Field, *see* Castor.

Paulerspury. Buildings and pavement. Illust. Lond. News,
1850, I. 214; V.C.H. Bucks. II. 11. (Under Stony Stratford.)

Peterborough. Traces of buildings. V.C.H. I. 188, 189.

Piddington. Buildings and pavement. Lewis, III. 545; V.C.H.
I. 198 ; Whellan, 277.

Raunds. Foundations. Bridges, II. 190; Gough's Camden, II. 275;
Lewis, III. 644 ; Morton, 516; V.C.H. I. 194 ; Whellan, 925.

Ringstead, *see* Raunds.

Sibson, *see* Castor.

Stanwick. Pavement. Bridges, II. 194 ; Britton and Brayley,
XI. 188; V.C.H. I. 194.

Sutton Field, *see* Castor.

Sutton, King's. Foundations (?). V.C.H. I. 201.

Thenford. Buildings. Baker, I. 717 ; Bridges, I. 203 ; Morton,
529 ; V.C.H. I. 201 ; Whellan, 498.

Thornhaugh, *see* Castor.

Thorpe, *see* Longthorpe.

Towcester. Buildings and pavement. Antiquary, VIII. 87 ;
B.A.A. Jour. II. 355 ; V.C.H. I. 184 (plan).

Wansford, *see* Castor.

Weekley. Buildings and pavement. V.C.H. I. 194.

Weldon. Buildings and pavement. Britton and Brayley, XI.
207; Gibson, 172 (plan); Gough's Camden, II. 284 (plan),
and Brit. Topog. II. 48 ; King's Mun. Antiq. II. 174 ; Lewis,
IV. 490 ; Lond. S.A. Minute Book, III. 204, 206, 208 (plan),
244, and Topog. Colls., red portfolio (plan, etc.); Lysons'
Reliquiae, I. pt. iv. 4 and pl. VII; Stukeley's Letters, I. 466,
III. 40, 41, 42, 58, 61; V.C.H. I. 193 (plan).

Whilton. Foundations. Baker, I. 236; Morton, 532 ; V.C.H.
I. 186.

Whittlebury. Buildings and pavement. Arch. Jour. VII. 172 ;
B.A.A. Jour. VI. 73, 87, 157, VII. 107 (plan); V.C.H. I. 199
(plan). One pav. relaid in dairy at Windsor Castle.

Woodford.   Pavement.   Bridges, II. 265 ; Gough's Camden, II.
   282; Lewis, IV. 641 ; Morton, 529 ; V.C.H. I. 194.
Yarwell, *see* Castor.

NORTHUMBERLAND

Brand.   Brand, J.   History of Newcastle-on-Tyne, 2 vols., 1789.
Bruce's Rom. Wall.   Bruce, J. Collingwood.   The Roman Wall, 3rd ed.,
   1867.
Bruce's Handbook.   Bruce, J. C.   Handbook to the Roman Wall, 6th ed.,
   1909.
Budge.   Budge, E. A. Wallis.   An account of the Roman Antiquities
   in the Museum at Chesters, etc., 2nd ed., 1907.
Durham and Northumb. Arch. Soc. Trans.   Durham and Northumberland
   Architectural and Archaeological Society Transactions, I.—V. 1870—
   1907.
Hodgson.   Hodgson, J.   History of Northumberland, 3 vols., 1820—58.
Maclauchlan.   Maclauchlan, H.   Memoir on the Roman Wall, 1858.
Maclauchlan's Watling Street.   Maclauchlan, H.   Memoir on the Watling
   Street, 1852.
Maclauchlan's East Branch of Watling Street.   Maclauchlan, H.   Memoir
   on the Eastern Branch of the Watling Street, 1864.
Newcastle S.A.   Newcastle Society of Antiquaries.
   (*a*)   Archaeologia Æliana, I.—IV. (1816—55), N.S. I.—XXV. (1857—
          1903), 3 S. I.—VI. (1904—10).
   (*b*)   Proceedings, I.—X. (1883—1902), 3 S. I.—III. (1903—09).
   (*c*)   Lapidarium Septentrionale, 1870.
Northumberland, Hist. of.   Northumberland, History of, issued by the
   County History Committee, 9 vols., 1893—1909.
Warburton.   Warburton, J.   Vallum Romanum, 1753.

Æsica, *see* Chesters, Great.

Benwell (*Condercum*).   Station, buildings, etc.   Brand, I. 606
   (plan) ; Britton and Brayley, XII. i. 72 ; Bruce's Rom. Wall,
   107 (plan), and Handbook, 49 ; Gordon, 71, and pl. XXVI ;
   Gough's Camden, III. 474, 511 ; Hodgson, III. ii. 175, 316 ;
   Horsley's Brit. Rom. 105, 138 ; Lond. S.A. Topog. Colls.
   Brit. Rom. III. (plans and drawings) ; Maclauchlan, 12 ;
   Newcastle S.A. Lapid. Septen. 22 ; Oxford Archit. and
   Hist. Soc. Proc. N.S. I. 215.

Borcovicus, *see* Housesteads.

Bremenium, *see* Rochester, High.

Brinkburn. Bridge piers. Maclauchlan's East Branch of Watling Street, 12, 15.

Busy Gap (near). Hypocaust. Phil. Trans. No. 278, 1131.

Bywell. Bridge piers. Newcastle S.A. Lapid. Septen. 338.

Caervoran (*Magna*). Station, buildings, etc. Brand, I. 611; Britton and Brayley, XII. i. 117; Bruce's Rom. Wall, 241 (plan), and Handbook, 189; Gordon, 79, and pl. XXIX; Gough's Camden, III. 482, 503; Hodgson, III. ii. 135, 204, 316; Horsley's Brit. Rom. 107, 151; Lewis, I. 270; Lond. S.A. Archaeologia, XXIV. 352; Maclauchlan, 47, 48; Mag. Brit. 1738, III. 638; Newcastle S.A. Proc. 3 S. II. 306; Stukeley's Itin. Curios. II. 59.

Carrawburgh (*Procolitia*). Station, buildings, excavations, well, etc. Brand, I. 609; Britton and Brayley, XII. i. 128; Bruce's Rom. Wall, 169 (plan), and Handbook, 126; Budge, 145; Coll. Antiq. VII. 115; Glasgow Arch. Soc. Trans. I. 117; Gordon, 74, and pl. XXVII; Gough's Camden, III. 478, 505; Hodgson, III. ii. 183; Horsley's Brit. Rom. 106, 145; Lond. S.A. Proc. 2 S. VI. 105; Maclauchlan, 34; Newcastle S.A. Arch. Æliana, N.S. VIII. 1, 20 (plan of well), 42, 60, XXIV. 19; Warburton, 55.

Castle Nick. Mile castle. Bruce's Rom. Wall, 225, and Handbook, 176; Maclauchlan, 44.

Cawfields. Mile castle and turret. Antiquary, XLI. 365; Bruce's Rom. Wall, 230, and Handbook, 180; Maclauchlan, 44; Newcastle S.A. Arch. Æliana, IV. 54, N.S. VI. 54, IX. 211, and Proc. 3 S. II. 286.

Chesterholm or Little Chesters (*Vindolana*). Station, buildings, excavations, etc. Brand, I. 610; Britton and Brayley, XII. i. 122; Bruce's Rom. Wall, 210 (plan), and Handbook, 169; Glasgow Arch. Soc. Trans. I. 113; Gough's Camden, III. 480, 504; Hodgson, III. ii. 195, 316; Horsley's Brit. Rom. 106, 148; Lewis, IV. 434 (under Wall-Town); Maclauchlan, 40; Newcastle S.A. Arch. Æliana, N.S. XXIV. 20; Stukeley's Itin. Curios. II. 60; Warburton, 66.

Chesters (*Cilurnum*). Station, buildings, excavations, etc. Arch. Jour. XLI. 442; B.A.A. Jour. N.S. VII. 71; Berwickshire Nat. Club Proc. VIII. 224; Brand, I. 609; Britton and

Brayley, XII. i. 132; Bruce's Rom. Wall, 149 (plans), and
Handbook, 88 (plans); Budge, 87 (plans); Coll. Antiq. II.
183; Cumb. and West. Arch. Soc. Trans. N.S. I. 84 (plan),
IV. 243 (plan); Dorset Field Club Proc. XIV. 34; Gent.
Mag. 1868, i. 84, and Lib. Rom. Brit. Rem. i. 246; Glasgow
Arch. Soc. Trans. I. 118; Gordon, 73; Gough's Camden,
III. 477, 508; Hodgson, III. ii. 180; Horsley's Brit. Rom.
105, 143; Illust. Archaeologist, I. 250; Lanc. and Ches.
Antiq. Soc. Trans. VI. 195; Lond. S.A. Archaeologia, XLVI.
1 (plans), and Proc. 2 S. VII. 66; Maclauchlan, 27, 32; Newcastle S.A. Arch. Æliana, III. 142, N.S. VII. 171, VIII. 211
(plans), XII. 124 (plans), XIII. 374, XXIII. 9 (plans), XXIV. 19,
Proc. 3 S. II. 284, and Lapid. Septen. 68, 470; Warburton,
50; Wright's Celt, Roman and Saxon, 208.

Bridge. Arch. Jour. XIX. 359; Brand, I. 609; Britton and
Brayley, XII. i. 133; Bruce's Rom. Wall, 144 (plan), and
Handbook, 72 (plan); Budge, 136 (plan); Coll. Antiq. II.
183; Cumb. and West. Arch. Soc. Trans. N.S. I. 88; Dorset
Field Club Proc. XIV. 35; Durham and Northumb. Arch.
Soc. Trans. IV. 5, 15; Godwin's Arch. Handbook, 34;
Gordon, 73; Gough's Camden, III. 508; Hodgson, III. ii.
181; Horsley's Brit. Rom. 143; Maclauchlan, 26; Newcastle
S.A. Arch. Æliana, N.S. V. 142, 148, VI. 19, 80 (plan), XVI.
328 (plan), XXIV. 28, and Proc. 3 S. II. 283; Northumber-
land, Hist. of, IV. 164 (plan); Warburton, 50.

Chesters, Great (*Æsica*). Station, buildings, excavations, etc.
Antiquary, XXX. 208, XXXI. 300, XXXIII. 321, 361; Archaeo-
logia Oxoniensis, 1892—95, 321; B.A.A. Jour. 2 S. XII. 275;
Brand, I. 610; Britton and Brayley, XII. i. 120; Builder,
LXVII. 196, LXXII. 543, 552, LXXIV. 557, 569; Bruce's Rom.
Wall, 232 (plan), and Handbook, 183; Durham and
Northumb. Arch. Soc. Trans. II. xvii; Gordon, 78, and
pl. XXVIII; Gough's Camden, III. 481, 503; Hodgson, III. ii.
202; Horsley's Brit. Rom. 107, 150; Lewis, IV. 434 (under
Wall-Town); Lond. S.A. Proc. 2 S. XVII. 29 (plan of baths);
Maclauchlan, 45; Newcastle S.A. Arch. Æliana, N.S. XXIV.
19 (plans, etc.), and Proc. 3 S. II. 287; Stukeley's Itin. Curios.
II. 59; Warburton, 71.

Chesters, Halton (*Hunnum*). Station, buildings, etc. Arch. Jour. XIV. 5; Brand, I. 608; Britton and Brayley, XII. i. 173; Bruce's Rom. Wall, 133 (plan), and Handbook, 63; Gough's Camden, III. 476, 510; Hodgson, III. ii. 179, 316 (plan of baths); Horsley's Brit. Rom. 105, 142; Maclauchlan, 21.

Cilurnum, *see* Chesters.

Condercum, *see* Benwell.

Corbridge (*Corstopitum*). Town, buildings, excavations, etc. Arch. Jour. LXIV. 39, LXV. 121, 334, LXVI. 53; B.A.A. Jour. 2 S. XII. 202, XIII. 196, XIV. 1, 214, XV. 1 (plan), 115, XVI. 1; British Curiosities in Art and Nature, 1721, 119; Britton and Brayley, XII. i. 171; Bruce's Rom. Wall, 339, and Handbook, 77; Builder, XCV. 320, XCVII. 36, 244; Coll. Antiq. IV. 146; Cumb. and West. Arch. Soc. Trans. N.S. VIII. 381; Gough's Camden, III. 509; Hodgson, III. ii. 243, 316; Horsley's Brit. Rom. 397; Lond. S.A. Proc. 2 S. XXII. 300, 410, 411, 521, XXIII. 112, 213; Maclauchlan's Watling Street, 21; Newcastle S.A. Arch. Æliana, 3 S. III. 161 (plans), IV. 205 (plans), V. 305 (plans), VI. 205 (plans), Proc. 3 S. III. 98, 101, 107, 163, 279, 313, and Lapid. Septen. 330; Reliquary and Illust. Arch. N.S. XV. 294.

    Bridge. B.A.A. Jour. N.S. XII. 205 (plan), XIII. 125; Coll. Antiq. IV. 146; Durham and Northumb. Arch. Soc. Trans. V. ccvii; Godwin's Arch. Handbook, 34; Hodgson, III. ii. 244; Maclauchlan's Watling Street, 20; Newcastle S.A. Arch. Æliana, N.S. VI. 18, XXII. 82, 3 S. III. 177; Stukeley's Letters, III. 132; Warburton, 151.

Habitancum, *see* Risingham.

Halton Chesters, *see* Chesters, Halton.

Haltwhistle Burn. Camp, buildings, etc. B.A.A. Jour. N.S. XIII. 130; Bruce's Handbook, 181; Maclauchlan, 46; Newcastle S.A. Arch. Æliana, 3 S. V. 213 (plans), and Proc. V. 157, 3 S. III. 40, 79, 162, 218.

Housesteads (*Borcovicus*). Station, buildings, excavations, etc. Antiquary, XXXV. 71; B.A.A. Jour. 2 S. XII. 272; Brand, I. 609; Britton and Brayley, XII. i. 125; Bruce's Rom. Wall, 179 (plan), and Handbook, 143; Budge, 174; Cheshire

Arch. Soc. Trans. III. 333; Cymmrodorion Soc. Trans.
1908—9, 72 (plan); Durham and Northumb. Arch. Soc.
Trans. III. cii, v. clxxxvi; Glasgow Arch. Soc. Trans. I.
114; Gordon, 75; Gough's Camden, III. 480, 504; Hodgson,
III. ii. 185, 316; Horsley's Brit. Rom. 106, 148, 219; Lanc.
and Ches. Antiq. Soc. Trans. VI. 197; Leicester Arch. Soc.
Trans. I. 303; Lewis, IV. 332 (under Thorngrafton); Mac-
lauchlan, 38, 92; Newcastle S.A. Arch. Æliana, I. 263, N.S.
XXIV. 20, XXV. 193 (plans), Proc. I. 186, 3 S. II. 285, and
Lapid. Septen. 90, 96; Scot. S.A. Proc. XXIV. 153; Stukeley's
Itin. Curios. II. 60; Warburton, 60; Wright's Celt, Roman
and Saxon, 178, 187.

Milecastles. Bruce's Rom. Wall, 201, and Handbook, 258;
Budge, 201; Gent. Mag. 1855, ii. 395, and Lib. Rom. Brit.
Rem. i. 251; Lond. S.A. Proc. 1 S. III. 67; Newcastle S.A.
Arch. Æliana, IV. 269.

Hunnum, *see* Chesters, Halton.

Limestone Bank, near Chesters. Milecastle and turret. Bruce's
Rom. Wall, 167, and Handbook, 123; Lond. S.A. Proc. 2 S.
VI. 104; Maclauchlan, 33; Newcastle S.A. Arch. Æliana,
N.S. VII. 256, and Proc. VII. 232.

Magna, *see* Caervoran.

Mucklebank Crag. Turret. Antiquary, XXVI. 2; Bruce's Handbook, 186; Newcastle S.A. Arch. Æliana, N.S. IX. 234, XXIV. 13.

Newcastle (*Pons Ælii*). The Wall. Britton and Brayley, XII.
i. 36; Bruce's Rom. Wall, 98, and Handbook, 43; Gough's
Camden, III. 473, 511; Hodgson, III. ii. 172; Horsley's Brit.
Rom. 104, 137; Maclauchlan, 11; Newcastle S.A. Arch.
Æliana, IV. 82, and Proc. IV. 270, VI. 66, IX. 214, 3 S. III.
192; Stukeley's Itin. Curios. II. 64.

Bridge. Brand, I. 35; Britton and Brayley, XII. i. 36; Bruce's
Rom. Wall, 102, and Handbook, 43; Durham and Northumb.
Arch. Soc. Trans. IV. 7; Gough's Camden, III. 512; Hodg-
son, III. ii. 173; Lond. S.A. Proc. 2 S. VI. 103; Newcastle
S.A. Arch. Æliana, N.S. X. 1 (sections), and Lapid. Septen.
15, 461 (sections).

Procolitia, *see* Carrawburgh.

Risingham (*Habitancum*). Station, buildings, etc. Britton and

Brayley, XII. i. 141; Bruce's Rom. Wall, 332, and Handbook, 248; Coll. Antiq. III. 153; Gough's Camden, III. 506; Hodgson, I. ii. 175, III. ii. 253; Maclauchlan's Watling Street, 27; Newcastle S.A. Arch. Æliana, III. 150, 158 (plan), and Lapid. Septen. 307.

Bridge. Britton and Brayley, XII. i. 141; Godwin's Arch. Handbook, 34; Maclauchlan's Watling Street, 28.

Rochester, High (*Bremenium*). Station, buildings, excavations, etc. Antiquary, IV. 169; Arch. Jour. XIV. 5, and Newcastle vol. 1852, I. 135 (plan); Britton and Brayley, XII. i. 149; Bruce's Rom. Wall, 313, 317 (plan), and Handbook, 248; Coll. Antiq. III. 153; Gough's Camden, III. 505; Hodgson, I. ii. 138, III. ii. 316; Lewis, III. 658; Maclauchlan's Watling Street, 34; Newcastle S.A. Arch. Æliana, N.S. I. 69 (plan), XXIV. 11 (plan), and Lapid. Septen. 280 (plan).

Rutchester (*Vindobala*). Station, etc. Brand, I. 608; Britton and Brayley, XII. i. 176; Bruce's Rom. Wall, 125 (plan), and Handbook, 57; Gordon, 72; Gough's Camden, III. 475, 513; Hodgson, III. ii. 177; Horsley's Brit. Rom. 105, 139; Maclauchlan, 15, 17; Newcastle S.A. Proc. X. 81; Warburton, 41.

Segedunum, *see* Wallsend.

Shields Lawe. Foundations. Bruce's Rom. Wall, 308, and Handbook, 179.

Vindobala, *see* Rutchester.

Vindolana, *see* Chesterholm.

Walbottle Dene. Milecastle. Bruce's Rom. Wall, 123, and Handbook, 53; Newcastle S.A. Arch. Æliana, N.S. VII. 2, and Proc. 3 S. II. 282.

Wallsend (*Segedunum*). Station, buildings, etc. Brand, I. 604; Britton and Brayley, XII. i. 78; Bruce's Rom. Wall, 88 (plan), and Handbook, 37; Gordon, 70; Gough's Camden, III. 472, 513; Hodgson, III. ii. 170, 316; Horsley's Brit. Rom. 104, 135; Maclauchlan, 6; Newcastle S.A. Proc. 3 S. I. 42 (plan), II. 278; Warburton, 24.

Walltown Crag. Turret. Bruce's Handbook, 186; Lond. S.A. Topog. Colls., red portfolio (drawing of section of wall); Newcastle S.A. Arch. Æliana, N.S. X. 57, XVI. 441.

Whitley Castle, near Alston. Station, buildings, etc. Britton and Brayley, XII. i. 107; Bruce's Rom. Wall, 354, and Handbook, 250; Hodgson, III. ii. 74, 316.

The Wall. General. Archaeological Review, IV. 81, 153; B.A.A. Jour. V. 201, N.S. VIII. 132, XII. 269, XV. 51; Bell, R., The Roman Wall, 1852; Brand, J., Hist. of Newcastle, 1789, I. Appendix; Bruce, J. Collingwood, The Roman Wall, 1st ed. 1851, 2nd ed. 1853, 3rd ed. 1867, The Wallet Book, afterwards Handbook to the Roman Wall, 1st ed. 1863, 2nd ed. 1884, 3rd ed. 1885, 4th ed. 1895, 5th ed. 1907, 6th ed. 1909, and Hadrian, the builder of the Roman Wall, 1853; Budge, E. A. Wallis, An account of the Roman Antiquities in the museum at Chesters, etc. 1907; Builder, XXXV. 564, 1023; Cambridge Antiq. Soc. Proc. IX. 177; Cheshire Arch. Soc. Trans. III. 331, N.S. I. 185; Coll. Antiq. II. 171; Cumb. and West. Arch. Soc. Trans. XIII. 453, XIV. 185, 413, XV. 172, 201, 337, 345, 365, XVI. 80, N.S. I. 75, II. 384, III. 328, IV. 239; Dorset Field Club Proc. XIV. 29; Gent. Mag. 1851, ii. 383; Ferguson, R. S., Popular History of Cumberland, 78; Gordon, A., Itinerarium Septentrionale, 1726, caps. viii, ix, x; Gough's Camden, III. 467; Hodgson, J., The Picture of Newcastle-on-Tyne, 1812, and History of Northumberland, 3 vols. 1820—58, I. i. 25, III. ii. 149; Horsley, J., Britannia Romana, 1732, caps. vii, viii, ix; Hutton, W., History of the Roman Wall, 2nd ed. 1813; Knight's Old England, I. 42; Lanc. and Ches. Antiq. Soc. Trans. VI. 194; Lewis, S., Topog. Dict. of England, III. 422; Lysons' Magna Britannia, IV. cxxix; Mackenzie, E., Hist. of Northumberland, 2nd ed. 1825, I. 177; Maclauchlan, H., Survey of the Roman Wall, 1857 (maps), and Memoir on the Roman Wall, 1858; Neilson, G., Per Lineam Valli, 1891; Newcastle S.A. Arch. Æliana, N.S. XIII. 85, 181, XVI. 447, XVIII. 83, XXIV. 1, Proc. II. 188, VII. 217, 3 S. II. 277, and Lapid. Septen.; Scarth, H. M., Roman Britain, 73; Stukeley, W., Itinerarium Curiosum, II. (Iter Boreale), 55, and Letters, III. (Surtees Soc. 80), 139; Wallis, J., Hist. of Northumberland, 2 vols. 1769, II. 1; Warburton, J., Vallum Romanum, 1753; Wellbeloved, C.,

Eburacum, 17; Wright, T., Celt, Roman and Saxon, 157, 191, 226.

NOTTINGHAMSHIRE

Dickinson. Dickinson, W. Antiquities of Nottinghamshire, pt. i. Southwell, 1801.

Thoroton. Thoroton, R. Antiquities of Nottinghamshire, with additions by John Throsby, 3 vols. 1797.

Thoroton Soc. Trans. Thoroton Society Transactions, vol. I.—XIII. 1897—1910.

V.C.H. Victoria History of the Counties of England. Nottinghamshire, II. 1910.

Barton-upon-Trent. Buildings and pavement. Arch. Jour. XLIII. 30; Athenaeum, Apr. 19, 1856; Gent. Mag. 1856, i. 506, and Lib. Rom. Brit. Rem. i. 259; Lewis, I. 155; Midland Counties Historical Collector, II. 142; Nottingham Review, Apr. 18, 1856; V.C.H. II. 23.

Bridgeford, East. Foundations. Arch. Jour. XLIII. 17, 18, 19; Gough's Camden, II. 400; Lewis, I. 355; Stukeley's Itin. Curios. I. 105; Times, Nov. 15, 1910; V.C.H. II. 15.

Brough (*Crococolana*). Foundations, etc. Arch. Jour. XLIII. 15; Gough's Camden, II. 404; Horsley's Brit. Rom. 439; Lewis, I. 646; Pointer's Brit. Rom. 41, 53; Stukeley's Itin. Curios. I. 103; V.C.H. II. 11.

Collingham, South, *see* Brough and Cromwell.

Cromwell. Bridge. Antiquary, X. 274; Arch. Jour. XLIII. 26; B.A.A. Jour. XL. 419, XLI. 43, 83 (plan); Builder, XLVIII. 258 (plan); Durham and Northumb. Arch. Soc. Trans. IV. 16; Notts. Daily Guardian, Feb. 20, 1877; V.C.H. II. 25.

Littleborough. Foundations and causeway. Arch. Jour. XLIII. 11, 12; Gough's Camden, II. 396, 404; Stukeley's Itin. Curios. I. 93; Trollope, E., Sleaford, 54; V.C.H. II. 19.

Mansfield Woodhouse. Buildings and pavement. Arch. Jour. XLIII. 28; B.A.A. Jour. VIII. 187; Britton and Brayley, XII. i. 396; Fowler, No. 16; Gent. Mag. 1786, ii. 616, and Lib. Rom. Brit. Rem. i. 260; Harrod, W., Hist. of Mansfield, 1801, 47 (plans); King's Mun. Antiq. II. 175, 179; Lewis,

III. 241, 443 ; Lincoln, A survey of the Antiquities of the city of, 1840—48, 27 ; Lond. S.A. Archaeologia, VIII. 363 (plan), IX. 193, 197, 203, Minute Book, XXI. 296, 472, and Topog. Colls., brown portfolio (drawing) ; Morgan, 72, 114, 121 ; Rooke, H., Description of two Roman Villas discovered near Mansfield Woodhouse, 1801 (plans); Thoroton, II. 173 (plan); V.C.H. II. 28 (plans, etc.).

Oldcotes, near Blythe (Styrrup). Buildings and pavement. Arch. Jour. XXVIII. 66, 71, XLIII. 32 ; V.C.H. II. 34.

Southwell. Foundations and pavement. Arch. Jour. XLIII. 26; Dickinson, 97 ; Lond. S.A. Archaeologia, IX. 199, and Minute Book, XXII. 422 ; Thoroton Soc. Trans. v. 58 ; V.C.H. II. 34.

Styrrup, *see* Oldcotes.

Thorpe. Buildings and pavement. Arch. Jour. XLIII. 30 ; Lewis, IV. 339 ; V.C.H. II. 35.

Willoughby. Pavement. Arch. Jour. XLIII. 21 ; Gough's Camden, II. 401 ; Lewis, IV. 569 ; Lond. S.A. Archaeologia, XXXV. 395 ; Stukeley's Itin. Curios. I. 107 ; V.C.H. II. 17.

Winthorpe. Bridge. Arch. Jour. XLIII. 25 ; B.A.A. Jour. VIII. 169; Dickinson, 92; V.C.H. II. 7, 36.

OXFORDSHIRE

Beesley. Beesley, A. History of Banbury, 2 vols. 1848.

Berks., Bucks. and Oxon. Arch. Jour. Berkshire, Buckinghamshire and Oxfordshire Archaeological Journal, I.—XV. 1895—1910.

Blomfield. Blomfield, J. C. History of the Deanery of Bicester, 1882.

Dunkin's Bicester. Dunkin, J. History and Antiquities of Bicester and Alchester, 1816.

Dunkin's Bullington. Dunkin, J. History and Antiquities of the Hundreds of Bullington and Ploughley, 2 vols. 1823.

Gardner. History, Gazetteer and Directory of the County of Oxford, printed and published by R. Gardner, 1852.

Hussey. Hussey, R. On the Roman road from Allchester to Dorchester, 1841.

Marshall's Hist. of Woodstock. Marshall, E. The Early History of Woodstock Manor, etc. 1875.

Oxford Archit. Soc. Proc. Oxford Architectural and Historical Society Proceedings, I.—III. 1840—59, N.S. I.—VI. 1860—1900.

North Oxford Arch. Soc. Trans. North Oxfordshire Archaeological Society Reports and Transactions, 1856—1910.

Plot. Plot, R. Natural History of Oxfordshire, 1677.

Pointer's Brit. Rom. Pointer, J. Britannia Romana, 1724.

Pointer's Stunsfield. Pointer, J. Account of a Roman Pavement at Stunsfield, 1713.

Skelton. Skelton, J. Antiquities of Oxfordshire, 1823.

Warton. Warton, T. History and Antiquities of Kiddington, 3rd ed. 1815.

Alchester. Foundations and pavement. Archaeologia Oxoniensis, 1892—95, 34; B.A.A. Jour. VI. 154, XII. 176; Blomfield, 22, 23, 24; Britton and Brayley, XII. ii. 536; Dunkin's Bicester, 187, 197, and Bullington, II. 174; Gardner, 776; Gough's Camden, II. 19; Hussey, 21, 29; Kennet, W., Parochial Antiquities, 1695, 693; Lond. S.A. Minute Book, X. 118; Oxford Archit. Soc. Proc. N.S. V. 355; Warton, 58.

Beaconsfield Farm, see Tew, Great.

Beckley. Buildings and pavement. Arch. Jour. XX. 73; Oxford Archit. Soc. Proc. N.S. I. 186 (plan).

Bloxham. Kiln (?). Beesley, 609; Gardner, 617.

Ditchley (Challow Hill). Pavement. Jordan, J., Hist. of Enstone, 1857, 51; Warton, 67.

Drayton. Pavement. Beesley, 44; Gardner, 624; North Oxford Arch. Soc. Trans. III. 17.

Enstone, see Ditchley.

Fawler. Buildings and pavement. Berks., Bucks. and Oxon. Arch. Jour. IV. 17.

Fencot-on-Otmoor. Kiln. B.A.A. Jour. VI. 60; Blomfield, 19; Dunkin's Bullington, I. 120; Hussey, 33, 34.

Fringford. Buildings and pavement. Blomfield, 17.

Hanwell. Buildings and pavement. Beesley, 44.

Harpsden. Buildings. Antiquary, XLV. 206.

Headington. Buildings and kiln (?). Arch. Jour. VI. 183; B.A.A. Jour. V. 159, VI. 52, 54 (plan); Berks., Bucks. and Oxon. Arch. Jour. IV. 20; Illust. Lond. News, April 14, 1849; Smith, C. Roach, Illust. Rom. Lond. 81.

Horton. Foundations. Arch. Jour. VIII. 313.

Northleigh. Buildings and pavement. Builder, XCIV. 747; Gardner, 682; Hakewill, H., Roman remains at Northleigh and Stonesfield, 1826, with map and plan of house; Jordan, J.,

Hist. of Enstone, 1857, 51 ; Lewis, III. 63 ; Lond. S.A. Archaeologia, XXXVII. 433 ; Marshall's Hist. of Woodstock, 12 ; Morgan, 111, 117 (plan of house) ; Oxford Archit. Soc. Proc. N.S. II. 346, III. 3, 37 ; Skelton (Wooton Hundred), 9, 11 (plan) ; Warton, 67 ; Wright's Celt, Roman and Saxon, 229, 243.

Otmoor, *see* Fencot.

Shotover. Kiln. B.A.A. Jour. VI. 60.

Steeple Aston. Pavement. Beesley, 45 ; Britton and Brayley, XII. ii. 9; Gardner, 659; Gough's Camden, II. 15 ; Mag. Brit. 1738, IV. 212, 381 ; Morgan, 113; Plot, 327; Pointer's Stunsfield, 34.

Steeple Barton. Pavement. Warton, 67.

Stonesfield or Stunsfield. Buildings and pavement. B.A.A. Jour. XXXVIII. 303; Britton and Brayley, XII. ii. 425; Fowler, No. 21 ; Gardner, 690; Gent. Mag. 1818, i. 364, and Lib. Rom. Brit. Rem. i. 261 ; Gough's Camden, II. 15, and Brit. Topog. II. 88; Hakewill, H., Roman remains at Northleigh and Stonesfield, 1826, 19; Hughson, D., Hist. of London, I. 36 ; King's Mun. Antiq. II. 169; Leland's Itin. VIII. ix ; Lond. S.A. Archaeologia, XXXVII. 434, Minute Book, XVII. 164, XVIII. 397, XIX. 193, and Topog. Colls., red portfolio (orig. drawings by W. Lewington) ; Marshall's Hist. of Woodstock, 12 ; Morgan, 33, 108, 116 ; Oxford, Ashmolean Museum (four drawings) ; North Oxford Arch. Soc. III. 118; Pointer's Brit. Rom. 47, and Stunsfield; Royal Soc. Archives, Classified Papers, XVI. 41 (original drawing of plan) ; Skelton (Wooton Hundred), 20; Stukeley's Itin. Curios. I. 47 ; Warton, 66.

Tew, Great (Beaconsfield Farm). Buildings and pavement. Beesley, 39, 40, 41, and pl. X (pavement) ; Britton and Brayley, XII. ii. 462 ; Gardner, 692; Gent. Mag. 1811, i. 388, and Lib. Rom. Brit. Rem. i. 261 ; Gough's Camden, II. 15; Lewis, IV. 316 ; Mag. Brit. 1738, IV. 212, 382 ; Morgan, 113; Plot, 327 ; Pointer's Stunsfield, 34; Warton, 67 (erroneously called Dunstew).

Water Eaton. Pavement. Marshall's Hist. of Woodstock, 10.

Wendlebury, *see* Alchester.

Wheatley. Buildings. Arch. Jour. II. 350 (plan), III. 92, and
Oxford vol. 1850, xix ; Athenaeum, Nov. 15, 1845 ; B.A.A.
Jour. XI. 65 ; Oxford Archit. Soc. Proc. N.S. III. 4.

Wigginton. Buildings and pavement. Beesley, 41, 42 (plan),
and pl. XI (pavement) ; Gardner, 632 ; Lewis, IV. 560 ;
North Oxford Arch. Soc. Trans. III. 17, 118 ; Skelton
(Bloxham Hundred), 9, 12 (plan).

Wood Eaton. Foundations (?). Hussey, 37, 38 ; North Oxford
Arch. Soc. III. 114.

Woodperry. Buildings. Arch. Jour. III. 116, 124 ; Lond. S.A.
Proc. 1 S. I. 107.

Woodstock. Buildings. Godwin's Arch. Handbook, 231 ;
Marshall's Hist. of Woodstock, 13.

RUTLAND

V.C.H. Victoria History of the Counties of England. Rutland, I. 1908.

Casterton, Great. Foundations. Britton and Brayley, XII. ii.
112 ; Stukeley's Itin. Curios. I. 84 ; Trollope, E., Sleaford,
43 ; V.C.H. I. 88.

Ketton. Pavement. Lond. S.A. Proc. 2 S. XIX. 194 ; V.C.H.
I. 90.

Market Overton and Thisleton. Foundations, kiln, etc. Arch.
Jour. XLI. 219 ; Lond. S.A. Proc. 2 S. XXII. 48 ; Stukeley's
Letters, III. 32 ; V.C.H. I. 90, 92, 93.

SHROPSHIRE

Arch. Cambrensis. Archaeologia Cambrensis of the Cambrian Archaeo-
logical Association, 1 S. I.—IV. 1846—49, 2 S. I.—V. 1850—54, 3 S. I.—
XV. 1855—69, 4 S. I.—XIV. 1870—83, 5 S. I.—XVII. 1884—1900, 6 S.
I.—X. 1901—10.

Hartshorne. Hartshorne, C. H. Salopia Antiqua, 1841.

Montgomery Colls. Collections Historical and Archaeological relating to
Montgomeryshire, published by the Powys-Land Club, I.—XXXV. 1868
—1910.

Shrops, Arch. Soc. Trans. Shropshire Archaeological and Natural History
Society Transactions, 1 S. I.—XI. 1878—88, 2 S. I.—XII. 1889—1900,
3 S. I.—IX. 1901—09.

V.C.H. Victoria History of the Counties of England. Shropshire, I. 1908.

Wright's Uriconium. Wright, T. Uriconium, 1872.

Acton Scott. Buildings. Lond. S.A. Archaeologia, XXXI. 339 (plan), and Proc. 1 S. 1. 73; Shrops. Arch. Soc. Trans. 1 S. II. 341, 2 S. XI. 166; V.C.H. I. 259 (plan); Wright's Uriconium, 29, 31 (plan).

Lea, see Pontesbury.

Linley Hall. Buildings. B.A.A. Jour. XIII. 174, 176, XVII. 213; Gent. Mag. 1856, ii. 500, and Lib. Rom. Brit. Rem. i. 264; Illust. Lond. News, Sept. 13 and Oct. 4, 1856; Shrops. Arch. Soc. Trans. 1 S. II. 343, 2 S. XI. 166; V.C.H. I. 257 (plan); Wright's Uriconium, 24, 25 (plan).

Okengates. Hypocaust(?). Gent. Mag. 1797, i. 111; Harts-horne, 132; Shrops. Arch. Soc. Trans. 1 S. II. 339, 2 S. XI. 165; V.C.H. I. 261.

Oswestry, Old. Pavement. Shrops. Arch. Soc. Trans. 1 S. II. 340, 2 S. XI. 165; Wright's Uriconium, 23.

Pontesbury (Lea). Buildings and pavement. Arch. Jour. LIV. 166; B.A.A. Jour. XXXVIII. 303; Dukes, T. F., MS. History of Uriconium, 1829, in Library of Soc. of Antiquaries, Lond. (coloured etching); Fowler, No. 18; Gent. Mag. 1793, ii. 1144; Lond. S.A. Archaeologia, XII. 92, Minute Book, XXV. 75, 226, and Topog. Colls., red portfolio (drawing of pave-ment); Montgomery Colls., XVII. 109; Morgan, 33, 107; Shrops. Arch. Soc. Trans. 1 S. II. 341, 2 S. V. 230, XI. 166; V.C.H. I. 258; Wright's Uriconium, 24.

Rushbury. Foundations(?). Shrops. Arch. Soc. Trans. 1 S. II. 345, 2 S. XI. 166; V.C.H. I. 261.

Weston. Foundations. Rawdenhurst, T., Hist. of Hawkstone, 53; Shrops. Arch. Soc..Trans. 1 S. II. 343, 2 S. XI. 165; V.C.H. I. 262.

Wroxeter (*Uriconium* or *Viroconium*). The city, walls, gates, buildings, pavements and excavations. Anderson, J. C., The Roman City of Uriconium, 1867, and Shropshire, its early History and Antiquities, 1867, 132; Antiquary, XII. 97, XXVI. 17, XXX. 208, XXXV. 365; Arch. Cambrensis, 3 S. V. 207, 257, VI. 312, XIII. 157, 6 S. VI. 181; Arch. Jour. XVI. 53, 264, 302, XVII. 54, 73, 240, 269, XIX. 80, XX. 196, 385, XXI. 121, 130, LIV. 123 (plans, etc.), and Winchester vol. 1845, under Porchester Castle, 9, 10; Athenaeum, Apr. 16

and June 18, 1859; Blakeway MSS. Bodleian Lib. Oxford ; B.A.A. Jour. XV. 205, 311, XVI. 158 (plans), 205, 342, XVII. 100, and Coll. Arch. I. 8 ; British Curiosities in Art and Nature, 1721, 92 ; Britton and Brayley, XIII. i. 185 ; Chester Arch. Soc. Jour. II. 309 (plans); Coll. Antiq. III. 29; Dukes, T. F., Antiquities of Shropshire, 1844, 148, and MS. History of Uriconium, 1829, in library of Soc. of Antiquaries, Lond.; Fox, G. E., Guide to Uriconium, 1898 (plans); Gent. Mag. 1813, i. 9, 1828, i. 255, 1859, i. 448, 625, ii. 219, 1862, i. 192, 398, ii. 598, 677, 1863, i. 302, 1867, ii. 514, 1868, i. 665, and Lib. Rom. Brit. Rem. i. 265; Gough's Camden, III. 5, 22, and Brit. Topog. II. 182 ; Hartshorne, 115 ; Horsley's Brit. Rom. 419; Illust. Lond. News, XXXIV. (1859), 377, 386, 426 ; Lewis, IV. 683 ; Lincoln, A survey of the Antiquities of the city of, 1840—48, 27 *n* ; Liverpool Arch. Soc. Trans. N.S. I. Sess. 13, 189, 192 ; Lond. S.A. Archaeologia, IX. 323 (plans), Proc. 1 S. IV. 275, 314, 2 S. I. 394, IV. 55 (plan), Minute Book, I. 51, and Topog. Colls., red portfolio (plans, etc.); Mag. Brit. 1738, IV. 638, 639, 640; Montgomery Colls. XXI. 38 ; Morgan, 96, 107 ; Phil. Trans. XXV. 2226; Reliquary, II. 151, III. 169; Royal Soc. Archives, Classified Papers, XVI. 40; Scarth's Rom. Brit. 135; Shaw's Staffs. I. Introd. 28; Shrops. Arch. Soc. Trans. 1 S. II. 317, 326, 2 S. X. xxxii, XI. vii, XII. v, 3 S. II. 163 (plan), III. xxxix ; Times, July 25, Sept. 3, 26, Oct. 19, 1859, Oct. 8, 1860, Oct. 8, 1861, Sept. 30, 1862 ; V.C.H. I. 220 (plans, etc.) ; Woolhope Field Club Trans. 1881—82, 239 ; Wright, T., Uriconium, 1872, Guide to the ruins of Uriconium, 1859, Celt, Roman and Saxon, 149, 188, 204, 212, and Wanderings of an Antiquary, 25.

Yarchester. Foundations. Shrops. Arch. Soc. Trans. 1 S. II. 339, 2 S. XI. 166; V.C.H. I. 261 ; Wright's Uriconium, 35.

SOMERSETSHIRE

Bath Field Club Proc.   Bath Natural History and Antiquarian Field Club
    Proceedings, I.—IX. 1867—1905.

Batten.   Batten, John.   Historical and Topographical Collections relating
    to parts of South Somerset, 1894.

Bristol and Glouc. Arch. Soc. Trans.   Bristol and Gloucestershire Archaeo-
    logical Society Transactions, I.—XXXII. 1876—1909.

Clifton Antiq. Club Proc.   Clifton Antiquarian Club Proceedings, I.—VI.
    1884—1908.

Collinson.   Collinson, J.   History of Somersetshire, 3 vols. 1791.

Hoare's Anc. Wilts.   Hoare, Sir R. C.   Ancient History of North Wiltshire,
    2 vols. 1819.

Hoare's Pitney Pavement.   Hoare, Sir R. C.   The Pitney Pavement, 1831.

Phelps.   Phelps, W.   History of Somersetshire, 2 vols. 1836—39.

Pownall.   Pownall, T.   Roman Antiquities at Bath, 1795.

Pulman.   Pulman, G. P. R.   Book of the Axe, 1875.

Rutter.   Rutter, J.   Delineations of the N.W. Division of Somerset, 1829.

Scarth's Rom. Bath.   Scarth, H. M.   Aquae Solis, or Notices of Roman
    Bath, 1864.

Somerset Arch. Soc. Proc.   Somersetshire Archaeological and Natural
    History Society Proceedings, I.—LV. 1851—1909.

Somerset and Dorset N. and Q.   Somerset and Dorset Notes and Queries,
    I.—X. 1890—1907.

V.C.H.   Victoria History of the Counties of England.   Somersetshire,
    I. 1906.

Warner.   Warner, R.   Roman Antiquities discovered at Bath, 1797.

Alcombe (Cheney Court).   Buildings.   Scarth's Rom. Bath
    119; Somerset Arch. Soc. Proc. XII. i. 25.

Ashton, Long.   Foundations.   Collinson, III. 141 ; V.C.H. I. 305.

Banwell.   Foundations.   Gent. Mag. 1811, ii. 105; Rutter, 144;
    V.C.H. I. 307.

Bath (*Aquae Sulis*).   The walls, gates, etc.   Arch. Jour. XLVIII.
    174; B.A.A. Jour. XIII. 259; Bath Herald, May 7, 1803;
    Bath Field Club Proc. IV. 138, VII. 114, 116; Collinson, I. 8;
    Gent. Mag. 1804, ii. 1006; Gibbs' Bath Guide, 1835, 4, 7 ;
    Gough's Camden, I. 116; Leland's Itin. II. 61; Pownall, 27;
    Scarth's Rom. Bath, 7, 108; Somerset Arch. Soc. Proc.
    XXXI. i. 31, ii. 15 ; Stukeley's Itin. Curios. I. 146 ; V.C.H. I.
    226; Warner, Introd. xii.

    Temple of Sul Minerva.   Arch. Jour. XXV. 159; Athenaeum,

Dec. 28, 1867; B.A.A. Jour. X. 153, XII. 303, XIII. 257, XVII. 8, XXIX. 190, 379; Bath Chronicle, Feb. 6, 1868, Apr. 8, 1869, Apr. 28, 1870; Bath Field Club Proc. II. 119, 348; Britton and Brayley, XIII. i. 362; Builder, XXVII. 303; Carter, J., Ancient Architecture, 1795, I. 8, pls. VII—X; Collinson, I. 8; Crutwell and Duffield's Bath Guides; Gent. Mag. 1791, i. 103, and Lib. Rom. Brit. Rem. i. 284; Gough's Camden, I. 116; King's Mun. Antiq. II. 215; Knight's Old England, I. 47; Lond. S.A. Archaeologia, X. 325, XXXVI. 187, and Minute Book, XXVIII. 352, 364; Lysons' Reliquiae, I. ii. pls. I—IX; Pownall; Scarth's Rom. Bath, 17, and Rom. Brit. 147; V.C.H. I. 229; Warner, 73; Wright's Celt, Roman and Saxon, 168; plans and drawings by J. T. Irvine in the National Museum at Edinburgh.

Baths. Antiquary, V. 226, VI. 274, XII. 132, XV. 159, XXVII. 154, XXVIII. 45, 139, 161, XXXI. 299; Arch. Jour. XXXV. 100, XXXVI. 323, XL. 263, XLII. 11, XLVII. 101, XLVIII. 177, LXI. 210, 214 (plan); B.A.A. Jour. XIII. 257, XVII. 8, XXXIV. 246, XXXV. 190, 427, XXXVI. 122, XXXVIII. 91, XXXIX. 407, XLI. 92, 378, XLII. 224, XLIII. 145, N.S. I. 97, XI. 62; Bath Field Club Proc. IV. 357, VI. i. 75, VII. ii. 118; Bristol and Glouc. Arch. Soc. Trans. VIII. 89, XXIII. 34; Builder, XLIII. 319, LI. 109, 510, LXVIII. 228, LXXIII. 328; Davis, C. E., Excavations of Roman Baths at Bath, 10th ed. 1895, A Guide to the Roman Baths, 16th ed. 1884, and The Mineral Baths at Bath, 1883; Gent. Mag. 1755, 376, and Lib. Rom. Brit. Rem. i. 284; Gough's Camden, I. 114 (plan); Lanc. and Ches. Antiq. Soc. Trans. II. 84, III. 263; Lewis, I. 164; Lond. S.A. Proc. 2 S. v. 282, VII. 403, VIII. 409, 458, XI. 130, 194, XVII. 28, XVIII. 346, XIX. 286, Minute Book, III. 283, VII. 212, 213, 216, 218, VIII. 159 (plan), 282, 339, 357, XXIII. 445, XXIV. 34, 77, 83, XXV. 18, 61, and Topog. Colls., red portfolio (orig. drawings), and eleven plans and sections by R. Mann; Lucas, C., Essay of Waters, 1756, III. 222 (plan); Morgan, 168; New Bath Guide, N.D. 10; Phelps, I. i. 155 (plan); Reliquary, XXI. 64, XXIII. 64; Scarth's Rom. Bath, 14 (plan), and Rom. Brit. 147; Somerset Arch. Soc. Proc. III. ii. 77, XXII. i. 35, ii. 20, 22, XXVII. i. 32, XXIX. i. 35, 36,

XXXIII. i. 19, XLI. i. 21 ; Spry, J. H., Practical Treatise on the Bath Waters, 1822, 14 (plan), 149; Sutherland, A., Attempts to Revive Ancient Medical Doctrine, 1763, I. 16 (plan); V.C.H. I. 243 (plan, etc.); Wright's Celt, Roman and Saxon, 168.

Abbey Green. Pavement. Omnium Gatherum, I. 25 ; V.C.H. I. 262.

Bluecoat School. Pavement. Bath and Cheltenham Gazette, June 9, 1859; Morgan, 91, 101; Scarth's Rom. Bath, 89 ; V.C.H. I. 261. Preserved in the school.

Mineral Water Hospital. Pavement. Antiquary, X. 229; B.A.A. Jour. XLI. 98, XLIV. 116; Bath and Cheltenham Gazette, May 11, 1859; Bath Field Club Proc. VI. i. 37; Building News, Sept. 12, 1884; Gent. Mag. 1862, ii. 209, and Lib. Rom. Brit. Rem. i. 288; Omnium Gatherum, I. 25 ; Scarth's Rom. Bath, 89, 94; Somerset Arch. Soc. Proc. XI. ii. 187, XII. i. 26; V.C.H. I. 261. Pavements preserved in hospital.

Norfolk Crescent. Pavement. Bath Chronicle, Oct. 15, 1818; V.C.H. I. 263.

Royal United Hospital. Pavement and foundations. B.A.A. Jour. XXIX. 379; Bath and Cheltenham Gazette, Aug. 1864; Bath Field Club Proc. IX. i. 56; Builder, XXII. 623; Intellectual Observer, VI. 217; Morgan, 91, 101; Scarth's Rom. Bath, 136; V.C.H. I. 262.

Walcot Street. Pavement and pier bases. Bath and Cheltenham Gazette, Nov. 20, 1816 ; Bath Field Club Proc. X. 316; Gent. Mag. 1815, i. 559, and Lib. Rom. Brit. Rem. i. 285; Lond. S.A. Minute Book, XXXIII. 160 ; V.C.H. I. 263.

Weymouth House Schools. Pavement. Antiquary, XXXIII. 231; Bath Chronicle, June 17 and 25, and July 22, 1897; Times, June 18, 1897 ; V.C.H. I. 262.

Bathampton. Kiln. Somerset Arch. Soc. Proc. XXIV. ii. 5, 15.

Bathford. Buildings and pavement. Arch. Jour. XXXVI. 329, 333 ; Bath Field Club Proc. V. i. 66; Britton and Brayley, XIII. i. 437 ; Collinson, I. 111; Gough's Brit. Topog. II. 226, and Camden, I. 118 ; Lewis, I. 169; Lond. S.A. Minute

Book, IV. 19, XX. 48; Scarth's Rom. Bath,119; Skrine, H. D., Bathford and Neighbourhood, 1871, 23; Somerset Arch. Soc. Proc. XXII. i. 51, XXIV. ii. 5, 14; V.C.H. I. 300.

Bathwick. Foundations and pavement. Bath Field Club Proc. II. 479; Scarth's Rom. Bath, 137; V.C.H. I. 263, 264.

Bawdrip. Building and pavement. Somerset Arch. Soc. Proc. LXIX. ii. 187; V.C.H. I. 329, 352.

Bayford, *see* Stoke Trister.

Bratton. Foundations. Phelps, I. 221; V.C.H. I. 320.

Brean Down. Foundations. Somerset Arch. Soc. Proc. XXIV. ii. 7, XXXI. ii. 13; V.C.H. I. 358.

Brislington. Buildings and pavement. Antiquary, XXXVI. 38, 106, 335 (plan); Barker, W. R., Account of Roman villa found at Brislington; Bristol and Glouc. Arch. Soc. Trans. XXIII. 263, 289 (plan), XXIV. 283; Builder, LXXVIII. 22, 45, LXXIX. 258, LXXXI. 179; Clifton Antiq. Club Proc. IV. 262, 306, V. 44, 78 (plan); Somerset Arch. Soc. Proc. XLVII. 56; Somerset and Dorset N. and Q. VII. 27; V.C.H. I. 303. Orig. pav. in Bristol Museum.

Burnett, *see* Corston.

Butleigh Wootton, *see* Street, near Glastonbury.

Cadbury, *see* Tickenham.

Camerton. Buildings and pavement. Arch. Jour. XXXVI. 334; Collinson, III. 329; Gent. Mag. 1827, i. 252; Phelps, I. 179; Somerset Arch. Soc. Proc. XI. ii. 174 (plan), XII. i. 25, XXIV. ii. 14; V.C.H. I. 289 (plan), 290 (plan), 291 (plan), 293.

Chard. Foundations and pavement. Arch. Jour. XXXVI. 334; Pulman, 460; Somerset Arch. Soc. Proc. XXII. ii. 30; V.C.H. I. 332.

Charlton Mackrell. Buildings. Arch. Jour. XXXVI. 334; Bath Field Club Proc. I. ii. 18; Hoare's Pitney Pavement, 6; Morgan, 88; Phelps, I. i. 168; Somerset Arch. Soc. Proc. LIII. 18; V.C.H. I. 323; Wright's Celt, Roman and Saxon, 228.

Chedzoy. Hypocaust. V.C.H. I. 352, 359.

Cheney Court, *see* Alcombe.

Chesterblade, near Evercreech. Foundations. V.C.H. I. 319.

Chew Stoke. Foundations. V.C.H. I. 309.

Chilton Polden, *see* Polden.

Coker, East. Buildings and pavements, found in 1753 and 1818. Arch. Cant. XV. 139; Arch. Jour. XXXVI. 329; B.A.A. Jour. XII. 300; Batten, 106; Coll. Antiq. II. 51; Collinson, II. 340, III. 204 (under Yeovil); Gent. Mag. 1753, 293, and Lib. Rom. Brit. Rem. i. 40 (under Coket, Devon); Gough's Brit. Topog. II. 226, and Camden, I. 91; Lewis, I. 637, IV. 701 (under Yeovil); Morgan, 89, 100; Phelps, I. i. 167; Public Advertiser, June 23, 1753; Royal Society Letters and Papers, Decade II. 361; Somerset Arch. Soc. Proc. IV. i. 7, V. i. 9, XIII. i. 62, XXII. ii. 30, XXIV. ii. 13, 15; V.C.H. I. 329; Wright's Celt, Roman and Saxon, 253; Yeovil General Evening Post, June 23, 1753. A portion of one pavement in Taunton Museum.

Coker, West. Foundations, found in 1861. Arch. Jour. XXIV. 181, 184, XXXVI. 334; B.A.A. Jour. XVIII. 392, XIX. 321; Batten, 107; V.C.H. I. 331.

Combe Down. Buildings. Arch. Jour. XI. 289, XXXVI. 334; B.A.A. Jour. XII. 304, XIX. 66; Scarth's Rom. Bath, 115; Somerset Arch. Soc. Proc. V. ii. 60, 145, XII. i. 24, XXIV. ii. 14; V.C.H. I. 309.

Combe St Nicholas (Wadeford). Buildings and pavement. Arch. Jour. XXXVI. 329, 336; B.A.A. Jour. XII. 300; Davidson, J., Brit. and Rom. Remains, near Axminster, 1833, 76; Lysons' Reliquiae, I. iv. pl. VIII; Phelps, I. i. 174; Pulman, 459; Somerset Arch. Soc. Proc. I. i. 28, V. i. 9, XIII. i. 61, 72 (plan), XXIV. ii. 15, 113, XXVIII. i. 44; V.C.H. I. 333 (plan).

Congresbury. Buildings. Clifton Antiq. Club Proc. II. 177; Somerset Arch. Soc. Proc. XXIII. ii. 9, XXXIII. ii. 5; V.C.H. I. 307.

Copley, *see* Kingweston.

Corston (Burnett). Buildings and pavement. Scarth's Rom. Bath, 126; V.C.H. I. 303.

Cranmore, West. Pavement. Hoare's Anc. Wilts. II. (Rom. Aera) 145 n; V.C.H. I. 319.

Curry Rivel and Drayton. Foundations. V.C.H. I. 328, 329.

Dinnington, *see* Seavington.

Discove. Pavement. Arch. Jour. XXXVI. 334; Collinson, I. 215; Gent. Mag. 1823, i. 585; Gough's Camden, I. 100; Lewis, I. 401; Somerset Arch. Soc. Proc. XXIV. ii. 14; V.C.H. I. 320.

Ditcheat. Buildings. Arch. Jour. XXXVI. 334; Phelps, II. 263; Somerset Arch. Soc. Proc. XXXVI. i. 61; V.C.H. I. 320.

Edington. Building and pavement. Arch. Jour. XXXVI. 329; Collinson, III. 433; Gough's Camden, I. 99, 103; Lewis, II. 145; Lond. S.A. Archaeologia, XIV. 91; Phelps, I. 176; Somerset Arch. Soc. Proc. XXIV. ii. 15; V.C.H. I. 352.

Kiln. Somerset Arch. Soc. Proc. I. ii. 55, 57; V.C.H. I. 353, 356.

Failand Hill, *see* Ashton, Long.

Farley Hungerford. Buildings and pavements. Arch. Jour. XXXVI. 334, 335; Bath Herald, Sept. 28, 1822; Collinson, III. 362; Gent. Mag. 1822, ii. 365, 1823, i. 113, and Lib. Rom. Brit. Rem. i. 289, ii. 350; Gough's Camden, I. 111; Jackson, J. E., Guide to Farley Hungerford; Phelps, I. i. 179; Scarth's Rom. Bath, 120; Somerset Arch. Soc. Proc. III. ii. 114, XII. i. 24, XXIV. ii. 14; Stukeley's Letters, I. 139; V.C.H. I. 300.

Flax Bourton. Building. Antiquary, XXXIII. 360.

Ham, High. Buildings and Pavements. Somerset Arch. Soc. Proc. XI. i. 33, XIII. i. 62, XXIV. ii. 14; V.C.H. I. 328. Drawings of pavements in Taunton Museum.

Ham Hill. Foundations. Somerset Arch. Soc. Proc. LIII. i. 87, ii. 179, 181. Plan in Taunton Museum.

Huntspill. Kilns. Arch. Jour. XXXVI. 328, 335; Somerset Arch. Soc. Proc. XXIV. ii. 5, 15; V.C.H. I. 352, 353.

Hurcot, near Somerton. Buildings and pavement. Arch. Jour. XXXVI. 335; B.A.A. Jour. XII. 300; Bath Field Club Proc. I. ii. 18; Hoare's Pitney Pavement, 6; Morgan, 88, 99; Phelps, I. i. 168; Somerset Arch. Soc. Proc. XXIV. i. 74; V.C.H. I. 322; Wright's Celt, Roman and Saxon, 228.

Ilchester. Buildings and pavement. Bath Field Club, I. ii. 18; Britton and Brayley, XIII. i. 515; Collinson, III. 298; Gough's Camden, I. 93; Phelps, I. i. 166 (plan); Somerset Arch. Soc. Proc. XXII. ii. 30, XXIV. ii. 6, LI. 150; Somerset

Record Soc. XV. 204; Somerset and Dorset N. and Q. I. 26 Stukeley's Itin. Curios. I. 155; V.C.H. I. 294.

Kingsdon. Buildings. Bath Field Club, I. ii. 18; Hoare's Pitney Pavement, 6; Morgan, 88; Phelps, I. i. 168; V.C.H. I. 325; Wright's Celt, Roman and Saxon, 228.

Kingweston (Copley Wood). Foundations. Arch. Jour. II. 209; Bath Field Club Proc. I. ii. 18; Hoare's Pitney Pavement, 7; Morgan, 88; Phelps, I. i. 168; Somerset Arch. Soc. Proc. XXIV. i. 74; V.C.H. I. 322; Wright's Celt, Roman and Saxon, 228.

Knoll Hill, near Chedzoy. Pavement. V.C.H. I. 329 n, 352 n.

Langford, Lower. Buildings and Pavement. Gent. Mag. 1856, ii. 108, and Lib. Rom. Brit. Rem. i. 291; Somerset Arch. Soc. Proc. XXIV. ii. 15; V.C.H. I. 308. *See also* Wrington.

Langridge. Foundations. Arch. Jour. XI. 408; Scarth's Rom. Bath, 104, 125; Somerset Arch. Soc. Proc. XII. i. 25; V.C.H. I. 301.

Lansdown. Buildings. Antiquary, XLIV. 5; Arch. Jour. XXVII. 64; B.A.A. Jour. 2 S. XII. 289, XIII. 251, XIV. 216; Bath Field Club Proc. I. ii. 16; Bath Herald, Sept. 20, 1905; Lond. S.A. Proc. 2 S. XXII. 34; Somerset Arch. Soc. Proc. XXIV. ii. 14, L. 105; V.C.H. I. 301.

Littleton. Buildings. Arch. Jour. XXXVI. 335; Bath Field Club Proc. I. ii. 18; Gent. Mag. 1827, ii. 113, and Lib. Rom. Brit. Rem. i. 289; Hoare's Pitney Pavement, 7; Morgan, 88; Phelps, I. i. 168 (plan); Somerset Arch. Soc. Proc. XXIV. i. 74; V.C.H. I. 323; Wright's Celt, Roman and Saxon, 228.

Lyte's Cary. Buildings. Arch. Jour. XXXVI. 335; Bath Field Club Proc. I. ii. 18; Hoare's Pitney Pavement, 6; Morgan, 88; Phelps, I. i. 168; Somerset Arch. Soc. Proc. XXIV. i. 74; V.C.H. I. 326; Wright's Celt, Roman and Saxon, 228.

Mendip Hills. Foundations. Arch. Jour. XVI. 153; B.A.A. Jour. XXXI. 133; Cardiff Naturalists' Soc. Trans. VII. 1; Hoare's Anc. Wilts. II. 42; Lond. S.A. Proc. 2 S. XI. 30; V.C.H. I. 335.

Newton St Loe. Buildings and pavement. Arch. Jour. XXXVI. 329, 335; Dorset Field Club Proc. XXI. 166; Lond. S.A.

Proc. 2 S. XX. 248 ; Morgan, 91, 102 ; Nichols, Rev. W. L., Horae Romanae, 1838, and Description of the Roman Villa discovered at Newton St Loe ; Scarth's Rom. Bath, 114 ; Somerset Arch. Soc. Proc. XII. i. 24, XXII. i. 37, 64, XXIV. ii. 5, 14 ; V.C.H. I. 302.

Norton Fitzwarren. Kiln. Somerset Arch. Soc. Proc. XXIV. ii. 5, 15 ; V.C.H. I. 365.

Norton St Philips. Building. Hoare's Anc. Wilts. II. (Rom. Aera) 109.

Norton-sub-Hamdon. Tesserae and well. Trask, C., Norton-sub-Hamdon, 1898, 19, 240 ; V.C.H. I. 331.

Paulton. Buildings. V.C.H. I. 315 (plan).

Petherton, South. Buildings and pavement. Arch. Jour. XXXVI. 335 ; Collinson, III. 106, 107 ; Somerset Arch. Soc. Proc. XXIV. ii. 15 ; V.C.H. I. 331.

Pitney. Buildings and pavements. Arch. Jour. XXXVI. 329, 335 ; B.A.A. Jour. XII. 300, XXXVIII. 303 ; Bath Field Club Proc. I. ii. 18 ; Gent. Mag. 1828, ii. 361, 1830, i. 17, 1833, i. 148, 1836, i. 194, and Lib. Rom. Brit. Rem. i. 291 ; Hoare's Pitney Pavement, 10 (plan) ; Lewis, III. 552 ; Lond. S.A. Topog. Colls., red portfolio (drawings of pavements) ; Morgan, 33, 98 ; Phelps, I. i. 169 (plan) ; Rutter, 170 n ; Somerset Arch. Soc. Proc. V. i. 9, XI. i. 23, XIII. i. 62, XXII. ii. 30, XXIV. ii. 5, 13, 15 ; V.C.H. I. 326 (plan), 328 ; Wright's Celt, Roman and Saxon, 228.

Polden. Kiln. Arch. Jour. XXXVI. 328, 329; Somerset Arch. Soc. Proc. I. ii. 59, XXIV. ii. 5, 15 ; V.C.H. I. 353.

Portbury, see Seavington.

Radstock. Foundations. Somerset Arch. Soc. Proc. XXX. i. 102, ii. 77 ; V.C.H. I. 316.

Seavington (Dinnington and Portbury). Buildings and pavements. Arch. Jour. XXXVI. 335 ; Collinson, III. 141 ; Gent. Mag. 1862, i. 298 ; Gough's Camden, I. 107; Lewis, III. 574; Norris, H., South Petherton in the Olden Time, 1882, 15; Phelps, I. i. 177; Pulman, 68, 69; Scot. S.A. Proc. VI. 334; Somerset Arch. Soc. Proc. XXIV. ii. 11, 15, XXXVII. i. 26; V.C.H. I. 332. Frag. of pavement in Taunton Museum.

Sedgemoor, King's. Building. V.C.H. I. 325.

Shepton Mallet. Buildings. Somerset Arch. Soc. Proc. LIII.
18; V.C.H. I. 317, 318.

   Kilns. Arch. Jour. XXII. 163, XXXVI. 328; Bristol and Glouc.
Arch. Soc. Trans. XXVI. 329; Coll. Antiq. VI. 194; Gent.
Mag. 1864, ii. 770, and Lib. Rom. Brit. Rem. i. 293; Somerset
Arch. Soc. Proc. XIII. i. 12, ii. 1, XXIV. ii. 5, 15, XXX. ii. 130,
LIII. 18; V.C.H. I. 318.

Shipham. Foundations. Phelps, I. i. 135; V.C.H. I. 308.

Somerton. Buildings and pavement. Arch. Jour. XXXVI. 335;
Hoare's Pitney Pavement, 7; Lewis, IV. 139; Phelps, I. i.
168; Somerset Arch. Soc. Proc. XXII. ii. 30, XXIV. i. 74;
V.C.H. I. 324, 325; Wright's Celt, Roman and Saxon, 228.

Stanchester, *see* Curry Rivel.

Stoke, North. Buildings. Bath Field Club Proc. IX. i. 50
(plan), 89; Bath Chronicle, Dec. 8, 1887; Scarth's Rom.
Bath, 126; Somerset Arch. Soc. Proc. XXXIII. ii. 146;
V.C.H. I. 302.

Stoke Trister (Bayford). Foundations. V.C.H. I. 320.

Street, near Glastonbury (Butleigh Wootton). Buildings. Arch.
Jour. XXXVI. 333; Hoare's Pitney Pavement, 10; Morgan,
88; Phelps, I. i. 169; Somerset Arch. Soc. Proc. XXIV. i. 74;
V.C.H. I. 322; Wright's Celt, Roman and Saxon, 228.

Temple Cloud. Foundations. Somerset Arch. Soc. Proc. XXIV.
i. 74; V.C.H. I. 367.

Tickenham (Cadbury). Foundations. Arch. Jour. XXXVI. 336;
Rutter, 234; Seyer's Bristol, I. 162; Somerset Arch. Soc.
Proc. XXIV. ii. 8, 14.

Tiverton. Buildings. B.A.A. Jour. IX. 74.

Wadeford, *see* Combe St Nicholas.

Warley, *see* Bathford.

Watergore, *see* Petherton, South.

Wellow. Buildings and pavements. Arch. Jour. IV. 356;
XXXVI. 329, 336; B.A.A. Jour. XII. 300, XXXVIII. 99;
Collinson, III. 325; Dorset Field Club Proc. XXIII. 113;
Gent. Mag. 1787, ii. 961, 1807, ii. 969, 1846, ii. 633, and Lib.
Rom. Brit. Rem. i. 295, ii. 596; Gough's Camden, I. 111;
King's Mun. Antiq. II. 168, 178; Lewis, IV. 493; Lond. S.A.
Archaeologia, XIX. 45 and note, Minute Book, III. 53, 56,

XXXI. 379, Vet. Mon. I. pls. L—LII, and Topog. Colls., red portfolio (plan and pavements); Morgan, 34, 90, 100; Phelps, I. i. 164 (plan); Scarth's Rom. Bath, 112; Somerset Arch. Soc. Proc. III. i. 11, XII. i. 24, XXII. i. 38, XXIV. ii. 5, 14; Warner's Bath Guide, 1811, 133; Wilts. Arch. Soc. Mag. XXII. 237; V.C.H. I. 312—15 (plans, etc.).

Wemberham, *see* Yatton.

Whatley, near Frome. Buildings and pavement. Arch. Jour. XXXVI. 329, 336, and Bristol vol. 1851, lxviii; Gent. Mag. 1838, i. 435, 1839, ii. 77, and Lib. Rom. Brit. Rem. i. 297; Lewis, I. 408, IV. 526; Somerset Arch. Soc. Proc. I. i. 38, XII. i. 26, XXIV. ii. 5, 15, XXXIX. i. 37; V.C.H. I. 317.

Whitestaunton. Buildings. Academy, Sept. 1, 1883; Antiquary, VIII. 217, 226; Builder, XLV. 283; Clifton Antiq. Club Proc. III. 79; Dorset Field Club Proc. IX. xxviii; Somerset Arch. Soc. Proc. XXVIII. i. 15, 43, XXIX. i. 35, ii. 98; V.C.H. I. 334.

Wick, *see* Lansdown.

Wigborough, *see* Petherton, South.

Wincanton. Pavement (?). Somerset Arch. Soc. Proc. XVI. i. 5, 14, XXIV. ii. 15; V.C.H. I. 369 (probably mediaeval).

Wiveliscombe. Foundations. Britton and Brayley, XIII. i. 555; Collinson, II. 488.

Woolavington (Coombe). Foundations. Stradling, W., Priory of Chilton Polden, 1839, 12; V.C.H. I. 369.

Wrington. Buildings. Arch. Jour. XXXVI. 329, 336; Lond. S.A. Proc. 2 S. VII. 159, XI. 30; Somerset Arch. Soc. Proc. XXII. ii. 30, XXIII. ii. 10, XXIV. ii. 15, XXXIII. ii. 4; V.C.H. I. 308. *See also* Langford, Lower.

Yanley. Foundations. Arch. Jour. XXXVI. 336; Collinson, II. 304; V.C.H. I. 305 n.

Yatton (Wemberham). Buildings and pavement. B.A.A. Jour. XL. 126, XLIII. 104, 353 (plan); Bristol and Glouc. Arch. Soc. Trans. XII. 324; Builder, XLIX. 820; Clifton Antiq. Club Proc. I. 157; Lond. S.A. Proc. 2 S. XI. 29; Somerset Arch. Soc. Proc. XXIV. ii. 15, XXXI. i. 18, 23, ii. 1 64 (plan); V.C.H. I. 306 (plan).

Yeovil, *see* Coker, East.

STAFFORDSHIRE

Plot. Plot, R. History of Staffordshire, 1686.
Shaw. Shaw, S. History of Staffordshire, 2 vols. 1798—1801.
V.C.H. Victoria History of the Counties of England. Staffordshire, I. 1908.

Madeley. Foundations. V.C.H. I. 191.
Rocester. Foundations. Shaw, I. Introd. 34 n; V.C.H. I. 192.
Sedgley. Foundations (?). V.C.H. I. 192.
Stafford (near). Pavement. Gent. Mag. 1818, i. 78, and Lib.
    Rom. Brit. Rem. ii. 302.
Tettenhall. Foundations (?). Plot, 394; Shaw, II. 194; V.C.H.
    I. 193.
Wall (*Etocetum*). Foundations. B.A.A. Jour. XXIX. 53, 116,
    XLVI. 227; Birmingham and Midland Instit. Trans. IV. 38;
    Gough's Camden, II. 495, 504; Horsley's Brit. Rom. 420;
    Mag. Brit. 1738, V. 25; Plot, 401; Shaw, I. Introd. 18, 19,
    356; Stukeley's Itin. Curios. I. 61; V.C.H. I. 193.
Wetton. Foundations. Bateman, T., Ten Years' Diggings, 193;
    Reliquary, V. 217; V.C.H. I. 196.

SUFFOLK

Kirby. Kirby, J. The Suffolk Traveller, 2nd ed. 1764.
Page. Page, A. History of Suffolk, 1847.
Suckling. Suckling, A. History of Suffolk, 2 vols. 1846—48.
Suff. Arch. Instit. Proc. Suffolk Institute of Archaeology Proceedings,
    I.—XIII. 1853—1909.

Aldeburgh. Traces of buildings. Builder, XCII. 701; Suff. Arch.
    Instit. Proc. XIII. 24.
Barham (Shrubland Park). Buildings. Lewis, I. 136.
Burgh, near Woodbridge. Traces of buildings. Antiquary,
    XXXVII. 342; Arch. Jour. LVII. 91; Report on excavations
    at Castle Field, Burgh, by the Woodbridge Field Club,
    1900—01.
Burgh Castle (*Garianonum*). Fort, walls, towers, etc. Anti-
    quary, XLV. 210; Arch. Jour. XLVI. 348, 366, LIII. 358, LVII.
    120, 124 (plan), 136, Norwich vol. 1847, 196, and Winchester

vol. 1845, under Porchester Castle, 10, 11; B.A.A. Jour.
I. 46, 49, XIV. 164, 197, XXXVI. 98, 213, and Coll. Arch.
II. 244; Blome's Britannia, 217; Britton and Brayley, XIV.
393; Builder, VIII. 442; Coll. Antiq. VII. 161; Gent. Mag.
1846, ii. 638, 1850, ii. 418, and Lib. Rom. Brit. Rem. ii. 303,
304; Godwin's Arch. Handbook, 36; Gough's Camden,
II. 157, 172; Ives, J., Remarks on the Garianonum of the
Romans, 2nd ed. 1803; King's Mun. Antiq. II. 52; Lewis.
I. 421; Lond. S.A. Archaeologia, XII. 134 n, XXIII. 363, XLI.
428, and Proc. I S. III. 227 (plan); Mag. Brit. 1738, V. 229;
Norf. Arch. V. 146 (plan); Royal Instit. Proc. XVI. i. 40;
Spelman's Icenia, 155; Stukeley's Itin. Curios. I. 132 (plan),
and Letters, III. 200; Suckling, I. 328 (plan); Suff. Arch.
Instit. Proc. XI. 308; V.C.H. Norfolk, I. 305; Wright's
Arch. Album, 93, and Celt, Roman and Saxon, 173, 188.

Coddenham. Foundations. Arch. Jour. LVII. 140; Gent. Mag.
1825, i. 292, and Lib. Rom. Brit. Rem. ii. 306.

Eye. Buildings. Arch. Jour. LVII. 92, 143; East Anglian N.
and Q. I S. I. 249.

Felixstow (Walton Castle). Fort, walls, etc., but submerged
since 1740. Arch. Jour. LVII. 114, 143; B.A.A. Coll. Arch.
II. 246, 247; Britton and Brayley, XIV. 272; Grose, vol. VI.;
Gough's Camden, II. 166; Kirby, 89; Lond. S.A. Proc. 2 S.
XI. 12, and Minute Book, I. 71; Martin, T., Church Notes,
I. 185; Tour in the Whole Island of Britain, by a gentleman,
3rd ed. 1742, 39.

Icklingham. Buildings and pavement. Arch. Jour. LVII. 94,
111, 148; B.A.A. Jour. XIX. 281, XXXIII. 221, 258, XXXIV. 12
(plan); Lewis, II. 591.

Ipswich, see Whitton.

Ixworth. Buildings and pavement. Arch. Jour. LVII. 92, 151;
B.A.A. Coll. Arch. II. 248; Page, 787; Suff. Arch. Instit.
Proc. I. 74, 77 (plan of hypo.), 78.

Pakenham. Pavement. Arch. Jour. LVII. 155; B.A.A. Coll.
Arch. II. 248; Britton and Brayley, XIV. 191; Gough's
Camden, II. 162; Suckling, I. xx; Suff. Arch. Instit. Proc.
I. 74.

Rougham. Foundations, etc. Arch. Jour. LVII. 93, 98, 156;

Gent. Mag. 1843, ii. 524, 1844, ii. 369, and Lib. Rom.
Brit. Rem. ii. 308 ; Suff. Arch. Instit. Proc. IV. 262, 271.

Stow, West. Kilns. Antiquary, XXIV. 20 ; Arch. Jour. LVII.
104, 161 ; B.A.A. Jour. XXXVII. 152, XLVII. 94 ; Builder,
LI. 441.

Walton Castle, *see* Felixstow.

Wattisfield. Pavement. East Anglian Miscellany, Feb. 1,
1902.

Whitton, near Ipswich. Buildings and pavement. Arch. Jour.
LVII. 93, 164 ; Athenaeum, Jan. 20, 1855 ; B.A.A. Coll.
Arch. II. 248 ; Gent. Mag. 1855, i. 179, and Lib. Rom. Brit.
Rem. ii. 317 ; Illust. Lond. News, Feb. 10, 1855 ; Lond. S.A.
Proc. 1 S. III. 199, and Topog. Colls., red portfolio (drawing
of pavement) ; Suff. Arch. Instit. Proc. II. 211. Orig. pav.
in Ipswich Museum.

SURREY

Aubrey. Aubrey, J. Natural History and Antiquities of Surrey, 5 vols.
1719.

Brayley. Brayley, E. W. Topographical History of Surrey, 5 vols. 1850.

Kempe. Kempe, A. J. The Loseley Manuscripts, 1835.

Manning and Bray. Manning, O. and Bray, W. History of Surrey, 3 vols.
1804—14.

Surrey Arch. Colls. Surrey Archaeological Collections, published by the
Surrey Archaeological Society, I.—XXXIII. 1858—1910.

Abinger. Buildings. B.A.A. Jour. XXXIII. 501, XXXIV. 110,
243 ; Builder, XXXVI. 19 (plan) ; Lond. S.A. Proc. 2 S. VIII.
213, XIII. 248 ; More Letters of Chas. Darwin, II. 213 n.

Albury (Farley Heath). Buildings. Arch. Jour. X. 166 ;
Aubrey, IV. 79; B.A.A. Jour. IV. 158 ; Brayley, I. 20, V. 152 ;
Britton and Brayley, XIV. 222 ; Gough's Camden, I. 251 ;
Kempe, xi n ; Manning and Bray, II. 122 ; Surrey Arch.
Colls. XII. 147 ; Tupper, M.F., Farley Heath, 1850, 25,
26.

Beddington. Buildings. Arch. Review, IV. 68 ; B.A.A. Jour.
XXVII. 514, and pl. 26 (plan) ; Lond. S.A. Proc. 2 S. V. 149,
VIII. 212, and Topog. Colls., brown portfolio (plan of site
and buildings); Surrey Arch. Colls., VI. 118 (plan).

Bletchingley (Pendhill). Buildings. Brayley, I. 21, IV. 111 n; Gent. Mag. 1814, i. 86, and Lib. Rom. Brit. Rem. ii. 318; Lewis, I. 271; Lond. S.A. Archaeologia, XXXII. 403, and Proc. 1 S. I. 146, 2 S. XIII. 248; Manning and Bray, III. Appendix, cxxi, and pl. XXVI (plan).

Broadstreet Green, see Worplesdon.

Chiddingfold. Buildings. Antiquary, VII. 276, VIII. 84; Lond. S.A. Proc. 2 S. IX. 307, 308, 334; Surrey Arch. Colls. XIV. 215.

Colley Farm, see Reigate.

Coombe Hill, see Kingston.

Earlswood Common. Foundations. Lond. S.A. Minute Book, XXXIV. 69.

Ewell. Shafts. Lond. S.A. Archaeologia, XXXII. 451, XLVI. 446, and Proc. 2 S. I. 309.

Farley Heath, see Albury.

Farnham. Kiln. Surrey Arch. Colls. XX. 228 (plan).

Fetcham. Foundations. Surrey Arch. Colls. XX. 1.

Kingston (Coombe Hill). Foundations (?). Brayley, I. 21; Gough's Camden, I. 254; Leland's Itin. VI. 23; Manning and Bray, I. 329.

Pendhill, see Bletchingley.

Puttenham. Pavement. Surrey Arch. Colls. XII. 149.

Reigate (Colley Farm). Foundations. Lond. S.A. Proc. 2 S. XIII. 248.

Southwark, see London.

Tilford (Whitmead). Kiln. Surrey Arch. Colls. XII. 151.

Titsey. Buildings. Arch. Jour. XXXV. 70; Gower, G. L., Handbook to the parish of Titsey, 1869, 16; Lond. S.A. Archaeologia, LIX. 214 (plan), and Proc. 2 S. VIII. 211, 213, XIII. 248; Surrey Arch. Colls. IV. xiv, xv, 214 (plan).

Tongham. Foundations(?). Gough's Camden, I. 248; Stukeley's Itin. Curios. I. 203 n.

Walton-on-the-Hill. Buildings and pavement. Brayley, I. 22, IV. 388; Britton and Brayley, XIV. 180; Lond. S.A. Archaeologia, IX. 108, Proc. 2 S. IX. 110, and Minute Book, XXXIII. 346; Manning and Bray, II. 644; Morgan, 208; Surrey Arch. Colls. II. 1 (plan).

Whitmead, *see* Tilford.

Worplesdon (Broadstreet Green). Buildings and pavement. Kempe, xi n ; Lewis, IV. 672 ; Lond. S.A. Archaeologia, XXIII. 398 (plan), and Topog. Colls., red portfolio (plan) ; Morgan, 206.

SUSSEX

Allen. Allen, T. History of Surrey and Sussex, 2 vols. 1829.

Dallaway. Dallaway, J. and Cartwright, E. History of Sussex, 2 vols. 1815—30.

Horsfield's Lewes. Horsfield, T. W. History and Antiquities of Lewes, 1824.

Horsfield's Sussex. Horsfield, T. W. History of Sussex, 2 vols. 1835.

Parry. Parry, J. D. An Historical and Descriptive Account of the coast of Sussex, 1833.

Sussex Arch. Colls. Sussex Archaeological Collections, published by the Sussex Archaeological Society, I.—LIII. 1849—1910.

Angmering. Buildings. Dallaway, II. i. 366; Horsfield's Sussex, II. 141 ; Sussex Arch. Colls. XLVI. 157.

Arundel. Buildings. Sussex Arch. Colls. XL. 283, XLVI. 157.

Bignor. Buildings and pavements. Arch. Cantiana, XV. 132 ; Arch. Jour. XLI. 172, XLVII. 270; Athenaeum, June 14, 1879; B.A.A. Jour. X. 153, XXXII. 486, XXXVIII. 303, XLI. 422, XLII. 57, 212; Britton and Brayley, XIV. 88; Dallaway, II. i. 221 (plan); Gent. Mag. 1811, ii. 183, 515, 1812, ii. 437, 1845, ii. 122, and Lib. Rom. Brit. Rem. ii. 328; Godwin's Arch. Handbook, 56, 58; Horsfield's Sussex, I. 54, II. 151, and Lewes, 63; Knight's Old England, I. 54 ; Lewis, I. 233; Lond. S.A. Archaeologia, XVIII. 203 (plans), XIX. 176 (plan), Proc. 2 S. XVIII. 26, XXI. 161, 234, XXII. 275, Minute Book, XXXIII. 45, 51, 60, 293, 297, 316, and Topog. Colls., red and brown portfolios (drawings); Lysons' Reliquiae, III. 1—6, and pls. I—XXXII, Remains of a Roman Villa at Bignor, also An Account of a Roman Villa found at Bignor in 1811, 1st ed. 1815, 2nd ed. 1820; Morgan, 33, 199, 200 (plan), 203 ; Parry, 375 ; Sussex Arch. Colls. XI. 136, XXX. 63 ; Wright's Celt, Roman and Saxon, 243, 253, and Wanderings of an Antiquary, 272.

Blatchington, West. Buildings. Gent. Mag. 1818, ii. 107, and
Lib. Rom. Brit. Rem. ii. 332; Horsfield's Sussex, I. 157;
Lewis, I. 268; Sussex Arch. Colls. XXVII. 70.

Bosham. Foundations. Sussex Arch. Colls. XVIII. 1, 2, 3, 4,
LIII. 272.

Bramber. Bridge (?). Sussex Arch. Colls. II. 63, 73; Wright's
Wanderings of an Antiquary, 263.

Brighton. Foundations. Antiquary, XLII. 164.

Chanctonbury Ring. Buildings. Arch. Jour. XLI. 172; Sussex
Arch. Colls. LIII. 131, 134 (plan), and pl. 13 (plan).

Chichester (*Regnum*). City walls, buildings, pavements, etc.
Allen, I. 84, 87; B.A.A. Jour. XXIII. 88, XLII. 96, 119 (plan),
XLIII. 14; Britton and Brayley, XIV. 33, 48, 54; Coll. Antiq.
VII. 205; Dallaway, I. 2, 5; Gough's Camden, I. 277;
Horsfield's Sussex, I. 41, and Lewes, 52; Lewis, I. 573;
Lond. S.A. Proc. 2 S. VII. 292, and Minute Book, VI. 35;
Stukeley's Itin. Curios. I. 200, 202; Sussex Arch. Colls.
VIII. 291, XV. 167, XIX. 198, XXXII. 230.

Chilgrove. Foundations. Sussex Arch. Colls. X. 169.

Clayton. Buildings. Lewis, I. 608; Sussex Arch. Colls. II. 315,
XIV. 178.

Densworth, *see* Funtington.

Duncton. Buildings. Britton and Brayley, XIV. 90; Gent.
Mag. 1812, i. 381, 1816, ii. 17, and Lib. Rom. Brit. Rem. ii.
336; Horsfield's Sussex, II. 170; Lewis, II. 100; Lond. S.A.
Topog. Colls., red portfolio (drawing); Sussex Arch. Colls.
II. 315.

Eastbourne. Buildings and pavement. Allen, I. 88; Arch.
Jour. IV. 209; B.A.A. Jour. XXXIV. 218; Britton and Brayley,
XIV. 32, 163; East-Bourne, 1787, Appendix; Gough's
Camden, I. 296, and Brit. Topog. II. 292; Horsfield's Sussex,
I. 49, and Lewes, 53, 56, 58; Horsley's Brit. Rom. 488;
King's Mun. Antiq. II. 173; Lewis, I. 304; Parry, 198;
Phil. Trans. XXX. 549, 783; Stukeley's Letters, III. 212;
Sussex Arch. Colls. II. 257, III. ix, IV. viii, IX. 156, XIV. 125,
XVI. 308, XXXVIII. 160.

Fishbourne. Buildings and pavement. Dallaway, I. 100; Gent.
Mag. 1805, ii. 926, and Lib. Rom. Brit. Rem. ii. 334;

Horsfield's Sussex, II. 52; Lewis, II. 235; Sussex Arch. Colls. X. 169.

Funtington (Densworth). Walled sepulchral remains (?). Sussex Arch. Colls. X. 168, 175 (plan).

Harting, South. Foundations. Sussex Arch. Colls. XXXIX. 226.

Hurstpierpoint. Buildings. Lond. S.A. Archaeologia, XLII. 42; Sussex Arch. Colls. X. 210, XIV. 178 (plan).

Lancing. Buildings and pavement. Arch. Jour. XII. 279, XLI. 172; Coll. Antiq. I. 92; Dallaway, II. ii. 388; Gent. Mag. 1828, ii. 631, 1830, ii. 17, and Lib. Rom. Brit. Rem. ii. 341; Horsfield's Sussex, II. 207; Lewis, III. 15; Parry, 349, 363; Sussex Arch. Colls. XLVI. 157.

Littlehampton. Buildings. Sussex Arch. Colls. XLVI. 157.

Newhaven. Foundations. Arch. Jour. IX. 285; Sussex Arch. Colls. V. 263.

Penhurst (Towncreep). Foundations. Sussex Arch. Colls. XXXVIII. 21.

Pevensey (*Anderida*). Fort, walls, towers, and excavations. Allen, II. 602; Arch. Jour. XL. 443, LXV. 125 (plans), Chichester, vol. 1853, 41 (plan), and Winchester, vol. 1845, under Porchester Castle, 7, 8; B.A.A. Jour. N.S. XIII. 253; Birmingham and Midland Instit. Trans. VI. 26; Britton and Brayley, XIV. 158; Builder, LXXXIX. 433, 633, 646; Coll. Antiq. VII. 166; Gough's Camden, I. 296; Horsfield's Sussex, I. 309; King's Mun. Antiq. II. 38 (plan); Lewis, III. 542; Lond. S.A. Archaeologia, XLI. 437, and Proc. 2 S. XXI. 410, XXII. 151, 274; Parry, 255; Royal Instit. Proc. XVI. 40; Salzman, L. F., and Ray, J. E., Report on the excavations in 1906—07, and 1907—08 (plans, etc.); Smith, C. Roach, Report on the excavations in 1852 (plans, etc.); Stukeley's Letters, III. 224; Sussex Arch. Colls. VI. 103, 265, 274 (plan), LI. 99 (plans), LII. 83 (plans); Wright's Celt, Roman and Saxon, 169, 177, and Wanderings of an Antiquary, 146.

Portslade. Buildings. Sussex Arch. Colls. XLVI. 157.

Preston. Buildings. B.A.A. Jour. XXXIII. 518; Lond. S.A. Proc. 2 S. VII. 293, 294.

Pulborough. Buildings. Dallaway, II. i. 321; Horsfield's Sussex,

II. 164; Lond. S.A. Proc. 2 S. XVIII. 294, XXIII. 121 (plan); Sussex Arch. Colls. XI. 141 (plan), 143.

Slindon. Pavement. Sussex Arch. Colls. XXVI. 267.

Southwick. Buildings. Horsfield's Sussex, II. 218; Sussex Arch. Colls. I. ix, XIII. 3.

Towncreep, *see* Penhurst.

Upmarden. Pavement. Sussex Arch. Colls. XL. 283.

Wiston. Buildings. B.A.A. Jour. IV. 386; Sussex Arch. Colls. II. 313 (plan).

Worthing. Buildings. Antiquary, XXXVI. 334; Sussex Arch. Colls. XLVI. 157.

WARWICKSHIRE

Dugdale. Dugdale, Sir W. Antiquities of Warwickshire, 2nd ed. edited by W. Thomas, 2 vols. 1730.

V.C.H. Victoria History of the Counties of England. Warwickshire, I. 1904.

Alchester. Foundations. Arch. Jour. XLIV. 55; Britton and Brayley, XV. i. 267; Dugdale, II. 761; Gent. Mag. 1785, ii. 941, and Lib. Rom. Brit. Rem. ii. 343; V.C.H. I. 236.

Coventry. Pavement (?). Britton and Brayley, XV. i. 98; Gent. Mag. 1793, ii. 787; V.C.H. I. 246 (probably mediaeval).

Hartshill. Kilns. Antiquary, XXXIII. 231; Britton and Brayley, XV. i. 310; Builder, LXXII. 325; Lond. S.A. Proc. 2 S. XVI. 405; V.C.H. I. 234, 246.

High Cross, *see* Leicestershire.

Mancetter. Foundations. Britton and Brayley, XV. i. 309; Nichols' Leicester, IV. 1027; V.C.H. I. 233.

Monk's Kirby. Foundations. Britton and Brayley, XV. i. 58; Dugdale, I. 74; Gough's Camden, II. 451; V.C.H. I. 238.

Wilmecote. Stone-lined well. B.A.A. Jour. XXIX. 41; Gent. Mag. 1841, ii. 81, and Lib. Rom. Brit. Rem. ii. 343; V.C.H. I. 249.

WESTMORLAND

Arch. Survey.   An Archaeological Survey of Cumberland and Westmorland,
   by R. S. Ferguson, printed in Archaeologia, LIII. (1893), 485—531.
Cumb. and Westm. Arch. Soc. Trans.   Cumberland and Westmorland
   Antiquarian and Archaeological Society Transactions, 1 S. I.—XVI.
   1874—1900, N.S. I.—X. 1901—10.
Nicolson and Burn.   Nicolson, J. and Burn, R.   History of Westmorland
   and Cumberland, 2 vols. 1777.

Bowes Moor, *see* Maiden Castle.
Brougham.   Pavement.   Arch. Survey, 522 ;   Stukeley's Itin.
   Curios. II. 45.
Burton (the Quamps), *see* Dalton-near-Warton, Lanc.
Kirkby Thore.   Foundations and pavement.   Arch. Survey, 526;
   Britton and Brayley, XV. i. 89 ;   Gough's Camden, III. 411 ;
   Lond. S.A. Proc. 1 S. I. 79 ;   Phil. Trans. XIV. 555 ;   Watkin's
   Rom. Lanc. 30.
Low Burrow Bridge, Tebay.   Buildings and pavement.   Anti-
   quary, IX. 25 ;   Arch. Survey, 526;   B.A.A. Jour. VIII. 40, 41 ;
   Britton and Brayley, XV. i. 207 ;   Cumb. and Westm. Arch.
   Soc. Trans. VIII. 1 ;   Lond. S.A. Proc. 2 S. X. 30 ;   Watkin's
   Rom. Lanc. 29, 30.
Maiden Castle on Stainmoor.   Walls.   Arch. Jour. XIX. 358 ;
   Arch. Survey, 527;   Cumb. and Westm. Arch. Soc. Trans. V.
   69;   Gent. Mag. 1862, ii. 47, and Lib. Rom. Brit. Rem. i. 65;
   Nicolson and Burn, I. 8, 578.
Watercrook, near Kendal.   Buildings.   Arch. Survey, 531 ;
   Britton and Brayley, XV. i. 204;   Cumb. and Westm. Arch.
   Soc. Trans. N.S. VIII. 102 ;   Gough's Camden, III. 404 ;
   Lewis, III. 353 (under Natland);   Nicolson and Burn, I. 105;
   Stukeley's Itin. Curios. II. 41.

WILTSHIRE

Aubrey and Jackson.   Aubrey, J. and Jackson, J. E.   Wiltshire Collections,
   1862.
Hoare's Anc. Wilts. II. (Rom. Aera).   Hoare, Sir R. C.   Ancient History of
   North Wiltshire, II. (Roman Aera), 1819.

Hoare's Mod. Hist. South Wilts. Hoare, Sir R. C. Modern History of
South Wiltshire, 5 vols. 1822—44.
Smith. Smith, A. C. Guide to the British and Roman Antiquities of the
North Wiltshire Downs, 1884.
Wilts. Arch. Soc. Mag. Wiltshire Archaeological and Natural History
Society Magazine, I.—XXXVI. 1854—1910.
Wilts. N. and Q. Wiltshire Notes and Queries, I.—VI. 1893—1910.

Baydon. Foundations. Gent. Mag. 1866, ii. 335, and Lib. Rom.
Brit. Rem. ii. 346; Wilts. Arch. Soc. Mag. X. 104 (plan).
Bedwyn, Great. Buildings and pavement. Bath Field Club
Proc. I. ii. 12; Lewis, I. 190; Lond. S.A. Minute Book, I.
232; Wilts. Arch. Soc. Mag. VI. 261, XIX. 86.
Bishopstrow, near Warminster (Pitmead). Buildings and pave-
ments. Britton and Brayley, XV. ii. 316; Gent. Mag. 1786,
ii. 990, 1787, i. 221, and Lib. Rom. Brit. Rem. ii. 352;
Hoare's Anc. Wilts. II. (Rom. Aera) 111—117 (plans);
King's Mun. Antiq. II. 169, 171, 174; Lewis, I. 256, IV. 464;
Lond. S.A. Minute Book, XXI. 464, XXII. 23, and Vet. Mon.
II. 43; Morgan, 105; Wilts. Arch. Soc. Mag. XXV. 196,
XXXIII. 111, XXXIV. 276, 433.
Bowood. Foundations. B.A.A. Jour. XXXVII. 111; Hoare's
Anc. Wilts. II. (Rom. Aera) 124; Wilts. Arch. Soc. Mag.
XXIV. 170.
Box. Buildings and pavements. Antiquary, XXXVIII. 376;
Arch. Jour. LXI. 1 (plans, etc.); B.A.A. Jour. XVI. 340,
XLII. 83, XLIII. 47 (plan); Bath Field Club Proc. V. i. 50,
IX. ii. 172, X. 257; Gent. Mag. 1831, i. 595, 1833, i. 357, and
Lib. Rom. Brit. Rem. ii. 347, 583; Illust. Lond. News,
Nov. 8, 1902; Lewis, I. 310; Scarth's Rom. Bath, 119;
Somerset Arch. Soc. Proc. XII. i. 24, 25, XXIV. ii. 14; Wilts.
Arch. Soc. Mag. III. 21, V. 5, XXVI. 405, XXVIII. 258, XXXIII.
236 (plans, etc.).
Bromham. Buildings and pavement. B.A.A. Jour. XXXVII. 83,
88, 109 (plan), 172; Bath Field Club Proc. V. i. 36; Britton
and Brayley, XV. ii. 436; Gent. Mag. 1796, i. 472, ii. 564,
1840, ii. 528, 1841, i. 81, and Lib. Rom. Brit. Rem. ii. 348;
Gough's Camden, I. 162, and Brit. Topog. II. 384; Hoare's
Anc. Wilts. II. (Rom. Aera) 123 (plan); Lewis, I. 383;

Lond. S.A. Minute Book, x. 63 ; Morgan, 106 ; Smith, A. C., Guide to the British and Roman Antiquities of the North Wilts. Downs, 1884, 29 ; Wilts. Arch. Soc. Mag. III. 21, IX. 19, XIX. 299 (plan), XXIV. 170, XXV. 194 ; Wright's Celt, Roman and Saxon, 253.

Broomgrove, *see* Milton.

Calne, *see* Studley.

Clarendon Wood, near Salisbury. Buildings. Arch. Jour. II. 86 ; B.A.A. Jour. I. 57 ; Wilts. Arch. Soc. Mag. XIII. 34.

Colerne. Buildings and pavement. Arch. Jour. XII. 89, XIII. 328 (plan) ; Lewis, I. 643 ; Scarth's Rom. Bath, 120 ; Somerset Arch. Soc. Proc. XII. i. 24, XXIV. ii. 12, 14 ; Wilts. Arch. Soc. Mag. III. 14, 21, XXV. 196.

Cricklade, *see* Latton.

Dean, West. Buildings and pavement. Arch. Jour. II. 82, 86 ; B.A.A. Jour. I. 53, 57, 62, and Winchester vol. 1846, 239 ; Britton and Brayley, XV. ii. 211 ; Gough's Camden, I. 154, and Brit. Topog. III. 384 ; Hoare's Mod. Hist. of South Wilts. v. 30 ; Lewis, II. 22 ; Lond. S.A. Minute Book, IV. 103, 107 ; Morgan, 94, 106 ; V.C.H. Hampshire, I. 311 ; Wilts. Arch. Soc. Mag. XIII. 39, 276 (plan), XXII. 243 (plan), XXIX. 90 ; Woodward's Hants. III. 196.

Devizes. Pavement (?). Arch. Jour. XLIV. 54 (nothing known of this locally).

Ditteridge (Hasilbury Farm). Buildings and pavement. Scarth's Rom. Bath, 120 ; Seyer's Memoirs of Bristol, I. 174 ; Somerset Arch. Soc. Proc. XII. i. 25.

Easton Grey. Buildings and pavement. Arch. Jour. XLIV. 54 ; Aubrey and Jackson, 85 n ; Britton and Brayley, XV. ii. 597 ; Collinson's Somerset, I. 100.

Folly Farm, *see* Mildenhall.

Foxley Park. Buildings (unexcavated). Hoare's Anc. Wilts. II. (Rom. Aera) 101.

Froxfield (Rudge). Pavement. Arch. Jour. XIV. 282 ; Britton and Brayley, XV. ii. 698 ; Gent. Mag. 1838, i. 192, and Lib. Rom. Brit. Rem. ii. 448 ; Gough's Camden, I. 163 ; Hoare's Anc. Wilts. II. (Rom. Aera) 121 (plan) ; Lond. S.A. Archaeologia, VIII. 98, XV. 189, Minute Book, I. 129, 131,

165, and Topog. Colls., red portfolio (drawing of pavement);
Morgan, 105 ; Newbury Field Club Trans. IV. 202.
Fyfield. Pavement. Hoare's Anc. Wilts. II. (Rom. Aera) 89;
Smith, 170.
Grittleton. Foundations. Aubrey and Jackson, 128 n.
Hannington Wick. Buildings and pavement. Wilts. Arch. Soc.
Mag. XXV. 232 (plan).
Hasilbury Farm, see Ditteridge.
Heddington. Foundations. Aubrey and Jackson, 5, 45 ;
Britton and Brayley, XV. ii. 435 ; Hoare's Anc. Wilts. II.
(Rom. Aera) 124 ; Mag. Brit. 1738, VI. 69 ; Marsh, A. E. W.,
Hist. of Calne, 260.
Iford. Buildings. Wilts. Arch. Soc. Mag. V. 5.
Latton, near Cricklade. Pavement. Aubrey and Jackson, 152;
Lewis, III. 31 ; Wilts. Arch. Soc. Mag. IX. 232, XII. 127.
Littlecote. Pavement. B.A.A. Jour. XXXVIII. 303 ; Britton
and Brayley, XV. ii. 698 ; Fowler, No. 20; Gent. Mag. 1838,
i. 192, and Lib. Rom. Brit. Rem. ii. 448 ; Gough's Camden,
I. 163, and Brit. Topog. II. 384; Hoare's Anc. Wilts. II.
(Rom. era) 117 (plans); Lewis, III. 100; Lond. S.A.
Archaeologia, VIII. 97, and Minute Book, I. 232, 238;
Lysons' Reliquiae, I. iv. pls. IX and X; Morgan, 33, 96,
104; Newbury Field Club Trans. IV. 202 ; Stukeley's
Letters, III. 254, 256 ; Wilts. Arch. Soc. Mag. XXV. 194 ;
Wright's Celt, Roman and Saxon, 253.
Malmesbury. Hypocaust (?). Arch. Jour. XLIV. 53 ; Lanc. and
Ches. Antiq. Soc. Trans. III. 264.
Marlborough, Folly Farm, see Mildenhall.
Mildenhall (Folly Farm). Foundations and pavement. Britton
and Brayley, XV. ·ii. 682 ; Hoare's Anc. Wilts. II. (Rom.
Aera) 71, 72 ; Smith, 221 ; Wilts. Arch. Soc. Mag. XIX. 86.
Milton (Broomgrove). Kilns. Wilts. Arch. Soc. Mag. XXVII.
294.
Netheravon. Buildings and pavement. Lond. S.A. Proc. 2 S.
XXII. 275 ; Wilts. Arch. Soc. Mag. XXXV. 533.
Oliver's Camp, near Devizes. Buildings. Wilts. Arch. Soc.
Mag. XXXV. 441.
Pitmead, see Bishopstrow.

Rotherley. Foundations. Pitt-Rivers, Lt.-Gen., Excavations in Cranborne Chase, II. 55, 114 (plan).

Roundway Down, near Devizes. Buildings (?). Wilts. Arch. Soc. Mag. XXXV. 441.

Rudge, *see* Froxfield.

Savernake. Buildings and pavement. Bath Field Club Proc. I. iii. 91 ; Wilts. Arch. Soc. Mag. XIX. 16, 86.

Silver Street, near Bromham. Buildings. B.A.A. Jour. XXXVII. 111 ; Hoare's Anc. Wilts. II. (Rom. Aera) 124.

Studley, near Calne. Buildings. B.A.A. Jour. XXXVII. 111 ; Hoare's Anc. Wilts. II. (Rom. Aera) 124 ; Lond. S.A. Minute Book, VII. 50 ; Stukeley's Letters, III. 270 ; Wilts. Arch. Soc. Mag. XXIV. 170.

Swindon. Buildings. Wilts. Arch. Soc. Mag. XXX. 90, 217 (plan).

Tottenham Park. Buildings. Wilts. Arch. Soc. Mag. VI. 262.

Wanborough. Foundations. Aubrey and Jackson, 194 ; Hoare's Anc. Wilts. II. (Rom. Aera) 94.

Warleigh. Buildings. Wilts. Arch. Soc. Mag. V. 5.

Warminster, *see* Bishopstrow.

Westbury. Buildings and pavement. Wilts. Arch. Soc. Mag. XXV. 36.

Wick. Buildings. Wilts. N. and Q. III. 3.

Wraxhall, North. Buildings. Arch. Jour. XVII. 160, XVIII. 146 ; Aubrey and Jackson, 117 n ; Bath Field Club Proc. I. ii. 14 ; Gent. Mag. 1860, ii. 157, and Lib. Rom. Brit. Rem. ii. 354, 584 ; Scarth's Rom. Bath, 121 ; Somerset Arch. Soc. Proc. XII. i. 24, XXIV. ii. 14 ; Wilts. Arch. Soc. Mag. VII. 59 (plan), XXV. 196.

WORCESTERSHIRE

Allies. Allies, J. British, Roman and Saxon Antiquities of Worcestershire, 2nd ed., 1852.

Nash. Nash, T. History of Worcestershire, 2 vols. 1781—99.

V.C.H. Victoria History of the Counties of England, Worcestershire, I. 1901.

Dorn, near Blockley. Foundations. Allies, 87, 355 ; Gough's Camden, II. 489 ; Lewis, II. 73 ; Nash, I. 101 ; V.C.H. I. 221.

Droitwich. Buildings and pavement. Allies, 98 ; Arch. Jour. IV. 146 ; B.A.A. Jour. III. 119, XXXVII. 432 ; Bainbridge's Droitwich Salt Springs, 1873, 45, 46 ; Gent. Mag. 1847, ii. 72, and Lib. Rom. Brit. Rem. ii. 356 ; V.C.H. I. 208. Orig. pav. in Worcester Museum.

Eckington. Buildings. Allies, 74 ; V.C.H. I. 211.

Kempsey. Foundations. Allies, 54 ; V.C.H. I. 210.

Soddington-in-Mamble. Pavement (?) and kiln (?). Allies, 146 ; Britton and Brayley, XV. i. 277 ; Gent. Mag. 1807, ii. 1009, and Lib. Rom. Brit. Rem. ii. 356 ; V.C.H. I. 220.

Worcester. Foundations. Allies, 1, 15, 23 ; Gent. Mag. 1834, i. 96, 1860, ii. 159, and Lib. Rom. Brit. Rem. ii. 357 ; V.C.H. I. 203, 205, 207.

Kilns. Antiquary, XLI. 82 ; Builder, LXXXVIII. 156; Lond. S.A. Proc. 2 S. I. 148 ; Norfolk Archaeology, VI. 155 ; V.C.H. I. 207, 208.

YORKSHIRE

Allen. Allen, T. History of Yorkshire, 6 vols. 1828—31.

Drake's Ebor. Drake, F. Eboracum, or the History of York, 1736.

E. R. Antiq. Soc. Trans. East Riding Antiquarian Society Transactions, I.—XVII. 1893—1910.

Wellbeloved. Wellbeloved, C. Eburacum, or York under the Romans, 1842.

Whitaker's Craven. Whitaker, T. D. History of Craven, 3rd ed. by A. W. Morant, 1878.

Whitaker's Richmond. Whitaker, T. D. History of Richmondshire, 2 vols. 1823.

York Mus. Handbook. York Museum Handbook, 8th ed., 1891.

Yorks. Arch. Jour. Yorkshire Archaeological Journal, I.—XX. 1870—1909.

Yorks. Phil. Soc. Proc. Yorkshire Philosophical Society Proceedings, 1855.

Yorks. Phil. Soc. Reports. Yorkshire Philosophical Society Reports, 1829—1910.

Acomb, near York. Pavement. York Mus. Handbook, 95. Part of orig. pav. in Museum.

Adel (Cookridge). Foundations. Gent. Mag. 1852, i. 269, and Lib. Rom. Brit. Rem. ii. 600; Phil. Trans. XXIII. 1285.

Stone aqueduct. Gough's Camden, III. 283; Mag. Brit. 1738, VI. 409.

Aldborough (*Isurium*). Town, walls, buildings and pavements. Arch. Jour. VI. 98, XLIV. 53; Athenaeum, Nov. 18, 1848; B.A.A. Jour. IV. 401, V. 73, 80, XX. 39, 189, XLVIII. 65, 66; Britton and Brayley, XVI. 670; Coll. Antiq. VI. 259; Drake's Ebor. 24; Gent. Mag. 1811, ii. 312, 1832, i. 452, 1848, ii. 633, and Lib. Rom. Brit. Rem. ii. 303, 361, 362; Fowler, No. 6; Gough's Camden, III. 299, and pl. XVI, fig. i. (plan); Illust. Lond. News, Jan. 20, 1849; Horsley's Brit. Rom. 402; Lanc. and Ches. Antiq. Soc. IV. 275; Leland's Itin. I. 96; Lewis, I. 25, 294; Lond. S.A. Archaeologia, IV. 76, Proc. 2 S. VII. 280, Minute Book, VIII. 18, XIV. 170, XVIII. 303, and Topog. Colls., red portfolio (lithographs of pavements); Mag. Brit. 1738, VI. 379; Morgan, 130, 140; Reliquary, VIII. 182, N.S. IV. 91; Smith, H. E., Reliquiae Isurianae, 1852; Thoresby, R., Ducatus Leodiensis, 1715, 558; Stukeley's Itin. Curios. II. 73, and Letters, III. 281, 302, 364; Wright's Celt, Roman and Saxon, 154, 192, and Wanderings of an Antiquary, 235; Yorks. Arch. Jour. X. 335, XII. 413. An orig. pav. in the museum of the Leeds Literary and Philosophical Soc.

Amotherby. Paved floors. Gent. Mag. 1868, i. 83, and Lib. Rom. Brit. Rem. ii. 362.

Bishop Burton, near Beverley. Pavements. E. R. Antiq. Soc. Trans. XIV. 60; Drake's Ebor. 30; Gent, T., Hist. of Ripon, 1733, 77; Gough's Camden, III. 319; Oliver, G., Hist. of Beverley, 1829, 18 n, 488; Poulson, G., Beverlac, 1829, I. 16; Thoresby, R., Ducatus Leodiensis, 558.

Boroughbridge, *see* Aldborough.

Bowes. Buildings. Arch. Jour. VI. 350; Lewis, I. 307; Yorks. Arch. Jour. VII. 84.

Bradley (Grimscar Wood). Hypocaust. Gent. Mag. 1852, i. 269, and Lib. Rom. Brit. Rem. ii. 599; Lond. S.A. Archaeologia, XXXII. 24; Yorks. Arch. Jour. II. 138. *See also* Greteland.

Bridlington, *see* Rudston.

Burgh, near Bainbridge. Buildings. Mag. Brit. 1738, VI. 614.

Castle Dykes, *see* Stainley, North.

Castleford. Foundations. Stukeley's Itin. Curios. II. 76.

Castleshaw, near Delph. Station, buildings and excavations.
B.A.A. Jour. N.S. XIII. 198, XIV. 213; Bruton, F. A., First
Interim Report on the excavations of the Roman Forts at
Castleshaw, 1908 (plans, etc.); Lanc. and Ches. Antiq. Soc.
Trans. XVI. 151 ; Yorks. Arch. Jour. XX. 100 (plan).

Catterick. Station, buildings, &c. Arch. Jour. VI. 213, 215;
B.A.A. Jour. XLIII. 105, 238 ; Britton and Brayley, XVI.
292 ; Gough's Camden, III. 336; Horsley's Brit. Rom. 399;
Lond. S.A. Proc. 2 S. XI. 317 ; Mag. Brit. 1738, VI. 609 ;
Reliquary, N.S. I. 106 ; Stukeley's Itin. Curios. II. 72 ;
Whitaker's Richmond, II. 22.

Clementhorpe. Pavement. Yorks. Phil. Soc. Report, 1854, II.
26.

Collingham (Dalton Parlours). Buildings and pavements.
Antiquary, XXIX. 68 ; Gent. Mag. 1862, i. 607, and Lib.
Rom. Brit. Rem. ii. 419, 420 ; Scarth's Rom. Brit. 101 ;
York Mus. Handbook, 94 ; Yorks. Phil. Soc. Proc. I. 270,
and pl. 7 (plan), also Report, 1854, II. 26. Portion of orig.
pav. in York Museum.

Cookridge, *see* Adel.

Dalton Parlours, *see* Collingham.

Easingwold. Pavement. Yorks. Phil. Soc. Reports, 1854,
II. 26.

Elslack, near Skipton. Station, walls, gates, etc. Antiquary,
XLIV. 409, XLV. 201 ; B.A.A. Jour. N.S. XIV. 213, XV. 50 ;
Builder, XCVI. 656.

Etton, near Beverley. Hypocaust or kiln. Mortimer, J. R.,
Forty years Researches in British, etc. Burial Mounds in
East Yorks. 1905, 342.

Filey. Building. B.A.A. Jour. XLIV. 355 ; Scarborough Philosophical and Archaeological Society, 26th Report, 1857, 18
(plan); Yorks. Arch. Jour. IV. 68 (plan).

Gargrave. Foundations and pavement. Allen, VI. 46; Lewis,
II. 276; Whitaker's Craven, 229.

Greta Bridge. Bridge. Gough's Camden, III. 338.

  Buildings. Lond. S.A. Minute Book, XVI. 442.

Greteland, near Halifax. Foundations. Yorks. Arch. Jour. II.
139; *see also* Bradley.

Grimscar Wood, *see* Bradley.

Harpham. Pavement. Antiquary, XL. 322; Athenaeum, Feb.
25, 1905; E.R. Antiq. Soc. Trans. XII. xxi, XIII. ii. 141
(plan), XIV. 59; Hull Scientific and Field Nat. Club Trans.
III. 173; Hull Museum Publications, Nos. 22 and 23; Lond.
S.A. Proc. 2 S. XX. 215. Portions of orig. pavs. in Hull
Museum.

Hartlington Burnsall (Upper Wharfedale). Kiln. Reliquary
and Illust. Arch. N.S. IV. 47.

Hovingham. Buildings and pavements. Gough's Brit. Topog.
II. 467, and Camden, III. 328; King's Mun. Antiq. II. 169;
Lond. S.A. Archaeologia, XXVII. 404, and Minute Book, V.
151; Morgan, 142; Stukeley's Letters, III. 354, 356.

Ilkley. Foundations. Antiquary, XI. 36; Whitaker's Craven, 286.

Kilham, *see* Rudston.

Langtoft, near Driffield. Hypocaust or kiln. Mortimer, J. R.,
Forty years Researches in British, etc. Burial Mounds in
E. Yorks. 1905, 341.

Langton. Building. E.R. Antiq. Soc. Trans. X. 71 (plan);
Yorks. Phil. Soc. Reports, 1863, 21.

Malton (Mosley Bank). Pavement. Lond. S.A. Archaeologia,
XXVII. 404; Morgan, 142.

Middleham. Foundations. Antiquary, IV. 274; B.A.A. Jour.
N.S. XII. 288; Yorks. Arch. Jour. VII. 459.

Millington. Buildings. E.R. Antiq. Soc. Trans. VII. 44; Gough's
Camden, III. 313; Lewis, III. 305; Lond. S.A. Minute Book,
V. 62; Phil. Trans. No. 483, 541; Poulson, G., Beverlac,
1829, I. 10.

Mosley Bank, *see* Malton.

Oulston, near Easingwold. Building and pavement. Antiquary,
XXIX. 68; Lond. S.A. Proc. 1 S. III. 135; Newcastle S.A.
Proc. IV. 57; York Mus. Handbook, 93. Portion of orig.
pav. in York Museum.

Rotherham, *see* Templeborough.

Rudston and Kilham (between). Pavement. Athenaeum, Sept. 14, 1839; Gent. Mag. 1839, ii. 410, and Lib. Rom. Brit. Rem. ii. 364.

Slack, near Huddersfield. Station, buildings, etc. Antiquary, XLIV. 165 ; Arch. Jour. XXIII. 66, XXIV. 289 (plan); B.A.A. Jour. XX. 209, N.S. XIV. 141 ; Gent. Mag. 1824, i. 261, 1840, i. 521, 1866, i. 37, and Lib. Rom. Brit. Rem. ii. 371, 372 ; Gough's Camden, III. 274; Lewis, III. 168; Lond. S.A. Archaeologia, XXXII. 20; Whitaker's Manchester, I. 128 ; Yorks. Arch. Jour. I. 1 (plan), II. 134.

Stainley, North (Castle Dykes). Buildings. Arch. Jour. XXXII. 135 (plan), 251, and Ripon Manual (Yorks. Arch. and Topog. Assoc. 1874), 38.

Tadcaster. Bridge. Godwin's Arch. Handbook, 34 ; Lond. S.A. Proc. 1 S. II. 187 ; Wright's Celt, Roman and Saxon, 226.

Templeborough, near Rotherham. Buildings. Arch. Jour. XXXV. 66, 101 ; B.A.A. Jour. XXXIII. 503 (plan), XXXIV. 243, 248, 249 n; Builder, XXXV. 1139; Coll. Antiq. VII. 99 (plan); Gough's Camden, III. 266; Guest, J., Hist. of Rotherham, 1879, 593 ; Horsley's Brit. Rom. 482 ; Lond. S.A. Proc. 2 S. VII. 330 ; Yorks. Arch. Jour. V. 477.

Well, near Bedale. Foundations and pavement. Antiquary, XXV. 91 ; B.A.A. Jour. XLII. 433 ; Gough's Brit. Topog. II. 467, and Camden, III. 334; Lond. S.A. Minute Book, II. 148; Newcastle S.A. Proc. 3 S. II. 326 n ; Reliquary, N.S. I. 108 ; Yorks. Arch. Jour. VII. 284.

York (*Eboracum*). City, gates, walls, multangular tower, etc. Allen, II. 45 ; Arch. Jour. XXXI. 221, Norwich vol. 1847, 131, and Winchester vol. 1845, under Porchester Castle, 9 ; Britton and Brayley, XVI. 109 ; Drake's Ebor. 56, 57 ; Godwin's Arch. Handbook, 36; Gough's Camden, III. 303; Halfpenny, J., Fragmenta Vetusta, 1807, pls. 1, 2; Lewis, IV. 703; Mag. Brit. 1738, VI. 337 ; Phil. Trans. XIII. 1683 ; Scarth's Rom. Brit. 98 ; Stukeley's Letters, III. 378, 379 ; Wellbeloved, 47—59 (plans, etc.); Wright's Celt, Roman and Saxon, 173, 188, and Wanderings of an Antiquary, 212 ; Yorks. Arch. Jour. IV. 4 ; Yorks. Phil. Soc. Reports, 1860, 10, 30, 1893, 8 ; York Herald, June 7, 1910.

York. Bridge. Stukeley's Letters, III. 378.

Cherry Hill (Clementhorpe). Pavement. Arch. Jour. X. 166; Gent. Mag. 1851, ii. 418, and Lib. Rom. Brit. Rem. ii. 382 ; York Mus. Handbook, 94. Original drawing in the Museum.

Clifton. Pavement. Antiquary, VI. 35 ; Wellbeloved, 68.

Davygate and Lendal (between). Foundations. Allen, II. 29; Gough's Camden, III. 303.

Dowgate. Foundations. Lond. S.A. Archaeologia, II. 181.

Fishergate postern. Arches of gritstone. Allen, II. 44.

Fossbridge (near). Pavements. Gent. Mag. 1825, ii. 75, and Lib. Rom. Brit. Rem. ii. 379.

Friar's garden. Foundations. Allen, II. 27; Gent. Mag. 1770, 391, 1833, i. 357, and Lib. Rom. Brit. Rem. ii. 378, 379 ; Gough's Camden, III. 302; Wellbeloved, 70, 71, 72, 76, 91.

Goodramgate. Foundation. Gent. Mag. 1860, ii. 222, 1861, i. 48, and Lib. Rom. Brit. Rem. ii. 383.

Micklegate Bar. Pavement. Allen, II. 33 ; Antiquary, XXIX. 66 ; Fowler, 2nd Appendix, No. 4 ; Wellbeloved, 66 ; York Mus. Handbook, 95. Part of orig. pav. in Museum.

The Mount. Sepulchral chamber. Allen, II. 32; Lond. S.A. Archaeologia, XVI. 340 ; Wellbeloved, 107.

The Mount. Bath. Arch. Jour. X. 64.

North Street. Buildings. Yorks. Phil. Soc. Report, 1893, 8.

St Mary in Castlegate. Pavement. York Mus. Handbook, 95. Coloured rubbing in Museum.

Tanner Row. Pavement. Arch. Jour. X. 166; York Mus. Handbook, 94. A portion of orig. pav. in Museum.

Toft Green. Pavements. Gent. Mag. 1853, i. 398, and Lib. Rom. Brit. Rem. ii. 383 ; York Mus. Handbook, 28, 94. Orig. pav. in Museum.

SCOTLAND

Chalmers' Caledonia. Chalmers, G. Caledonia, 2 vols., 1807—10.
Christison. Christison, D. Early Fortifications in Scotland, 1898.
Gordon. Gordon, A. Itinerarium Septentrionale, 1726.
Hodgson's Northumb. Hodgson, J. History of Northumberland, 3 vols.,
    1820—58.
Maitland. Maitland, W. History and Antiquities of Scotland, 2 vols.,
    1757.
Macdonald. Macdonald, G. The Roman Wall of Scotland, 1911.
Roy. Roy, W. Military Antiquities of the Romans, 1793.
Scot. S. A. Scotland, Society of Antiquaries of:
    (a) Archaeologia Scotica, 1792—1890.
    (b) Proceedings, I.—XLII. 1855—1909.
Stuart. Stuart, R. Caledonia Romana, 2nd ed., 1852.

DUMBARTONSHIRE

Auchindavy. Fort. Gordon, 54; Hodgson's Northumb. III. ii.
    266; Horsley's Brit. Rom. 169; Macdonald, 182; Roy, 159,
    160, and pl. XXXV; Stuart, 326.
Bar Hill. Fort, buildings, excavations, etc. Builder, LXXXVI.
    389; Gordon, 54; Hodgson's Northumb. III. ii. 265;
    Horsley's Brit. Rom. 169; Macdonald, 96, pl. V, 187—202,
    pl. XXII (plan); Newcastle S.A. Proc. 3 S. III. 231; Re-
    liquary and Illust. Arch. N.S. XII. 4; Roy, 160, and pl.
    XXXV; Scot. S.A. Proc. XL. 403 (plans, etc.); Stuart, 336.
Castle Hill. Fort. Gordon, 52; Hodgson's Northumb. III. ii.
    268; Macdonald, 160; Roy, 158; Stuart, 305.
Dumbarton. Tower (?). Gough's Camden, IV. 92; Stuart, 174.
Duntocher or Duntochter. Fort and buildings. Gordon, 51;
    Gough's Camden, IV. 102; Hodgson's Northumb. III. ii. 268;
    Horsley's Brit. Rom. 164; Knox, J., View of Scotland,
    3rd ed. 1785, II. 611; Macdonald, 155, 157; Roy, 158,
    and pl. XXXV; Stuart, 295, 302 (plan).

Kilpatrick or Kirkpatrick, New or East. Fort. Gordon, 53 ;
    Hodgson's Northumb. III. ii. 267 ; Macdonald, 162 ; Roy,
    158 ; Stuart, 312.
Kilpatrick or Kirkpatrick, Old or West. Fort and building.
    Bruce, J., History of the Parish of West or Old Kilpatrick
    (1893), 36 ; Gordon, 50 ; Hodgson's Northumb. III. ii. 268 ;
    Macdonald, 154 ; Roy, 157 ; Stuart, 287, 294.
Kirkintilloch. Fort, buildings, etc. B.A.A. Jour. XLIV. 389 ;
    Gibson's Camden (1695), 959 ; Gordon, 54 ; Hodgson's
    Northumb. III. ii. 266 ; Horsley's Brit. Rom. 168 ; Mac-
    donald, 174 ; Roy, 159, and pl. XXXV ; Stuart, 322.
Westerwood. Fort. Gordon, 56 ; Hodgson's Northumb. III. ii.
    265 ; Macdonald, 205 ; Roy, 160 ; Stuart, 343.
The Wall. Arch. Jour. XV. 25 ; B.A.A. Jour. XLV. 131 ;
    Gordon, cap. VI. 50 ; Hodgson's Northumb. III. ii. 260 ;
    Horsley's Brit. Rom. cap. X. 158 ; Lanc. and Ches. Antiq.
    Soc. XI. 170 ; Lond. S.A. Proc. 1 S. I. 7 ; Newcastle S.A.
    Proc. 3 S. III. 229 ; Roy, cap. IV. 148 ; Stuart, cap. IV. 271.

DUMFRIESSHIRE

Avon Valley. Foundations. Athenaeum, Jan. 2, 1847 ; Dum-
    fries Courier.
Birrens. Fort, buildings, excavations, etc. Antiquary, I. 91,
    XXXI. 301 ; Christison, 72 ; Gordon, 18 ; Gough's Camden,
    IV. 61 ; Hodgson's Northumb. III. ii. 251 ; Lond. S.A. Proc.
    2 S. XVI. 193 ; Maitland, I. 291 ; Reliquary and Illust.
    Arch. N.S. XII. 7 ; Roy, 118, 119, and pl. XXIV ; Scot. S.A.
    Proc. XXX. 81 (plans, etc.) ; Stuart, 122 ; Stukeley's Letters,
    III. 400.
Birrenswark. Fort, buildings, excavations, etc. Christison, 85 ;
    Gordon, 16 ; Gough's Camden, IV. 62 ; Lond. S.A. Proc.
    2 S. XVIII. 373 ; Maitland, I. 292 ; Roy, 72, 119, and
    pl. XVI ; Scot. S.A. Proc. XXXIII. 198 (plans, etc.) ; Stuart,
    132.
Middleby. Buildings. Bruce's Rom. Wall, 359 ; Stukeley's
    Letters, II. 87.

ELGINSHIRE

Burghead. Fort, etc. Chalmer's Caledonia, I. viii. 130; Christison, 150, 254; Roy, 131, and pls. XXXIII—IV; Scot. S.A. Proc. IV. 353 (plan), XXIV. 147 (plan), XXV. 435; Stuart, 213.

FIFESHIRE

Carpow, near Newburgh. Buildings. Small, A., Roman Antiquities in Fife, 1823, 175.

LANARKSHIRE

Bemulie. Fort, buildings, etc. Gordon, 53; Hodgson's Northumb. III. ii. 267; Horsley's Brit. Rom. 167; Macdonald, 165; Roy, 159, and pl. XXXV; Stuart, 317.

Cadder, or Calder. Fort(?). Gordon, 21, 54; Macdonald, 169—73; Roy, 159; Scot. S.A. Proc. I. 170; Stuart, 321.

Carstairs. Buildings. Stuart, 139, 141.

LINLITHGOWSHIRE

Inveravon. Fort, buildings, etc. Macdonald, 241; Hodgson's Northumb. III. ii. 264; Stuart, 361.

MID-LOTHIAN

Cramond. Fort and buildings. Gordon, 116; Gough's Camden, IV. 57; Hodgson's Northumb. III. ii. 263; Maitland, I. 203; Stuart, 165.

Inveresk. Buildings. Chambers, R., Domestic Annals of Scotland, 1858, I. 33; Gough's Camden, IV. 47; Scot. S.A. Arch. Scot. II. 159, and Proc. VI. 179; Stuart, 156, and pl. IV (plan).

PEEBLESSHIRE

Lyne. Fort, buildings, excavations, etc. Christison, 82; Reliquary and Illust. Arch. N.S. XII. 16; Roy, 122, and pl. XXVIII; Scot. S.A. Proc. XXXV. 154 (plans, etc.); Stuart, 154.

PERTHSHIRE

Ardoch. Fort, buildings, excavations, etc. Antiquary, XXXIII.
19; Blair Drummond Papers, Historical MSS. Commission,
10th Report, pt. i. 130; Christison, 73; Gordon, 41; Gough's
Camden, IV. 121; Lond. S.A. Proc. 2 S. XVIII. 371; Maitland, I. 191; Reliquary and Illust. Arch. N.S. XII. 8; Roy,
82, 126, and pls. X, XXX; Scot. Hist. Soc. Publications, 1892,
258 (Memoirs of Sir John Clerk of Penicuick); Scot. S.A.
Proc. XXXII. 399 (plans, etc.); Sibbald, Sir R., Hist. Inquiries
concerning Roman Antiquities in Scotland, 1707, 37; Stuart,
188.

Inchtuthil. Fort, buildings, excavations, etc. Athenaeum, Sept. 7,
1901; Chalmer's Caledonia, I. 132; Curle, J., The Fort at
Newstead, 1911, 91 (plan of baths); Cymmrodorion Soc.
Trans. 1908—9, 72 (plan of baths); Gough's Camden, IV.
138; Maitland, I. 199; Reliquary and Illust. Arch. N.S. XII.
15; Roy, 75, 133, and pl. XVIII; Scot. S.A. Proc. XXXVI. 182
(plans, etc.); Stuart, 210.

ROXBURGHSHIRE

Jedburgh (Cappuck Farm). Foundations. Reliquary, N.S. I.
177; Reliquary and Illust. Arch. XII. 17.

Newstead, near Melrose. Fort, buildings, excavations, etc.
Antiquary, XLI. 284, 321, 405, 468; B.A.A. Jour. 2 S. XII.
286, XIV. 69, 214; Berwickshire Nat. Club Proc. V. 8;
Builder, XCII. 111; Curle, J., A Roman Frontier Post and
its people: The Fort at Newstead, 1911 (plans, etc.); Lond.
S.A. Proc. 2 S. XXI. 163; Reliquary and Illust. Arch. N.S.
XII. 17; Roy, 115, and pl. XXI; Scot. S.A. Arch. Scotica,
IV. 422, and Proc. I. 28, 213; Stuart, 262.

Ruberslaw. Buildings. Scot. S.A. Proc. XXXIX. 219.

STIRLINGSHIRE

Bankier, West. Fort, buildings, etc. Gordon, 20.

Camelon, near Falkirk. Fort, buildings, excavations, etc. Antiquary, XXXV. 249; Builder, LXXVI. 282; Gordon, 29; Horsley's Brit. Rom. 172; Lond. S.A. Archaeologia, I. 231; Macdonald, 250; Maitland, I. 206; Newcastle S.A. Proc. X. 217, 231 (plan); Reliquary and Illust. Arch. N.S. XII. 8; Roy, 126, and pl. XXIX; Scot. S.A. Proc. XXXV. 329 (plans, etc.); Stuart, 180.

Arthur's Oon, or Oven. Gordon, cap. III. 24; Gough's Camden, IV. 96, 103; Horsley's Rom. Brit. 174; Lond. S.A. Archaeologia, V. 252; Maitland, I. 208; Newcastle S.A. Proc. X. 217; Reliquary and Illust. Arch. N.S. XII. 10; Roy, 153, and pl. XXXVI; Stuart, 183; Stukeley's Letters, III. 414, 432.

Castlecary. Fort, buildings, excavations, etc. Antiquary, XXXVIII. 176, 324, 377; Gordon, 57; Hodgson's Northumb. III. ii. 264; Horsley's Brit. Rom. 170; Macdonald, 207, pl. XXVII (plan); Newcastle S.A. Proc. X. 225; Reliquary and Illust. Arch. N.S. XII. 10; Roy, 123, 160, 200, and pls. XXXV, XXXIX (plan of house); Scot. S.A. Proc. XXXVII. 271 (plans, etc.); Stuart, 343.

Mumrills. Fort. Macdonald, 239; Maitland, I. 172.

Roughcastle. Fort, buildings, excavations, etc. Antiquary, XXXIX. 321; Gordon, 59; Hodgson's Northumb. III. ii. 264; Horsley's Brit. Rom. 172; Macdonald, 96, pl. V, 220, pl. XXXIII (plan); Newcastle S.A. Proc. X. 230, 3 S. III. 230; Nimmo's Hist. of Stirlingshire, 1777, 8; Reliquary and Illust. Arch. N.S. XII. 13; Roy, 161, and pl. XXXV; Scot. S.A. Proc. XXXIX. 442 (plans, etc.); Stuart, 353.

Watling Lodge, near Falkirk. Guard House. Macdonald, 248 (plan).

The Wall, *see* Dumbartonshire.

WALES

Arch. Cambrensis. Archaeologia Cambrensis, published by the Cambrian
Archaeological Association, I.—IV. 1846—49, 2 S. I.—v. 1850—54, 3 S.
I.—XV. 1855—69, 4 S. I.—XIV. 1870—83, 5 S. I.—XVII. 1884—1900,
6 S. I.—X. 1901—10.

Cymmrodorion Soc. Trans. Cymmrodorion Society Transactions, 1908—9.

Hoare's Giraldus Cambrensis. Hoare, Sir R. C. Giraldus Cambrensis,
2 vols., 1806.

Lewis. Lewis, S. A Topographical Dictionary of Wales, 3rd ed., 2 vols.,
1845.

Montgomery Colls. Montgomeryshire Collections, published by the Powys-
Land Club, I.—XXXV. 1868—1910.

Pennant's Tour. Pennant, T. Tour in Wales, 2 vols., 1784.

Wyndham. Wyndham, H. P. Tour through Monmouthshire and Wales,
2 ed., 4to., 1781.

BRECKNOCKSHIRE

Coelbren. Fort, with brick floors and stone pitchings. Arch.
Cambrensis, 6 S. VII. 135; Builder, XCI. 330; Cymmrodorion
Soc. Trans. 1908—9, 149.

Cwmdu, *see* Penygaer.

Gaer Bannan, near Brecknock. Fort, buildings, etc. Arch.
Cambrensis, 4 S. IX. 235, 6 S. III. 174; Britton and Brayley,
XVIII. 3; Cymmrodorion Soc. Trans. 1908—9, 115 (plan),
187; Gough's Camden, III. 102; Hoare's Giraldus Cambrensis, I. cxlix; Jones, T., Hist. of Brecknockshire, 1805—9,
II. 102; Lond. S.A. Archaeologia, I. 294, II. 21, 22, VI. 8,
and Minute Book, XI. 97; Wyndham, 196.

Llanvrynach (Penypentre Farm). Buildings and pavement.
Cymmrodorion Soc. Trans. 1908—9, 125 n; Jones, T., Hist.
of Brecknockshire, 1805—9, II. 599 (plan); Lewis, II. 151;
Lond. S.A. Archaeologia, VII. 205 (plan).

Penygaer, near Crickhowel (Cwmdu). Fort, buildings, etc.

Cymmrodorion Soc. Trans. 1908—9, 126; Jones' Brecknock, II. 499 (plan); Lewis, II. 138; Scot. S.A. Archaeologia Scotica, III. 91 (plan).

CARDIGANSHIRE

Llanio. Fort and buildings. Arch. Cambrensis, 3 S. XIV. 450, 4 S. IV. 113, 5 S. V. 297; Cymmrodorion Soc. Trans. 1908—9, 106; Gough's Camden, III. 158; Meyrick, S. R., Hist. of Cardiganshire, 1810, x, 272.

CARMARTHENSHIRE

Abercover, near Carmarthen. Pavement. B.A.A. Jour. XXIV. 113.

Carmarthen. Buildings. Antiquary, XXXIII. 231; Lond. S.A. Proc. 2 S. XVI. 409.

Cwmbrwyn. Fort and buildings. Arch. Cambrensis, 5 S. VII. 334, 6 S. VII. 175 (plans, etc.); Cymmrodorion Soc. Trans. 1908—9, 162 (plan); Lond. S.A. Proc. 2 S. XVI. 409.

Dolau-Cothy (Tre-Gôch). Buildings and pavement. Arch. Cambrensis, 4 S. IX. 320, 5 S. V. 298, X. 90; Cymmrodorion Soc. Trans. 1908—9, 111.

Llandovery. Fort (?) and buildings (?). Arch. Cambrensis, 4 S. IV. 125; Cymmrodorion Soc. Trans. 1908—9, 112.

CARNARVONSHIRE

Caerhun. Fort and buildings. B.A.A. Jour. XXIV. 110, N.S. IV. 83, 86; Britton and Brayley, XVII. 475; Cymmrodorion Soc. Trans. 1908—9, 81 (plan); Gent. Mag. 1797, i. 296; Gough's Camden, III. 190; Hartshorne's Salopia Antiqua, 117 n; Lewis, I. 145; Lond. S.A. Archaeologia, XVI. 127 (plan).

Carnarvon. Fort and buildings. Arch. Cambrensis, I. 77, 177 (plan), 284 (plan), 5 S. X. 190 (plan), 276; Arch. Jour. III. 69; B.A.A. Jour. N.S. I. 21, XII. 210; Cymmrodorion Soc. Trans.

1908—9, 83, 84; Hoare's Giraldus Cambrensis, II. 94; Lond. S.A. Archaeologia, VI. 8; Wright's Celt, Roman and Saxon, 150.

Glasfryn, near Tremadoc. Buildings. Arch. Cambrensis, 6 S. VIII. 287, IX. 473, 477 (plans, etc.); B.A.A. Jour. N.S. XII. 206.

Llanbeblig, *see* Carnarvon.

DENBIGHSHIRE

Abergele. Pharos. B.A.A. Jour. XXXIV. 434.

Holt. Hypocaust. Arch. Cambrensis, 6 S. VI. 238; Watkin's Rom. Cheshire, 305.

Pont Ruffyd. Buildings (?). Arch. Cambrensis, 5 S. IV. 345; Cymmrodorion Soc. Trans. 1908—9, 79.

Vale Crucis Abbey. Hypocaust (?). Antiquary, XXXVI. 106; Arch. Cambrensis, 5 S. XI. 220.

FLINTSHIRE

Garreg, near Holywell. Pharos. Antiquary, XL. 292; Arch. Jour. LX. 210, 247; Britton and Brayley, XVII. 737; Pennant, T., Hist. of Whiteford and Holywell, 1796, 111.

Hope (Estyn). Buildings. Arch. Cambrensis, 4 S. II. 98; B.A.A. Jour. XXXIV. 431; Cymmrodorion Soc. Trans. 1908—9, 76; Gough's Camden, III. 222; Hartshorne's Salopia Antiqua, 117 n; Lewis, I. 429; Watkin's Rom. Cheshire, 306 n.

Pentre-ffwrndan, near Flint. Walls, and lead works. Arch. Cambrensis, 3 S. II. 306.

Wrexham. Buildings. B.A.A. Jour. XXXIV. 434; Lewis, II. 441.

GLAMORGANSHIRE

Barry Island. Stone well. B.A.A. Jour. N.S. I. 358.

Cardiff. Fort, buildings, and excavations. Antiquary, XXXIV. 233; Arch. Cambrensis, 3 S. VIII. 253 n, 5 S. XVII. 283, 6 S. I. 70 (plan, etc.), VIII. 29 (plan, etc.), 227; B.A.A. Jour.

XLIX. 220, 308, N.S. VII. 27; Cymmrodorion Soc. Trans. 1908—9, 154 (plan, etc.); Lond. S.A. Archaeologia, II. 10, LVII. 335 (plan, etc.); Public Advertiser, Oct. 9, 1777.

Cardiff (Ely Racecourse). Buildings. Antiquary, XXIX. 234, XXX. 46, 208; Arch. Cambrensis, 5 S. XI. 326; B.A.A. Jour. L. 326; Builder, LXVII. 244; Cymmrodorion Soc. Trans. 1908—9, 159 n.

Gellygaer. Fort, buildings, and excavations. Antiquary, XXXVI. 106, XXXVII. 13, XLIV. 245; Arch. Cambrensis, 3 S. XV. 86, 6 S. III. 14; Cymmrodorion Soc. Trans. 1908—9, 130 (plan, etc.); Lewis, I. 354; Ward, J., The Roman Fort of Gellygaer, 1903 (plans, etc.), also issued as vol. XXXV. of The Trans. of the Cardiff Naturalists Society.

Llantwit Major. Buildings and pavement. Antiquary, XIX. 33; Athenaeum, Oct. 20, 1888; Arch. Cambrensis, 5 S. V. 413; Arch. Review, II. 254; B.A.A. Jour. XLIV. 69; Cymmrodorion Soc. Trans. 1908—9, 159 n; Pitt-Rivers, Lt. Gen., Excavations in Bokerley Dyke and Wansdyke, 288.

Loughor or Llychwr. Buildings. Cymmrodorion Soc. Trans. 1908—9, 160; Lewis, II. 181.

Pennydarren, near Merthyr Tydfil. Fort, buildings, and pavement. Antiquary, XXXVIII. 324, 377, XLI. 244, XLII. 45, 361; Arch. Cambrensis, 6 S. VI. 193 (plans, etc.); Cymmrodorion Soc. Trans. 1908—9, 142; Wilkin, C., Hist. of Merthyr Tydfil, 1867, 2.

MERIONETHSHIRE

Aberglaslyn Pass. Fort, foundations of guardhouse. B.A.A. Jour. XXXIV. 110, 460.

Caergai, near Bala. Fort, buildings, etc. Arch. Cambrensis, 5 S. II. 196; Cymmrodorion Soc. Trans. 1908—9, 95 (plan).

Tomen-y-mur. Fort, buildings, etc. Arch. Cambrensis, 2 S. I. 327, 3 S. XIV. 474, 4 S. II. 190, 5 S. I. 334; B.A.A. Jour. XXIV. 117, XXVII. 278; Britton and Brayley, XVII. 932; Cymmrodorion Soc. Trans. 1908—9, 90 (plan, etc.); Hoare's Giraldus Cambrensis, I. cliii.

MONTGOMERYSHIRE

Caersws. Fort, buildings, etc. Antiquary, XLV. 333 (plan); Arch.
Cambrensis, III. 91, 3 S. III. 151, 309, 4 S. III. 75; Arch.
Jour. XIV. 84; Britton and Brayley, XVII. 838; Cymmrodorion
Soc. Trans. 1908—9, 100 (plan); Gough's Camden, III. 164;
Hoare's Giraldus Cambrensis, I. clvii; Montgomery, Colls.
II. 46, 54, 56 (plan); Pennant's Tour, II. 362.

Pennal. Fort, buildings, etc. Arch. Cambrensis, 3 S. XII. 542;
Cymmrodorion Soc. Trans. 1908—9, 98.

PEMBROKESHIRE

Ambleston (Castle Flemish?). Foundations. Cymmrodorion
Soc. Trans. 1908—9, 164; Lond. S.A. Proc. 2 S. XVI. 409.

Ford. Buildings. Britton and Brayley, XVIII. 737; Cymmrodorion Soc. Trans. 1908—9, 195; Fenton, R., Tour through
Pembrokeshire, 1811, 331; Lond. S.A. Proc. 2 S. XVI. 409.

RADNORSHIRE

Castell Collin, near Llandrindod. Fort, foundations, etc. Arch.
Cambrensis, 3 S. II. 32, 4 S. I. 58, 6 S. XI. 411; Britton and
Brayley, XVIII. 874; Cymmrodorion Soc. Trans. 1908—9,
105; Hoare's Giraldus Cambrensis, I. clvi; Lond. S.A.
Archaeologia, I. 303, IV. 5, VI. 8, XVII. 168, and Minute
Book, XI. 101; Williams, J., Hist. of Radnorshire, 1859, 48,
50.

INDEX

CAMBRIDGE : PRINTED BY JOHN CLAY, M.A. AT THE UNIVERSITY PRESS.

For EU product safety concerns, contact us at Calle de José Abascal, 56–1°,
28003 Madrid, Spain or eugpsr@cambridge.org.

www.ingramcontent.com/pod-product-compliance
Ingram Content Group UK Ltd.
Pitfield, Milton Keynes, MK11 3LW, UK
UKHW012341130625
459647UK00009B/454